Exploring Translatic

Exploring Translation Theories presents a comprehensive analysis of the core contemporary paradigms of Western translation theory.

The book covers theories of equivalence, purpose, description, uncertainty, localization, and cultural translation. This second edition adds coverage on new translation technologies, volunteer translators, non-lineal logic, mediation, Asian languages, and research on translators' cognitive processes. Readers are encouraged to explore the various theories and consider their strengths, weaknesses, and implications for translation practice. The book concludes with a survey of the way translation is used as a model in postmodern cultural studies and sociologies, extending its scope beyond traditional Western notions.

Features in each chapter include:

- An introduction outlining the main points, key concepts, and illustrative examples.
- Examples drawn from a range of languages, although knowledge of no language other than English is assumed.
- Discussion points and suggested classroom activities.
- A chapter summary.

This comprehensive and engaging book is ideal both for self-study and as a textbook for translation theory courses within Translation Studies, Comparative Literature, and Applied Linguistics.

Anthony Pym is Professor of Translation and Intercultural Studies at the Rovira i Virgili University, Spain. He is also President of the European Society for Translation Studies, a fellow of the Catalan Institution for Research and Advanced Studies, and Visiting Researcher at the Monterey Institute of International Studies. His publications include *The Status of the Translation Profession in the European Union* (2013) and *On Translator Ethics* (2012).

Exploring Translation Theories

Second edition

ANTHONY PYM

Routledge
Taylor & Francis Group

LONDON AND NEW YORK

First published 2010, this edition published 2014
by Routledge
2 Park Square, Milton Park, Abingdon, Oxon OX14 4RN

and by Routledge
711 Third Avenue, New York, NY 10017

Routledge is an imprint of the Taylor & Francis Group, an informa business

British Library Cataloguing in Publication Data
A catalogue record for this book is available from the British Library

Library of Congress Cataloging in Publication Data
Pym, Anthony, 1956–
    Exploring translation theories / Anthony Pym. – Second Edition.
       pages cm
    1. Translating and interpreting.   I. Title.
    P306.P95 2014
    418'.02 – dc23

                                                        2013022987

ISBN: 978-0-415-83789-7 (hbk)
ISBN: 978-0-415-83791-0 (pbk)
ISBN: 978-1-315-85763-3 (ebk)

Typeset in Berthold Akzidenz Grotesk
by RefineCatch Limited, Bungay, Suffolk
Printed and bound by CPI Group (UK) Ltd, Croydon, CR0 4YY

Contents

Illustrations

FIGURES

TABLES

Acknowledgements

I am grateful to the following publishers and authors for permission to adapt material of various kinds:

- John Benjamins Publishing Company for passages from my article "Natural and directional equivalence in theories of translation," published in *Target* 19/2 (2007) 271–94, which forms the basis for Chapters 2 and 3;
- Ricardo Muñoz Martín for Table 2.2;
- Christiane Nord, for Table 4.1 and Figure 4.1;
- Daniel Gouadec, for Table 4.2.

My sincere thanks to my colleagues Esther Torres Simón and Alberto Fuertes Puerta, who have revised the text, and to those who have helped revise parts of the text: Gideon Toury, Itamar Even-Zohar, Tal Golfajn, Christiane Nord, José Ramón Biau Gil, Christina Schäffner, John Milton, Serafima Khalzanova, Yukiko Muranaga, and Chie Okada. A good number of valuable points have been made by the translators of the book into Japanese (Kayoko Takeda), Portuguese (Fernando Ferreira Alves and Victor Ferreira), and Spanish (Esther Torres Simón, Humberto Burcet Rojas, and Ana Guerberof). Translators and their revisers are the closest readers.

Special thanks go to the many students and colleagues who have participated in the seminars that have comprised this course since it was first offered in 2003: at Monash University in Melbourne, Australia; in the PhD program in Translation and Intercultural Studies at the Rovira i Virgili University in Tarragona, Spain; and especially at the Monterey Institute of International Studies in the United States.

Further thanks are due to the reviewers of the first edition of this book: Dirk Delabastita, Brian Mossop, Hsin-hisn Tu, Shuhuai Wang, Peng Wang, Shaoshuang Wang, Ernst Wendland, Jonathan Downie, Arzu Eker Rodikakis, and Debbie Folaron. Useful comments have also been received from Ghodrat Hassani. This second edition responds to many of their observations and criticisms, although not all—I have not been allowed to make the book longer.

I am also extremely grateful for the editorial guidance provided by Louisa Semlyen and Eloise Cook, who are responsible for the book's title.

Preface

This is a course on the main paradigms of Western translation theories since the 1960s. It adopts a view of translation that includes interpreting (spoken translation) but does not give any special attention to its problems. The book is not primarily designed to make anyone a better translator; it is mainly for academic work, although it should be accessible to anyone interested in arguments about translation—and most translators are. The basic story is that all the theories respond in different ways to one central problem: translation can be defined by equivalence, but there are many reasons why equivalence is not a stable concept. So how can we think about translation beyond equivalence? The answers to that question have been more numerous than many suspect, and often creative and surprising.

The general view taken here is that theory is a field of struggle for or against particular ways of seeing translation. There is no neutral description in this. My mission will have been accomplished whenever anyone finds importance and perhaps pleasure in the contest of ideas, or better, whenever the issues of translation are debated, ideally as part of a pluralist learning project.

Since the first edition of this book, I have become acutely aware that these particular theories are focused on what I call the Western "translation form." They concern the kind of translation that a client might pay a translator to do in any Western country, underpinned by a set of unspoken assumptions about equivalence (see 5.4 below). However, there are many other cultures and situations in which notions of translation are not functionally separate from what we would call "adaptation" or "rewriting," and thus do not struggle with and against equivalence. So there are many other possible ways of theorizing translation, and many alternative narratives. I am only telling one of many possible stories. That said, the Western translation form has spread out over the world, as a peculiar traveling companion of modernity, and readers in all countries will nowadays be familiar with it, even as we strive to go beyond it.

This revised edition has added a few aspects to the original survey, particularly with respect to translation technologies, volunteer translators, non-lineal logic, mediation, Asian languages, and process research. But those are not major changes—just some small treats along the way.

This book accompanies some of the best introductory works in the field. Jeremy Munday's *Introducing Translation Studies* (third edition 2012) and Franz Pöchhacker's *Introducing Interpreting Studies* (2004) are indispensable guides. My aim here is to focus more squarely on the main *theories* that the other books cover, to leave aside much of the research and applications, and to make the theories engage with each other as directly as possible. This means presenting more criticisms than the introductory guides do. It also means that many fields of research, particularly those that have not made strong original contributions to translation theory, have been sidelined here. Some readers will be surprised to find no substantial treatment of empirical research on adaptation, multimedia, or the ways translation has been dealt with from the perspective of gender studies, for example. Those areas are very much part of Translation Studies; they have adopted many of the concepts and methods of neighboring disciplines, but they have not played key roles in debates over the translation form as such. I thus leave them to the companion volumes. Similarly absent is analysis of the possible social forces behind the various paradigms, and why they have developed historically. That kind of inquiry is also left for other places (for example, Pym 2011).

This book also accompanies *The Translation Studies Reader* (third edition 2012) edited by Lawrence Venuti, along with *The Interpreting Studies Reader* (2001) edited by Franz Pöchhacker and Miriam Shlesinger. Both those volumes are superb collections of key texts. My aim has not been to replace those texts: anyone who wants to know about translation theory must read the theorists, in context and in all their complexity. Only with first-hand engagement with the fundamental texts can you really follow the adventures of critical thought.

CHAPTER 1

What is a translation theory?

This chapter explains what I mean by the terms "theory" and "paradigm," and how theorization can be related to translation practice. I also detail the overall chapter plan of this book, some reasons for studying translation theory, and the ways the book can be used as part of a learning process.

1.1 FROM THEORIZING TO THEORIES

Translators are theorizing all the time. Once they have identified a translation problem, they usually have to decide between several possible solutions. Let's say you have to translate the English term "Tory," employed to designate the Conservative Party in Britain. According to the situation, you might consider things like using the English term and inserting information to explain it, or adding a footnote, or just giving a word-for-word equivalent of "Conservative Party," or naming the corresponding part of the political spectrum in the target culture, or just leaving out the problematic name altogether. All those options could be legitimate, given the appropriate text, purpose, and client. Formulating them (*generating* possible translations) and then choosing between them (*selecting* a definitive translation) can be a difficult and complex operation. Yet translators are doing precisely that all the time, in split seconds. Whenever they do it, whenever they decide to opt for one rendition rather than others, they bring into play a series of ideas about what translation is and how it should be carried out. They are theorizing.

The word "theory" probably comes from the Greek *theā*, view + *-horan*, to see—to theorize is to look at a view (the word *theater* has the same origins). A theory sets the scene where the generation and selection process takes place. Translators are thus not only constantly theorizing, but they are doing it in various kinds of conceptual scenes.

This private, internal theorizing becomes public when translators discuss what they do. They occasionally theorize out loud when talking with other translators or with clients, and sometimes with students or instructors. This out-loud theorizing might involve no more than a few shared terms for the things we are dealing with. For example, here I shall refer to the "**start text**" as the one we translate from, and to the "**target text**" as the translation produced. By extension, we can talk about the "start language" and the "target language," or the "start culture" and the "target culture." "**Translating**" would then be a set of processes leading from one side to the other.

Do these words mean that I am already using a theory? Such interrelated names-for-things do tend to form **models of translation**, and those models are never neutral—they often conceal some very powerful guiding ideas, which may form a scene coherent enough to be called a "theory." For instance, here I am saying "start text" where others say "source text," not just because it agrees with the possibilities of a few European languages (*Ausgangstext, texte de départ, texto de partida, testo di partenza*) but more importantly because it says something about other views of translation: How can we blithely assume that the text we translate from is not itself made up of translations, reworked fragments of previous texts, all tied up in never-ending translational networks? Why assume some kind of pristine or natural "source," somehow like a river bubbling up from the earth? Hence "start," as a word that can say something on the level of theory. But then, why stop there? Why, for example, should our terms reduce translation to an affair of just two sides ("start" and "target")? Surely each target is only a link toward further actions and aims, in further cultures and languages? For that matter, texts usually contain traces of more than one language and culture. In all these aspects, there are usually more than just two sides involved. And then, when we put the "start" and "target" ideas next to the "trans-" part of "translation," we see that the terms build a very *spatial* scene where our actions go from one side to the other. The words suggest that translators affect the target culture but not the source, thanks to a transitivity that happens in space. Is that not a strange assumption? The words are certainly starting to look like a theory.

Compare that scene with "**anuvad**," a Sanskrit and Hindi term for written translation that basically means, I am told, "repeating" or "saying later" (cf. Chesterman 2006; Spivak 2007: 274). According to this alternative term, the main difference between one text and the other could be not in space, but in time. Translation can then be seen as a constant process of updating and elaborating, rather than as some kind of physical movement across cultures.

Our interrelated names-for-things form scenes, and those scenes become theories about what a translation could be or should be.

This does not mean that all our inner theorizing is constantly turned into public theories. When translators talk with each other, they mostly accept the common terms without too much argument. Straight mistakes are usually fixed up quickly, through reference to usage, to linguistic knowledge, or to common sense. For instance, we might correct a translator who identifies the term "Tory" with extreme left-wing politics. Any ensuing discussion could be interesting but it will have no great need of translation theory. Only when there are **disagreements over different ways of translating** does private theorization tend to become public theory. If different translators have come up with different renditions of the term "Tory," one of them might argue that "translation should explain the source culture" (so they will use the English term and add a long footnote); another could say "translation should make things understandable to the target culture" (so they will just put "the main right-wing party"); a third might consider that "the translation should re-situate everything in the target culture" (so they would give the name of a conservative target-culture party); and a fourth will perhaps insist that since the start text was not primarily about politics, there is no need to waste time on an ornamental detail (so they might calmly eliminate the term).

When those kinds of arguments are happening, practical theorizing is turning into explicit theories. The arguments turn out to be between different theoretical positions. Sometimes the initially opposed positions will find they are compatible within a larger theory. Often, though, people remain with their fixed positions; they keep arguing. Or worse, they decide that everyone else is crazy: they stop arguing.

1.2 FROM THEORIES TO PARADIGMS

As theorizing turns into theory, some theories develop names and explanations for multiple aspects of translation, including names for the presumed blindness of other theories. When that stage is reached, it makes sense to talk about different "**paradigms**," here understood as sets of principles that underlie different groups of theories (cf. Kuhn 1962). This particularly occurs when we find general ideas, relations, and principles for which there is internal coherence and a shared point of departure. For example, one set of theories uses the terms "source," "target," and "equivalence." They agree that the term "equivalence" names a substantial relation between the "source" and the "target"; their shared point of departure is the comparison of start and target texts. People using those theories can discuss translation with each other fairly well; they share the same vague concepts and general ideas about the aims of a translation; they can even reach consensus about various kinds of equivalence. They are theorizing within the one paradigm.

On the other hand, we sometimes find people arguing about translation problems and reaching nothing but constant disagreement. In such cases, the terms are probably working within quite different paradigms, with different points of departure. For example, one kind of description works from comparisons between translations and non-translations (both in the same language). People engaged in that activity come up with results that could be of interest to psycholinguistics (the language used in translations is different from the language found in non-translations). But that finding seems almost totally irrelevant to anyone working within the equivalence paradigm. If the language in translations is different, the theorist of equivalence can still serenely argue that it *should not* be different. Each side thus continues the discussion without entertaining the other side's perspective. The paradigms enter into conflict. The outcome may be continued tension (debate without resolution), revolution (one paradigm wins out over the other), or mutual ignorance (people choose to travel along separate paths). My aim is to overcome some mutual ignorance.

1.3 HOW THIS BOOK IS ORGANIZED

This book is structured in terms of paradigms rather than individual theories, theorists, or schools. I will be talking about paradigms based on equivalence, purposes, descriptions, uncertainty, localization, and cultural translation. Equivalence is broken down into two sub-paradigms, corresponding to "natural" and "directional" flavors. I do this in order to underscore the complexity of equivalence, since some current theorists tend to dismiss it as naïve and outdated.

The **order of the paradigms** is very roughly chronological, starting around the 1960s and reaching the present day, except for the "uncertainty" paradigm, which was present all the way through. The fundamental conflict between uncertainty and equivalence would be the basic problem to which all the paradigms respond, each as a partial resolution.

This order does not mean the newer theories have replaced the older ones. If that were true, you would only have to read the last chapter. On the contrary, I spend a lot of time on equivalence precisely to indicate its complexity and longevity—a lot of equivalence theory lives on within the localization paradigm and in our technologies. Theories can, of course, become more exact in their descriptions and wider in their predictions, in accordance with an accumulation of knowledge. This sometimes happens in the field of translation, since the newer theories occasionally try to accommodate the perspectives of the older ones. For example, German-language *Skopos* theory can embed the equivalence paradigm as being appropriate to a "special case" scenario. That kind of accumulation is not, however, to be found with respect to the uncertainty paradigm (here including deconstruction), which would regard both equivalence and purpose as indefensible essentialisms. In such cases, we must indeed talk about quite different paradigms, without trying to fit one inside the other. Those paradigms differ right from the very basic questions of what translation is, what it can be, and how a translator should solve problems. When the paradigms clash, people are often using the word "translation" to refer to quite different things. Debate then becomes pointless, at least until someone attempts to go beyond their initial paradigm. Only then, when an attempt is made to understand a new view of translation, can there be productive public theorizing.

So you might have to read more than the last chapter.

1.4 WHY STUDY TRANSLATION THEORIES?

Why study these theories? Instructors and trainers sometimes assume that a translator who knows about theories will work better than one who knows nothing about them. As far as I know, there is no empirical evidence for that claim, and there are good reasons to doubt its validity. All translators theorize, not just the ones who can express their theories in technical terms. In fact, untrained translators may work faster and more efficiently because they know *less* about complex theories—they have fewer doubts and do not waste time reflecting on the obvious. On the other hand, awareness of different theories might be of practical benefit when confronting problems for which there are no established solutions, where significant creativity is required. The theories can pose productive questions, and sometimes suggest novel answers. Theories can also be significant agents of change, especially when moved from one professional culture to another, or when they are made to challenge endemic thought (think about the idea of translation as "saying later"). And public theories can help make people aware that translation is a very complex thing, hard enough to be studied seriously at university, thus enhancing the public image of translators and interpreters.

Awareness of a range of theories might also help the translation profession in a more direct way. When arguments occur, theories provide translators with valuable tools not just to defend their positions but also to find out about other positions. The theories might simply name things that people had not previously thought about. If a client complains that the term "Tory" has disappeared from the translation, you could say you have achieved "compensatory correspondence" by comparing the British party with a target-culture party two pages later in your target text. The client will probably not be entirely convinced, but they might start to realize that not everyone can solve problems the way you can. In fact, that bit of theory might be of as much practical use to the client as to the translator. The more terms and ideas you have, the more you and your client can explore the possibilities of translation.

Some knowledge of different theories can also be of assistance in the translation process itself. At the beginning of this chapter I presented a simple translation scene: a problem is identified, possible solutions are generated, and one solution is selected. That is a model (a set of related names-for-things), not a transcendent truth. In terms of my model, a plurality of theories can widen the range of potential solutions that translators think of. On the selective side, theories can also provide a range of reasons for choosing one solution and discarding the rest, as well as defending that solution when necessary. Some theories are very good for the ***generative*** side, since they criticize the more obvious options and make you think about a wider range of factors. Descriptive, deconstructionist, and cultural-translation approaches might all fit the bill there. Other kinds of theory are needed for the ***selective*** moment of translating, when decisions have to be made between the available alternatives. That is where reflections on ethics, on the basic purposes of translation, can provide guidelines. Unfortunately that second kind of theory, which should give reasons for selective decisions, has become unfashionable in some circles. That is why I indulge in plurality, to try to redress the balance.

1.5 HOW SHOULD TRANSLATION THEORIES BE STUDIED?

Since all translators are always theorizing, it would be quite wrong to separate the theory from the practice. The best uses of theory are in active discussions about different ways of solving translation problems. You can promote that kind of discussion on the basis of translations that you and others have already done. You will find that, at some points, one group of translators will disagree with another. If you are an instructor, get those groups to debate the point, then you suggest appropriate terms and concepts, once the students have found that they actually need those things. In this way, students come to theories only when they want to. Classes on individual theories or paradigms can then build on that practical basis.

Unfortunately our educational institutions tend to separate theory from practice, often demanding a separate course in "translation theory." If necessary, that can be done. However, the theories and their implications should still be drawn out from a series of practical tasks, structured as discovery processes. This book has been designed to allow such use. Toward the end of each chapter we list some "**frequently had arguments**," most of which do not have any clear resolution, and many of which are not really as frequent as we would like them to be. Then, at the end of each chapter we suggest some "**projects and activities**" that can be carried out in class or given as assignments. No solutions are given to the problems, and in many cases there *are* no correct solutions. Discussions and further suggested activities are available on the course website. Of course, the examples should always be adapted for use in a particular class. More important, the activities should be integrated into the learning process; they should probably come at the beginning of a class, rather than be used as appendage at the end.

In a sense, the challenge of this book is to work against its fixed written form. The real learning of theory, even for the self-learner, should be in dialogue and debate.

If anyone needs more, the **website associated with this course** (http://usuaris.tinet.cat/apym/publications/ETT/index.html) presents video lectures, supplementary materials, and links to social media where you can participate.

CHAPTER 2

Natural equivalence

This chapter begins from the idea that what we say in one language *can* have the same value (the same worth or function) when translated into another language. The relation between the start text and the translation is then one of equivalence ("equal value"), where "value" can be on the level of form, function, or anything in between. Equivalence does not say that languages are the same; it just says that values can be the same. The many theories that share that assumption can be fitted into a broad "equivalence paradigm," which can be broken down into two sub-paradigms. Here I focus on the sub-paradigm where the things of equal value are presumed to exist *prior* to anyone translating. In principle, this means it makes no difference whether you translate from language A into language B or vice versa: you should get the same value both ways. That "natural" equivalence will be opposed to what I will call "directional" equivalence in the next chapter. Natural equivalence stands at the base of a strong and robust body of thought, closely allied with Applied Linguistics. It is also close to what many translators, clients, and end-users believe about translation. It should be appreciated in all its complexity. On the one hand, theories of natural equivalence were an intellectual response to the structuralist concept of languages as world-views. On the other, they have produced lists of equivalence-maintaining solutions that try to describe what translators do. In this chapter I cover in some detail the list of translation solutions proposed by Vinay and Darbelnet (1958/1972). Such lists were, in their day, a substantial response to an important problem within structuralist linguistics.

The main points covered in this chapter are:

- Equivalence is a relation of "equal value" between a start-text segment and a target-text segment.
- Equivalence can be established on any linguistic level, from form to function.
- Natural equivalence is presumed to exist between languages or cultures prior to the act of translating.
- Natural equivalence should not be affected by directionality: it should be the same whether translated from language A into language B or the other way round.
- Structuralist linguistics, especially of the kind that sees languages as world-views, would consider natural equivalence to be theoretically impossible.

- The equivalence paradigm solves this problem by working at levels lower than language systems. This can be done by focusing on contextual signification rather than systemic meaning, by undertaking componential analysis, by assuming reference to a *tertium comparationis,* by assuming that deverbalization is possible, or by considering value to be markedness.

- Following Vinay and Darbelnet, there are several categorizations of the solutions by which equivalence can be maintained.

- The sub-paradigm of natural equivalence is historical, since it assumes the production of stable texts in languages that allow equal expressive capacity.

The term "equivalence," in various European languages, became a feature of Western translation theories in the second half of the twentieth century. Its heyday was in the 1960s and 1970s, particularly within the frame of structuralist linguistics. The term roughly assumes that, on some level, a start text and a translation can share the same value ("equivalence" means "equal value"), and that this assumed sameness is what distinguishes translations from all other kinds of texts. Within the paradigm, to talk about translations is to consider different kinds of equivalence. In the course of the 1980s, however, the equivalence paradigm came to be regarded as naïve or limited in scope. **Mary Snell-Hornby**, for example, jettisoned equivalence as presenting "an illusion of symmetry between languages which hardly exists beyond the level of vague approximations and which distorts the basic problems of translation" (1988: 22).

Here I take the unpopular view that the equivalence paradigm is richer than such quick dismissals would suggest. It merits a place alongside and within the more recent paradigms. This is because, if you look closely, the theorizing of equivalence has involved two competing conceptualizations, which here I call "natural" as opposed to "directional" equivalence. The intertwining duality of those notions allows for considerable subtlety in some past and present theories. It also creates confusion, not only in some of the theories of equivalence themselves but also in the many current arguments *against* equivalence.

2.1 NATURAL EQUIVALENCE AS A CONCEPT

Most discussions of equivalence concern typical misunderstandings. For instance, Friday the 13th is an unlucky day in English-language cultures but not in most other cultures. In Spanish, the unlucky day is *Tuesday* the 13th. So when you translate the name of that day, you have to know exactly what kind of information is required. If you are just referring to the calendar, then Friday will do; if you are talking about bad luck, then a better translation would probably be "Tuesday 13th" (actually "martes 13," or "martes y 13" in some varieties). The world is full of such examples. The color of death is mostly black in the West, mostly white in the East. A nodding head means agreement in western Europe, disagreement in Turkey. That is all textbook stuff.

The concept of equivalence underlies all these cases: they all presuppose that **a translation will have the same value** as (some aspect of) its corresponding start text. Sometimes the value is on the level of form (two words translated by two words); sometimes it is reference (Friday is always the day before Saturday); sometimes it is function (the function "bad luck on 13" corresponds to Friday in English, to Tuesday in Spanish). Equivalence need not say exactly which kind of value is supposed to be the same; it just says that equal value can be achieved on one level or another.

Equivalence is a very simple idea. Unfortunately it becomes quite complex, both as a term and as a theory.

As for the term, it seems that the first uses of "equivalence" in technical translation theory described the kind of relation that allows us to equate, more or less, the English "Friday the 13th" with the Spanish "martes 13." When Friday becomes Tuesday, the two terms are equivalent because they are considered to activate approximately the same cultural function. This is the sense in which **Vinay and Darbelnet** used the term *équivalence* in 1958, and **Vázquez-Ayora** referred to *equivalencia* in 1977. That is, for the initial period of equivalence theories, the term referred to only one kind of translation option (I shall soon look at the many alternative relations described by Vinay and Darbelnet). Equivalence was determined by function (the value "bad-luck day" in our example), which is precisely the opposite to what Snell-Hornby supposes when she talks about a "symmetry between languages." In this initial period, equivalence referred to what could be done at points where there was *no* symmetry between linguistic forms. Hence confusion.

Other theorists, particularly the American Bible scholar **Eugene Nida**, were soon formulating other kinds of equivalence. Nida might look at the Spanish "martes 13" and agree that there are two ways of rendering it: either as "Tuesday the 13th" or as "Friday the 13th." The first option would be "**formal equivalence**" (or "formal correspondence," since it corresponds to the *form* of what is said in Spanish), the second would be what Nida calls "**dynamic equivalence**" (or "functional equivalence," since it activates the same or similar cultural *function*). As soon as theorists started talking about different kinds of equivalence, the meaning of the term "equivalence" became much broader, referring to a relation of value on any level.

On the level of practice, things are scarcely simpler. Consider for a moment the television game shows that are popular all over the world. English audiences usually know a show called *The Price is Right*. In French this becomes *Le juste prix*, and in Spanish *El precio justo*. Equivalence between the names is not on the level of form (four words become three, and the rhyme has been lost), but it might operate on the level of function. In German the show became *Der Preis ist heiss*, which changes the semantics (it back-translates as "The price is hot," as in the children's game of rising temperatures when you approach an object). The German cleverly retains the rhyme, which could be what counts. It could be getting very warm in its approach to equivalence.

If you start picking up examples like this and try to say what stays the same and what has changed, you soon find that a translation can be equivalent to many different things. For example, in the game show *Who Wants to be a Millionaire?* the contestants have a series of "lifelines" in English, "jokers" in French and German, and a "comodín" (wild-card) in Spanish. Although those are all very different images or metaphors, they do have something in common. More intriguing is the fact that the reference to "millionaire" is retained even though different local currencies make the amount quite different. Given that the show format came from the United Kingdom, the American version should perhaps translate the pounds into dollars. This might give *Who Wants to Win $1,516,590?*—the title is decidedly less catchy. Equivalence was never really about exact values.

This is the point where it makes some sense to talk about what is "natural" in equivalence. Why does no one calculate the exact sum of money to be won? Because we need what is *usually* said in the target culture. If there is common agreement that the term "millionaire" functions only to say "more money than most of us can imagine possessing legally," then all you need is a common term corresponding to that very vague notion. The normal expression on one side should correspond to the normal expression on the other.

Of course, the theory becomes a little more sophisticated when we realize that not everything we find in texts is always "natural" or "common." If everything were common, the texts would be so boring there would be little reason to translate them. We might suppose that whatever is *uncommon* (or better, "marked") on one side can be rendered as something similarly rare ("marked") on the other. The notion of **markedness** says that some things are natural and others are less natural. It remains a theory of natural equivalence.

2.2 EQUIVALENCE VS. STRUCTURALISM

In the second half of the twentieth century, translation theorists dealt with this kind of problem against the background of structuralist linguistics. A strong line of thought leading from Wilhelm von Humboldt to Edward Sapir and Benjamin Whorf argued that **different languages express different views of the world**. This connected with the views of the Swiss linguist **Ferdinand de Saussure**, who in the early years of the twentieth century explained how languages form systems that are meaningful only in terms of the differences between the items. The word *sheep*, for example, has a value in English because it does not designate a cow (or any other animal) and it does not refer to *mutton*, which is the meat, not the animal (Saussure 1916/1974: 115). In French, on the other hand, the word *mouton* designates both the animal and the meat, both *sheep* and *mutton*.

Such relations between terms were seen as different "structures." Languages were considered to be systems comprising such structures. **Structuralism** said we should study those relations rather than try to analyze the things themselves. Do not look at actual sheep; do not ask what we want to do with those sheep. Just look at the relations, the structures. One should conclude, according to structuralist linguistics, that the words *sheep* and *mouton* have very different values. They thus cannot translate each other with any degree of certainty. In fact, since different languages cut the world up in very different ways, no words should be completely translatable out of their language system. Equivalence should not be possible.

That kind of linguistics is of little help to anyone trying to translate television game shows. It is not of greater help to anyone trying to understand how translations are actually carried out. So something must be wrong in the linguistics. As the French theorist **Georges Mounin** argued in the early 1960s, "if the current theses on lexical, morphological, and syntactic structures are accepted, one must conclude that translation is impossible. And yet translators exist, they produce, and their products are found to be useful" (1963: 5; my translation). Either translation did not really exist, or the dominant linguistic theories were inadequate. That is the point at which the main theories of equivalence developed. They tried to explain something that the linguistics of the day did not want to explain.

Think for a moment about the kinds of arguments that could be used here. What should we say, for example, to someone who claims that the whole system of Spanish culture (not just its language) gives meaning to "martes 13" (Tuesday the 13th) in a way that no English system could ever reproduce? *Martes y 13* was the stage name, for example, of a popular pair of television comedians. Or what do we say to a Pole who argues that, since the milk they bought had to be boiled before it could be drunk, their name for milk could never be translated by the normal English term *milk* (cf. Hoffman 1989)? In fact, if the structuralist approach is pushed, we can never be sure of understanding anything beyond our own linguistic and cultural system, let alone translating the little that we do understand.

Theories of equivalence then got to work. Here are some of the arguments used:

- **Signification**: Within linguistic approaches, close attention was paid to what is meant by "meaning." **Saussure** had actually distinguished between a word's "value" (which it has in relation to the language system) and its "signification" (which it has in actual use). To cite a famous example from chess, the *value* of the knight is the sum of all the moves it is allowed to make, whereas the *signification* of an actual knight depends on the position it occupies at any stage of a particular game. "Value" would thus depend on the language system (which Saussure called *langue*), while "signification" depends on the actual use of language (which Saussure termed *parole*). For theorists like **Coseriu**, those terms could be mapped onto the German distinction between **Sinn** (stable meaning) and **Bedeutung** (momentary signification). If translation could not reproduce the former, it might still convey the latter. French, for example, has no word for *shallow* (as in "shallow water"), but the signification can be conveyed by the two words *peu profond* ("not very deep") (cf. Coseriu 1978). The language structures could be different, but equivalence was still possible.
- **Language use**: Some theorists then took a closer look at the level of language use (*parole*) rather than at the language system (*langue*). Saussure had actually claimed there could be no systematic scientific study of *parole*, but theorists like the Swiss-German **Werner Koller** (1979/1992) were quite prepared to disregard the warning. If something like equivalence could be demonstrated and analyzed, then there were meaningful structures smaller than a *langue*.
- **Text levels**: Others stressed that translation operates not on isolated words but on whole texts, and texts have many linguistic layers. The Scottish linguist **John Catford** (1965) pointed out that equivalence need not be on all these layers at once, but could be "rank-bound." We might thus strive for equivalence to the phonetics of a text, to the lexis, to the phrase, to the sentence, to the semantic function, and so on. Catford saw that most translating operates on one or several of these levels, so that "in the course of a text, equivalence may shift up and down the rank scale" (1965: 76). This was a comprehensive and dynamic theory of equivalence.
- **Componential analysis**: A related approach, more within lexical semantics, was to list the values associated with a text item, and then see how many of them are found in the target-side equivalent. This kind of componential analysis might analyze *mouton* as "+ animal + meat − young meat (*agneau*)," *mutton* as "+ meat − young meat (lamb)," and *sheep* as "+ animal." You would make your translation selections in accordance with the components active in the particular text. We could go further: *lifeline* could be turned into something like "+amusing metaphor + way of solving a problem with luck rather than intelligence + no guarantee of success + need for human external support + nautical." The translations *joker* and *wild-card* reproduce at least three of the five components, and would thus be equivalent to no more than that degree. There is no

guarantee, however, that different people recognize exactly the same components, since values are constructed through interpretations.

All of those ideas are problematic. Yet all of them defended the existence of translation in the face of structuralist linguistics.

An example of comparative componential analysis

Comparative linguistics can provide ways of isolating semantic components. Bascom (2007) gives the following analysis of the potential equivalents *key* and the Spanish *llave*:

Wrench	Llave (inglesa)
Faucet	Llave (grifo)
Key	Llave (de casa)
Piano key	Tecla de piano
Computer key	Tecla de ordenador
Key of a code	Clave de un código
Key of music	Clave de música

According to this analysis, the Spanish *llave* would only correspond to the component "instrument for turning," *tecla* corresponds to the component "thing to press down," and *clave* is only an equivalent of *key* when an abstract or metaphorical sense is involved. This distinction between these components seems not to be made in English.

2.3 PROCEDURES FOR MAINTAINING NATURAL EQUIVALENCE

Another way to defend translation was to record and analyze the equivalents that can actually be found in the world. One of the most entertaining texts in translation theory is the introduction to **Vinay and Darbelnet**'s *Stylistique comparée du français et de l'anglais*, first published in 1958. The two French linguists are driving from New York to Montreal, noting down the street signs along the way:

> We soon reach the Canadian border, where the language of our forefathers is music to our ears. The Canadian highway is built on the same principles as the American one, except that its signs are bilingual. After SLOW, written on the road in enormous letters, comes LENTEMENT, which takes up the entire width of the highway. What an unwieldy adverb! A pity French never made an adverb just using the adjective LENT … But come to think of it, is LENTEMENT really the equivalent of SLOW? We begin to have doubts, as one always does when moving from one language to another, when our SLIPPERY WHEN WET reappears around a bend, followed by the French

GLISSANT SI HUMIDE. Whoal, as the Lone Ranger would say, let's pause a while on this SOFT SHOULDER, thankfully caressed by no translation, and meditate on this SI, this "if," more slippery itself than an acre of ice. No monolingual speaker of French would ever have come straight out with the phrase, nor would they have sprayed paint over the road for the sake of a long adverb ending in—MENT. Here we reach a key point, a sort of turning lock between two languages. But of course—*parbleu!*—instead of LENTEMENT [adverb, as in English] it should have been RALENTIR [infinitive, as in France]!

(1958/1972: 19; my translation)

What kind of equivalence is being sought here? The kind the linguists actually find is exemplified by the long French adverb "lentement," which says virtually the same thing as the English adverb "slow." It changes the length, but apparently there is room on the road. What worries the linguists is that the sign "Lentement" is not what the signs in France say. For them, the equivalent should be the verb "Ralentir," since that is what would have been used if no one had been translating from English (and if Canada were within France). This second kind of equivalence is thus deemed "natural." It is what different languages and cultures seem to produce from within their own systems. This natural equivalence is also ideally reciprocal, like ping-pong: "slow" should give "ralentir," which should give "slow," and so on.

Natural equivalents do exist, but rarely in a state of untouched nature. As the German theorist **Otto Kade** (1968) argued, they are mostly the stuff of terminology, of artificially standardized words that are *made* to correspond to each other. All specialized fields of knowledge have their terminologies; they unnaturally create "natural" equivalents. Vinay and Darbelnet, however, are seeking equivalents characterized as "natural" precisely because they are supposed to have developed without interference from meddling linguists, translators, or other languages. In terms of this naturalism, the best translations are found when you are not translating. You use this mode of thought whenever you look for solutions in "**parallel texts**" (non-translational target-language texts on the same topic as the source text).

In the late 1950s and 1960s, equivalence was often thought about in this way. The problem was not to show what the "thing" was or what you wanted to do with it (Vinay and Darbelnet probably should have asked what words were best at making drivers slow down). The problem was to describe ways equivalence could be attained in situations where there were no obvious natural solutions.

Vinay and Darbelnet worked from examples to define seven general "procedures" (*procédés*) that could be used. Since the things they classified were actually the textual *results* of the problem-solving process, here I shall call them "translation solutions." Table 2.1 is a version of the main solution types.

The seven solution types each come with examples on three levels of discourse. They go from the most literal (at the top) to the most re-creative (at the bottom). Vinay and Darbelnet describe this progression as being from the easiest to the most difficult, which makes some sense if we consider that the bottom situations are the ones where the translator probably has the most options to choose from.

Even though the linguists had no evidence of the steps a translator might take when solving translation problems, a simple model is nevertheless implied: the translator might first try the "literal" procedure, and if that does not work, they can either go up the table

Table 2.1 Vinay and Darbelnet's general table of translation solutions (my translation from Vinay and Darbelnet 1958/1972: 55)

	Lexis	Collocation	Message
1. Loan	Fr. Bulldozer Eng. Fuselage	Fr. Science-fiction Eng. À la mode	Fr. Five o'clock tea Eng. Bon voyage
2. Calque	Fr. Économiquement faible Eng. Normal School	Fr. Lutétia Palace Eng. Governor General	Fr. Compliments de la Saison Eng. Take it or leave it
3. Literal translation	Fr. Encre Eng. Ink	Fr. L'encre est sur la table Eng. The ink is on the table	Fr. Quelle heure est-il? Eng. What time is it?
4. Transposition	Fr. Expéditeur: Eng. From:	Fr. Depuis la revalorisation du bois Eng. As timber becomes more valuable	Fr. Défense de fumer Eng. No smoking
5. Modulation	Fr. Peu profond Eng. Shallow	Fr. Donnez un peu de votre sang Eng. Give a pint of your blood	Fr. Complet Eng. No vacancies
6. Correspondence (équivalence)	Fr. (milit.) La soupe Eng. (milit.) Tea	Fr. Comme un chien dans un jeu de quilles Eng. Like a bull in a china shop	Fr. Château de cartes Eng. Hollow triumph
7. Adaptation	Fr. Cyclisme Br.Eng. Cricket Am.Eng. Baseball	Fr. En un clin d'œil Eng. Before you could say Jack Robinson	Fr. Bon appetit! Am.Eng. Hi!

(closer to the start text) or down the table (closer to the target culture). This means that not all the solutions necessarily count as good ways to produce natural equivalence—in each case, translators are only required to do the best they can. For example, the use of **loans and calques** is only legitimate when there is not a more natural equivalent available (the examples in Table 2.1 are not meant to translate each other). "**Literal translation**," which here means fairly straightforward word-for-word processes, is quite possible between cognate languages but can also frequently be deceptive, since languages abound with "**false friends**" (lexical, phraseological and syntactic forms that look the similar but have different functions in different languages). Literalism is what gives the French *Lentement* as the equivalent of *Slow*, and that is not what Vinay and Darbelnet consider natural. The solutions of main interest to the linguists are **transposition** (where there is a switching of grammatical categories) and **modulation** (where adjustments are made for different discursive conventions). The remaining two solutions concern cultural adjustments: **correspondence** (actually called *équivalence* in the French version) would use all the corresponding proverbs and referents (like "Friday the 13th"), and **adaptation** would refer to different things with loosely equivalent cultural functions: cycling is to the French what cricket is to the British, or baseball to the Americans, we are told. At this end of the table there are many very vague equivalents available, and translators can spend hours exploring the possibilities (gardening is to the English what having lovers is to the Italians, perhaps). In all, Vinay and Darbelnet's solutions range from artificial or marked at one end to the vague but naturalistic at the other. The linguists were able to theorize the desirability of natural equivalence, but also implicitly recognized the practical need for translators to produce other kinds of solutions as well.

In addition to the list of general solutions, Vinay and Darbelnet outline a series of **"prosodic effects."** This gives a list of solutions operating closer to the sentence level. In most cases, the translator can be seen as following the constraints imposed by the target language, without many alternatives to choose between:

- **Amplification**: The translation uses more words than the source text to express the same idea. Example: "the charge against him" (four words) becomes "l'accusation portée contre lui" ("the charge brought against him," five words). When the amplification is obligatory, the effect is called **dilution**. Example: "le bilan" ("the balance") becomes "the balance sheet" (1958/1972: 183). This category also covers what Vinay and Darbelnet call **étoffement** (perhaps "completion" or "lengthening") (1958/1972: 109ff.), where a target-text word grammatically requires the support of another word. For example, "To the trains" becomes "Accès aux quais," where the preposition for "to" (à) grammatically needs the support of the noun meaning "access."
- **Reduction** (économie): The opposite of amplification (take the above examples in the opposite direction).
- **Explicitation**: The translation gives specifications that are only implicit in the start text (1958/1972: 9). Example: "students of St. Mary's" becomes "étudiantes de l'école St. Mary," where the French specifies that the students are women and St. Mary's is a school (1958/1972: 117).
- **Implicitation**: The opposite of explicitation (the directionality of the above example could be reversed, if it is common knowledge in the target culture that St. Mary's is a school for girls).
- **Generalization**: When a specific term is translated as a more general term. Example: "mutton" (the meat) becomes "mouton" (both the animal and the meat), or the American "alien" becomes "étranger" (which includes the concepts of both "foreigner" and "alien").
- **Particularization**: The opposite of *generalization* (reverse the above examples).

There are actually more terms than these in Vinay and Darbelnet. The above should nevertheless suffice to illustrate several points. First, the categories seem to be saying much the same thing: the translation can give more (amplification, explicitation, generalization) or less (reduction, implicitation, particularization). Second, these terms have been used throughout the equivalence paradigm, but in many different ways. **Kinga Klaudy** (2001), for example, uses **"explicitation"** to cover everything that is "more," and **"implicitation"** to cover everything that is "less." Third, the dominant factors in all these cases are the **systemic differences** between the start and the target languages. The individual translator does not really have a lot of choice. This is why the examples can all be read in both directions. Even when Vinay and Darbelnet claim that French is more "abstract" than English, so that there will be more generalization when translating into French, the difference is in order to preserve the equilibrium of the languages; it is not something that concerns the cognitive processes of the translator. To that extent, Vinay and Darbelnet consistently defend the virtues of natural equivalence.

There are quite a few theories that list solution types. Vinay and Darbelnet's work was inspired by **Malblanc** (1944/1963), who compared French and German. They in turn became one of the points of reference for **Vázquez-Ayora** (1977), who worked on Spanish and English. Different kinds of equivalence-maintaining procedures have been described in a Russian tradition including **Fedorov** (1953), **Shveitser** (1973/1987) and **Retsker** (1974), and by the American **Malone** (1988), all usefully summarized in Fawcett (1997). When Muñoz Martín compares several categorizations of translation solutions (Table 2.2), the most striking aspect is perhaps that there could be so many ways to cut up the same conceptual space. The terms for the solutions have clearly not been standardized. Then again, perhaps the best evidence for the existence of the sub-paradigm is the fact that these and many other linguists have agreed that this is the space where the terms and concepts are needed.

The lists of solution types tend to make perfect sense when they are presented along-side carefully selected examples. On the other hand, when you analyze a translation and you try to say exactly which solution types have been used where, you often find that several categories explain the same equivalence relation, and some relations do not fit comfortably into any category. Vinay and Darbelnet recognize this problem:

Table 2.2 Comparison of translation solution types, adapted from Muñoz Martín (1998)

Vinay and Darbelnet (1958)		Vázquez Ayora (1977)		Malone (1988)	
← more difficulty less →	Loan	Literal translation (← translation proper → less / more)		Matching	Equation $A \rightarrow E$
	Calque				Substitution $A \rightarrow S$
	Literal translation				
	Transposition	Oblique	Transposition	Reordering $AB \rightarrow BA$	
	Modulation		Modulation		
	Correspondence (équivalence)		Equivalencia		
	Adaptation		Adaptation		
Degree of difficulty not specified	Amplification	Secondary	Amplification	Recrescence	Amplification $A \rightarrow AB$
	Implicitation		Omission		Reduction $AB \rightarrow A$
	Compensation		Compensation		
	Explicitation		Explicitation	Repackaging	Diffusion $A \cap B \rightarrow A|B$
	Dilution				Condensation $A|B \rightarrow A \cap B$
	Particularization			Zigzagging	Divergence $A \rightarrow B/C$
	Generalization				Convergence $B/C \rightarrow A$

> The translation (on a door) of PRIVATE as DÉFENSE D'ENTRER [Prohibition to Enter] is at once a transposition, a modulation, and a correspondence. It is a transposition because the adjective *private* is rendered by a noun phrase; it is a modulation because the statement becomes a warning […] and it is a correspondence because the translation has been produced by going back to the situation without bothering about the structure of the English-language phrase.
>
> (1958/1972: 54; my translation)

If three categories explain the one phenomenon, do we really need all the categories? Or are there potentially as many categories as there are equivalents? This is a theoretical problem to which I will return in the next chapter.

Even more serious questions are raised when we try to apply these categories to translation between **European and Asian languages**. Let us go back to Table 2.1 and consider the classical list of solution types. Since they were working between French and English, Vinay and Darbelnet could more or less assume that the general default procedure is "literal translation," and only when that procedure does not work would the translator look for alternative solutions higher on the list ("loan" or "calque"), or harder solutions a little further down ("transposition," "modulation," etc.). Chinese, Japanese, and Korean, however, do not have the explicit syntactic relations of Germanic or Romance languages, so the default procedure is more usually at the level of "transposition" rather than "literal translation," and it is very difficult to make any consistent distinction between "transposition" and "modulation." At the same time, Japanese and Chinese (perhaps to a lesser extent Korean) are very open to borrowing when dealing with new "international" subject matter, so loans and calques become far more frequent and acceptable ways to produce equivalence in some fields. One of the results is that, if you are translating *from* Chinese into English in an international field, the source text seems to contain so many loans from English that it is hard to describe what you are doing with them—should we perhaps add a category for "loans returning to lender"? On the other hand, if we look at the top section of Table 2.1, the one term "loan" is clearly inadequate to situations where a translator might choose between transcription ("McDonald's" is written like that in many languages), script transformation ("Макдоналдс" is the name in Russian), and phonetic imitation (マクドナルド in Japanese). The classical linguistic theories of equivalence require more work if they are to be extended beyond cognate languages.

2.4 TEXT-BASED EQUIVALENCE

I have noted that **John Catford** (1965) saw equivalence as being mostly "**rank-bound**," in the sense that it is not established on all linguistic levels at the same time. As the translator moves along the text, the level of equivalence can shift up or down, from function to phrase to term to morpheme, for example, in accordance with the various constraints ensuing from the start text. Vinay and Darbelnet's catalogue of solution types (Table 2.1) does not contradict that view, since the solutions correspond to the same hierarchy of linguistic levels. Vinay and Darbelnet's preference is for movements downward, in order to enhance naturalness, but another theorist could legitimately argue for movements upward.

One of the most developed theories of this double-movement kind is by the Swiss-German theorist **Werner Koller**, whose textbook on "translation science" went through four editions and many reprints between 1979 and 1992. Koller proposes five frames for equivalence relations: **denotative** (based on extra-linguistic factors), **connotative** (based on the way the source text is expressed), **text-normative** (respecting or changing textual and linguistic norms), **pragmatic** (with respect to the receiver of the target text), and **formal** (the formal-aesthetic qualities of the source text). These categories suggest that the translator selects the type of equivalence most appropriate to the function dominant in the start text. This commanding role of the start text places Koller's general approach under the umbrella of "natural equivalence," since the start text determines when "pragmatic" equivalence is necessary.

The German theorist **Katharina Reiss** (1971/2000) was saying fairly similar things in the same years. Her approach recognizes three basic **text types** (informative, expressive, and operative) and she then argues that each type requires that equivalence be sought on the level corresponding to it (giving appropriate weight to content, form, or effect). Reiss's theory is traditionally classified as "functionalist" (see 4.2 below), but its basic approach is not entirely out of place here. As in Koller, the decisive factor is held to be none other than the nature of the source text.

2.5 REFERENCE TO A *TERTIUM COMPARATIONIS* AND THE "THEORY OF SENSE"

All these theories are rather vague about how natural equivalence works. They often assume there is a piece of reality or thought (a referent, a function, a message) that stands outside all languages and to which two languages can refer. That thing would be a third element of comparison, a **tertium comparationis**, available to both sides. The translator thus goes from the start text to this thing, then from the thing to the corresponding target text. Non-natural translations will result if you go straight from the source text to the target text, as when *Slow* is rendered as *Lentement*.

Perhaps the best-known account of this process was formulated by the Parisian theorist **Danica Seleskovitch**. For her, a translation can only be natural if the translator succeeds in forgetting entirely about the form of the start text. She recommends "listening to the sense," or "**deverbalizing**" the text so that you are only aware of the sense, which can be expressed in all languages. This is the basis of what is known as the **theory of sense** (*théorie du sens*) (Seleskovich and Lederer 1984). From our perspective, it is a process model of natural equivalence.

The great difficulty of this theory is that if a "sense" is deverbalized, how can we ever know what it is? As soon as we indicate it to someone, we have given it a semiotic form of some kind. And there are no forms (not even the little pictures or diagrams sometimes used) that can be considered truly universal. So there is no real way to prove that a "deverbalized sense" exists. "Listening to the sense" undoubtedly describes a mental state that simultaneous interpreters think they attain, but can what they are hearing really be a sense without form? This theory remains a weak metaphor with strong pedagogical virtues.

Note that process models like Seleskovitch's encourage translators *not* to look at linguistic forms in great detail, whereas the linguistic methods espoused by Vinay and Darbelnet and the like were based on comparing forms in two languages. Seleskovitch's ideal translator would move mentally from start form to universal sense, and then to the target form. Vinay and Darbelnet, however, implicitly model the translator as first selecting the translation that is closest to the start form, and only moving away from that literalism when necessary. Deverbalization or literalism, which model is the most correct? This might be the central argument of the natural equivalence paradigm. Research on the actual cognitive processes of translators might be able to decide the issue, but there are many factors involved: publicity might require something like deverbalization, technical translators might start from literalism, and work between European and Asian languages (operating at the default level of transposition and modulation) might require something between the two.

The sad fact is that not enough empirical research has been done to contrast and refine these very basic models. One of the reasons for this would seem to be that the "theory of sense" has been championed by the trainers of conference interpreters, while the comparative method has been developed almost exclusively by linguists, in a different academic world. The linguists would go on to compare not just isolated phrases and collocations, but also pragmatic discourse conventions and modes of text organization. Applied linguists like **Hatim and Mason** (1990, 1997) thus extend the level of comparison, but do not attempt to see what actually happens in the mind of the translator.

For the most idealistic natural equivalence, the ultimate aim is to find the pre-translational solution that reproduces all aspects of the thing to be expressed. Naturalistic approaches thus spend little time on defining translation; there is not much analysis of the limits of translation; there is no real consideration of translators having different aims. Those things have somehow been decided by equivalence itself. Translation is simply translation. But that is not always so.

2.6 THE VIRTUES OF NATURAL EQUIVALENCE

Natural equivalence is the basic theory in terms of which the other paradigms in this book will be defined. Its role is foundational, at least within the narrative that we are creating (soon we will see how historical the idea of natural equivalence actually is). All the following paradigms will be able to say bad things about natural equivalence. So let me quickly state a few of the good things that can be said about it:

1   In a context where structuralism seemed to make translation theoretically impossible, natural equivalence defended translation as a vital social practice.
2   In a period of abstract speculation about structures, systems, and meaning, the theorists of natural equivalence went out to see what could be done with actual language. If you look at virtually any of the theorists mentioned here, you find that their books are full of examples.
3   To give order to the data thus obtained, the theorists usually provided lists of solutions actually used by translators. These results have proved to be of use in the training of translators.
4   Although notions such as "same value," "*tertium comparationis*," or "deverbalization" are very idealistic, their operational functions correspond to some very widespread ideas about what a translation is. If there is a general consensus among professionals and clients that a translator should reproduce natural equivalence (no matter what the actual terms used), then a theory that expresses that expectation is serving a social function. Only when we have terms for the consensus can we start to test its viability.

2.7 FREQUENTLY HAD ARGUMENTS

Here I summarize the main debates touched on so far. You might like to decide whether you agree with these criticisms.

2.7.1 "Natural equivalence presupposes a non-existent symmetry"

At the beginning of this chapter we saw Mary Snell-Hornby criticize equivalence as presenting "an illusion of symmetry between languages." We might now like to see her criticism as stating the position of all the structuralist linguists that see different languages dividing up the world in different ways. Does natural equivalence deny that fact? Probably not, at least not if we look at the range of procedures formulated by Vinay and Darbelnet, or if we follow the theories of "marked" vs. "unmarked," or if componential analysis is used to describe the differences as well as the similarities between languages. On the other hand, Snell-Hornby might be referring to supposed symmetries of functions, in which case her point appears valid: theorists of natural equivalence tend to assume that all languages have the same expressive capacity (see 2.8 below).

2.7.2 "The tests of equivalence have no psychological basis"

Methods like componential analysis or the identification of solution types can to some extent explain the equivalent pairs that we find, but they cannot claim to represent the way translators actually think. As argued by **Jean Delisle** (1988: 72–3), they are linguistic explanations without any reference to translators' cognitive processes. This means that their use in pedagogical situations could be misleading and even counter-productive. Similar questions should be asked about the empirical status of "deverbalization."

2.7.3 "New information cannot be 'natural' "

If translations are supposed to bring in information that is *new* to a language or culture, then they cannot be expected to be "natural." Since new things will eventually require new terms and expressions, the translations are going to be marked in ways that their start texts are not. This argument usually becomes a question for terminology: should the translation use loans from the start text, or should new terms be invented from resources considered "natural" in the target language? The ideology of natural equivalence would certainly prefer the latter, but the speed of technological change and imbalances between languages are pushing translators to make use of loans and the like, particularly from English. There is little evidence that languages are suffering directly because of it. Languages tend to die when they receive no translations at all.

2.7.4 "Naturalness hides imperialism"

If a translation brings a culture a new way of thought, any attempt to present that thought as being "natural" is fundamentally deceptive. Can Nida really pretend that the Christian

God was already in the non-Christian cultures into whose languages the Bible is trans-lated? When the "lamb of God" becomes a "seal of God" for Inuit readers, the New Testament ceases to refer to first-century Palestine. The nature of the start text is thus concealed, the Inuit readers are deceived, and we have an ideological "illusion of symmetry" far stronger than anything Snell-Hornby was criticizing. At that point, translation has been reduced to the problem of marketing a product (for criticisms of Nida along these lines, see Meschonnic 1973, 2003 and Gutt 1991/2000).

2.7.5 "Naturalness promotes parochialism"

Although equivalence could conceivably be based on the literalist level of the source text or on "functions" of some kind, the sub-paradigm of natural equivalence mostly favors translations that do not read like translations. **Ernst-August Gutt** (1991/2000), for instance, argues that "equivalent function" produces an illusory naturalness, which mislead-ingly presents the translation as if it were a non-translation. It is better, for him, to look for equivalents that make the reader work. One variant of the anti-domestication argument is found in the American translator and critic **Lawrence Venuti** (particularly 1998), who is concerned not so much with the ways minor cultures are deceived but with the effects that naturalness ("fluency") has on the way major cultures see the rest of the world. If all cultures are made to sound like contemporary fluent English, then Anglo-American culture will believe that the whole world is like itself. For Venuti, a non-natural ("resistant") translation should therefore use forms that are not frequent in the target language, whether or not those forms are equivalent to anything in the source text. At that point the argument prima-rily concerns how one should write, and only secondarily how one should translate.

Most of these points will be developed in future chapters.

2.8 NATURAL EQUIVALENCE AS A HISTORICAL SUB-PARADIGM

To close this chapter, I should insist that natural equivalence is a profoundly historical idea. Notions of "equal value" presuppose that different languages do or can express values that can be compared in some itemized way. This need not mean that all languages look and sound the same; it need not involve an "illusion of symmetry." But it does assume that different languages are somehow on the same level.

That assumption is easily made with respect to our contemporary national languages: English, French, Russian, Arabic, Japanese, or Hindi are by no means symmetrical but they have roughly the same ranking in terms of expressive capacities. No one is seriously arguing that any of these are inherently inferior to the others. However, if we did believe that a language was inferior, or perhaps systematically less developed in some area of discourse, how could we defend natural equivalence as an ideal for translation into that language?

Belief in the equal values of languages was quite rare in European theorizing prior to the Renaissance. Much of medieval thinking assumed a **hierarchy of languages**, where some were considered intrinsically better than others. At the top were the languages of divine revelation (Biblical Hebrew, New Testament Greek, Arabic, sometimes Sanskrit), then the languages of divinely inspired translation (the Greek of the Septuagint, the Latin of the Vulgate), then the national vernaculars, then the patois or regional dialects. This usually meant that translation was seen as a way of **enriching the target language** with the values of a superior source language. Most translations went downward in the hierarchy, from Hebrew or Greek to Latin, or from Latin to the vernaculars. For as long as the hierarchy existed, claims to equivalence (certainly without the term) played little role in thought on translation.

For roughly parallel historical reasons, the basic idea of equivalence was difficult to maintain prior to the age of the **printing press**. Before printing, the start text was not a stable entity. Texts tended to undergo constant incremental changes in the process of copying (each copyist adapted and changed things), and those small changes followed the numerous variations of regional dialects, prior to the standardization of national vernaculars. There was usually not just one "source text" waiting to be translated. There would be a range of different manuscripts, with layer upon layer of different receptions inscribed in those manuscripts. Translation could be seen as an extension of that process. Why try to be equivalent if there is nothing stable to be equivalent to?

Printing and the rise of standardized vernaculars helped the conceptualization of equivalence. True, the term "equivalence" was not used. In its place you usually find talk of "fidelity," often to an author, but also to a sense, intention, or function that could be found in a fixed text.

In accordance with this same logic, the relative demise of equivalence as a concept could correspond to the electronic technologies by which contemporary texts are constantly evolving, primarily through updating (think of websites, software, and product documentation). Without a fixed text, what should a translation be equivalent to? For that matter, in the age of international English and strong national vernaculars, have we not created a new hierarchy of languages (see 7.8 below)?

Seen in this historical light, natural equivalence cannot really provide any guarantee of a "true" or "valid" translation. Yet its power as a concept remains strong.

SUMMARY

This chapter started by defending the equivalence paradigm against those who reduce it to a belief that all languages are structured the same way. The chapter nevertheless finishes with a rather negative assessment. I have indicated some of the things the sub-paradigm of natural equivalence tends to leave out; I have argued that the ideal of pre-existing equivalence is based on the historical conditions of print culture and national vernacular languages; we have seen that the commonsensical notion of "equal value" only had intellectual validity in opposition to the structuralist belief in languages as world-views; I have noted how natural equivalence can be described as illusory and deceptive. Those critical evaluations certainly do not mean that the concept of natural equivalence can simply be forgotten. Perhaps the most important things to retain from it are the solution types and modes of analysis. Terms like "modulation," "explicitation," "compensation," "markedness," and "componential analysis" form the basic metalanguage of linguistic approaches. They must be known and understood. Indeed, the debates over natural equivalence concern most of the central problems of the Western translation form, and do so in ways that are not always naïve. Once you have grasped its basic principles, all the other paradigms can be seen as responses to it.

SOURCES AND FURTHER READING

The third edition of *The Translation Studies Reader* (Venuti 2012) has only a text by Nida to represent equivalence (Vinay and Darbelnet and Catford were in earlier editions but disappeared), which might indicate how mainstream theory has moved away from the beliefs operative in professional practice. Munday (2012) places Vinay and Darbelnet and Catford in the chapter on "product and process," which for me belongs to the descriptive paradigm. The basic theories of natural equivalence are well summarized in Peter Fawcett's *Translation and Language: Linguistic Theories Explained* (1997). The classical texts are often still available and remain very readable. A good library should have Catford (1965), Vinay and Darbelnet (1958 and subsequent editions; English translation in 1995), and something of Nida (the general theory is in *Toward a Science of Translating*, 1964). Critics of natural equivalence are nowadays abundant. Very few of them, however, have taken the trouble to read the foundational texts in detail, or to understand the intellectual climate in which the sub-paradigm developed.

Suggested projects and activities

The following are general suggestions for what can be done in the classroom, or for fun. In some cases, the activities are aimed at consolidating awareness of the theories presented in this chapter. In other cases, they raise awareness of problems that will be picked up in the next few chapters.

1   Consider this definition of translation: "Translating consists in *reproducing* in the receptor language the *closest natural equivalent* of the source-language message" (Nida and Taber 1969: 12). What should happen when the start text contains items that are supernatural or specific to an ancient culture? Find examples in any passage from the Old Testament.

2   Consider the road signs in your language. Which of them result from natural equivalence? (Think about "Stop," for a start.)

3   The following is a Dominican friar giving orders in recently conquered Mexico:

   I hereby order that all friars in this house, whether in sermons, catechisms, private talk among themselves, with secular Spaniards or with Indians, shall refrain from using the name *Cabahuil* or *Chi*, or whatever else may be the case, but shall use the name *Dios* ["God" in Spanish] to explain to the natives the nature of the one true God.

   (Cited by Remesal 1966: 2.277; my translation)

   Which name *should* the missionaries have used for God?

4   Use Google Translate to do back-translations several times (e.g. moving from English to Chinese to English to Chinese, for the one text). What happens to equivalence? What translation procedures are involved? What procedures are needed to improve the translations?

5   Select a term you find complex and problematic. Locate or propose several possible translations of it. Now attempt a componential analysis of the term's

function in its context. How many of the components are found in the translations? How many have been lost? What gains have been made?

6   For the same term, select its most frequent equivalent and do a comparative analysis of both, as in the example of *key* vs. *llave* above. Does the comparative analysis reveal semantic components that were not clear when you only looked at the start language?

7   The Italian version of the game show *Who Wants to be a Millionaire?* was called *Chi vuol esser miliardario?* (Who Wants to be a Billionaire?) in 1999, then became *Chi vuol esser milionario?* (Who Wants to be a Millionaire?). Why the change? What kind of equivalence is this?

8   Check the names of game shows in your languages. How many of them look natural? Do a web search to see how many of them are actually translations. What kind of equivalence can explain them?

9   Consider the terms used in your languages for websites, webpages, and Internet technology. How many of these terms are obviously translations? How many would count as "natural" translations? Can you describe the procedures by which they were produced (check the terms used in Table 2.1 above)? Is there a difference between the official terms and the ones people commonly use?

10   Consider the terms used in your languages for a "USB drive," "pen drive," "memory stick," or combinations of these. Is there a standard English term from which your language has translated? Is "natural equivalence" still working when there are several competing terms in the start language? Who did the translations?

CHAPTER 3

Directional equivalence

This chapter looks at a set of theories that are based on equivalence but do *not* assume that the relation is natural or reciprocal. For these theories, if you translate from language A into language B, and then back-translate from language B into language A, the result in language A need not be the point you started from. This means that *directionality* is a key feature of translational equivalence, and that translations are thus the results of active *decisions* made by translators. Whereas the sub-paradigm of natural equivalence develops categories of translation solutions, the sub-paradigm of directional equivalence tends to have only two opposed poles, for two extreme ways of translating (usually "free" vs. "literal," although there are many variants). Since translators must decide how they are going to translate, there is no guarantee that two translations of the same text will ever be the same. This logic will be seen at work in theories of similarity, in Kade's typology of equivalence, and in the classical dichotomies of translation strategies. The chapter closes with a short presentation of relevance theory, which remains a theory of equivalence, and a consideration of equivalence as a functional social illusion: what people believe about equivalence may be more important than any actual testing of its existence.

The main points covered in this chapter are:

■ Directional equivalence is an *asymmetric* relation where the creation of an equivalent by translating one way does not imply that the same equivalence will be created when translating the other way.

■ Theories of directional equivalence allow that the translator has a choice between several translation solutions, and that those solutions are not wholly dictated by the start text.

■ The solutions for directional equivalence tend to be expressed in terms of two opposed poles, where one pole stays close to the start-text form and the other modifies that form. For example, "formal correspondence" is opposed to "dynamic equivalence."

■ Although there are usually more than two ways of translating, the reduction to two is part of the way translation has been seen in Western tradition. The two polarities ensue from an assumed cultural and linguistic border.

■ Directional equivalence can describe the way a translation represents its start text. This concerns categories like "illusory" vs. "anti-illusory"

(Levý), where an "illusory" translation does not show itself to be a translation.

- Relevance theory can be used to describe the beliefs that people have about translations. Equivalence is a belief in "interpretative resemblance" (Gutt).
- Equivalence can also be seen as a social fiction that promotes trust in cross-cultural communication.

I cheated in the previous chapter. I left out one of the very important solution types presented by Vinay and Darbelnet:

- **Compensation**: "Procedure whereby the tenor of the whole piece is maintained by playing, in a stylistic detour, the note that could not be played in the same way and in the same place as in the source" (1958/1972: 189). For example, French must choose between the intimate and formal second-person pronouns (*tu* or *vous*); contemporary English cannot. To render the distinction, where pertinent, the translator might opt for a switch from the family name to the given name, or to a nickname, as in "My friends call me Bill," to render "On se tutoie ..." (meaning, "We can use the intimate second-person pronoun ..."). Compensation can also be used to indicate various points of emphasis (for example, italics being used in English to render a syntactic emphasis in French), or to render a switch from one linguistic variety to another (examples can be found in Fawcett 1997).

I left compensation out because it stretches the limits of what might be considered "natural" equivalence. When the use of the intimate second person in French is rendered as "Call me Bill," there is an underlying faith that the two languages both have the capacity to express intimate vs. formal relations, but there is no guarantee that "Call me Bill" will be rendered back into French as "On se tutoie." It could be rendered in any number of ways. So here we have a new kind of problem: a certain kind of solution works in one direction, but not necessarily in the other. We are dealing with a peculiarly *directional* kind of equivalence.

When you look closely, this kind of directional equivalence can creep into other parts of Vinay and Darbelnet as well. Consider their example of **explicitation** where "students at St. Mary's" become explicitly female students in the French translation (since the language obliges the noun to be male or female). Compare this with a much-discussed example from **Hönig and Kussmaul** (1982/1996), where the term "Eton" is rendered into German as "eine der englischen Eliteschulen" ("one of the elite English schools"—see 4.4 below). This could be considered amplification, since it uses more words to convey the idea, and explicitation, since it makes explicit the information that English readers might attach to the term "Eton." The added information, though, is not really in search of natural equivalence, and it is not properly considered "explicitation" in the sense in which Vinay and Darbelnet use the term. This is because the **directionality** is not reciprocal (cf. Folkart 1989). You can get from the English to the German with some surety, but will the phrase "one of the elite English schools" necessarily bring you back to "Eton"? Probably not, given that there are quite a few schools to choose from. Directionality is playing a far more important role here, since we have started to think about what the *users* of the translation might actually need to know. That is something that theories of natural equivalence are aware of but do not systematically take into account—it is there in the examples but not picked up in the process of theorization. We are dealing with a kind of equivalence that has flourished in a slightly different kind of theorization.

3.1 TWO KINDS OF SIMILARITY

The English translation scholar **Andrew Chesterman** (1996, 2005) argues that the relation between translations and their start texts can be understood in terms of **similarity** rather than equivalence. He points out that there are different kinds of similarity. We might say, for example, that although translations are commonly supposed to be "like" their start texts, those start texts are not always held to be "like" their translations. This is strange. The relation "to be like" can be thought of in two ways. On the one hand, the same quality is considered to be equally present on both sides, so "Friday the 13th" in English is like "martes 13" in Spanish, and the same relation can be seen the other way round. On the other hand, we can say that a daughter is like her mother (in the sense that she "takes after" her mother), but we would not usually say that a mother is like her daughter (chronologically, it is unlikely that she would "take after" her daughter). In this second case, the relation is *asymmetric*, with different roles and expectations being placed on the two sides.

Chesterman sees these relations as two different kinds of similarity. He represents "**divergent similarity**" as:

$$A \rightarrow A', A'' \{\ldots\}$$

This might be the way the translator sees the task of translating: a new text is produced, which is like its start text in some respects, but it does not replace it (texts continue to exist), and it is only one of many possible representations (alternative renditions are imaginable, and there may be other translations in the future). What is most obvious here is the *directionality* that leads from start to translation, as from mother to daughter, and does not work the same way the other way round.

Chesterman then presents "**convergent similarity**" as:

$$A \leftrightarrow B$$

This might be the way a translation is seen by its receiver, in the expectation that what they seek in A is also in B. This is the case of "Friday the 13th" and "martes 13."

Chesterman suggests that these similarity relations might be able to replace theories of equivalence. We might also ask if theories of equivalence have long dealt with these kinds of relations, albeit without the names.

According to the ideals of "natural" equivalence, the relation between terms should work in the same way as "convergent similarity," operating equally well in both directions. You should be able to go from "Friday the 13th" to "martes 13" and then back exactly to "Friday the 13th." And yet there is surely another kind of equivalence that comes into play as soon as we allow that, under some circumstances, a translator could opt for "Tuesday the 13th" in English (perhaps to explain something about Hispanic culture). This might then be rendered back into Spanish as "martes 13" (Tuesday the 13th), but it could also conceivably lead to "viernes 13" (Friday the 13th). Whatever you put will be one of a series of possibilities. In this second set of circumstances, natural equivalence is no longer supplying the same measure of certitude. We have entered the world of asymmetric relations, where one-way movements look like Chesterman's "divergent similarity." I suspect there are many theories that see equivalence (not so much similarity) as being characterized by this same directionality.

If natural equivalence forms one side of the equivalence paradigm, "directional equivalence" would be the other.

3.2 DIRECTIONALITY IN DEFINITIONS OF EQUIVALENCE

From the late 1950s, many definitions of translation have referred to equivalence, especially within Applied Linguistics. We have already seen one of those definitions:

> Translating consists in *reproducing* in the receptor language the *closest natural equivalent* of the source-language message.
>
> (Nida and Taber 1969: 12; italics mine)

Consider this in terms of **directionality**. Note that the term "equivalent" is only "of the source-language message," so there is no question of that original message being the equivalent of the translation. In that sense, the concept of equivalence would appear to be directional. At the same time, however, the verb "reproducing" suggests that the natural equivalent actually exists prior to the act of translation, in the make-up of the languages or cultures themselves. To that extent, the definition retains some of the idealism of natural equivalence. In other words, the mode of thought seems to be both natural and directional, at the same time.

We can try this kind of analysis on a few more of the early definitions (italics mine):

> Translation may be defined as follows: the *replacement* of textual material in one language (SL) by *equivalent material* in another language (TL).
>
> (Catford 1965: 20)

> [Translation] *leads* from a source-language text to a target-language text which is *as close an equivalent as possible* and presupposes an understanding of the content and style of the original.
>
> (Wilss 1982: 62).

Look closely at the definitions. In each case, the term "equivalent" describes one side only, the target side. The processes ("replace," "lead," and "reproduce" in the example from Nida and Taber) are directional: translation goes from one side to the other, but not back again. Similar definitions abound. So the directionality that Chesterman finds in relations of similarity can also be found in some theories of equivalence.

I will use the term "directional equivalence" to refer to all those cases where an equivalent is located on one side more than the other, at least to the extent that the theories forget to tell us about movements that could go either way. "Natural equivalence" then refers to theories that assume the possibility of an equally balanced two-way movement.

Both kinds of theory would seem to fall within the one paradigm, since there appear to have been no major disputes between the two camps. For example, both naturalness and directionality have to be used if we are to cover all the things that happen to the names of game shows (check how often the term "millionaire" implicitly refers to English-language dreams). Or again, when Vinay and Darbelnet present their list of translation solutions (Table 2.1), the examples go roughly from directional at the top to naturalness at the bottom. The theorists wanted to focus on natural equivalence (and the inner natures of French and English), but they were quite happy to enlist examples that were telling a slightly different story.

Now, if we take the above definitions and we ask what the target-side equivalent is actually equivalent to, we find an interesting array of answers: "material," "the message," "source-language text." The theories in this group would seem to agree on some things (target-side equivalents, directionality) but not on others (the nature of the thing to translate). Their debates are not about equivalence itself, but about the nature and location of value.

In any theory, look for the definition of translation and try to see what it is assuming, then what it is omitting. What you find often indicates the strengths and weaknesses of the whole theory. In this case, the strength of the definitions, whether based on naturalness or directionality, is that they have the one term ("equivalent") that distinguishes translation from all the other things that can be done in interlingual communication (rewriting, commentary, summary, parody, etc.). The weakness is that they mostly do not explain why this relation should just be one-way in some cases, or two-way in others. Further, they are often in doubt as to whether the equivalent is equal to a value within a language, to a message, to a text with content and style, to an effect, or to all those things but at different times.

Do relations of equivalence really have to be one-way? The question was raised many years ago in an elegant piece of theorizing by the Leipzig scholar **Otto Kade**. Kade (1968) proposed that equivalence at the level of the word or phrase comes in four modes: "**one-to-one**," as in the case of stable technical terms; "**one-to-several**," when translators have to choose between alternatives (as in our "lifeline" example); "**one-to-part**," when the available equivalents are only partial matches, or "**one-to-none**," when translators have to create a new solution (coining neologisms or perhaps borrowing the foreign term, as in the upper part of Vinay and Darbelnet's table). Kade describes one-to-one relationships as "**total equivalence**" and considers the clearest examples to be technical terms—for me, they involve a decision process that is more pertinent to terminology and phraseology than to translating as such. Those relationships are obviously two-way: you can go from language A to language B and then back to A. They fit in with the ideal of natural equivalence. The "one-to-several" and "one-to-part" cases, however, should be **directional**, since there is no guarantee that the return will bring you back to the same place. Kade sees "one-to-several" equivalence as being "**choice-based**" (*fakultativ* in German), while "one-to-part" equivalence is considered "**approximate**" (*approximativ*). As for the "one-to-none" kind of problem, it should be even more directional.

Kade's overarching theory is ultimately of the directional type, since he limits absolute reciprocity to technical terms (probably the least "natural" pieces of language you can find). This effectively embeds "natural equivalence" as a special case within the "directional" model, incorporating one mode of theorization within the other. (Later we will see the *Skopos* approach do the same thing with the entire equivalence paradigm.)

Kade's types of equivalence

Kade (1968) proposes four types of equivalence. The following are our terms for the types, with possible examples:

■ *One-to-one* (*Eins-zu-Eins*): One start-language item corresponds to one target-language item: English *lion* corresponds to German *Löwe*, and this relation may be considered "total equivalence" for as long as neither culture has intimately different relations with lions. The surer examples are technical terms like the names of chemical elements.

■ *One-to-several or several-to-one* (*Viele-zu-Eins*): An item in one language corresponds to several in the other language. There are two ways to understand this. For example, the English word *key* corresponds to *llave, tecla*, and *clave* in Spanish (see 2.2 above). In context, however, the translator will usually know what kind of key is being referred to and will have few real choices to make. A different example would be the Spanish term *competencia* (domain of activity exclusive to a governmental or administrative organism), which could be rendered by "responsibility," "mandate," "domain," "competence," and so on. Unless a one-to-one equivalent has been established in a certain situation (e.g. *competencia = competence*), the translator will have to choose between the alternatives. The result will be "choice-based equivalence."

■ *One-to-part* (*Eins-zu-Teil*): Only partial equivalents are available, resulting in "approximate equivalence." For example, the English term *brother* has no full equivalent in Chinese, Japanese, or Korean, since the corresponding terms have to specify whether the brother is older or younger. Whichever choice is made, the equivalence will only be "approximate."

■ *One-to-none* (*Eins-zu-Null*): No equivalent is available in the target language. For example, most languages did not have a term for a *computer* a century ago. When that term had to be translated, the translators could use a circumlocution (a phrase to describe the object), they could generate a term from within the target language (e.g. French *ordinateur* and Iberian Spanish *ordenador*), or they could borrow the form of the English term (e.g. German *Computer*, Danish *computer*, Bulgarian *компютър*, or Latin American Spanish *computadora*). Some cultures prefer to import or represent foreign terms; others prefer to generate new terms from their own existing resources.

3.3 BACK-TRANSLATION AS A TEST

To see whether an equivalent is natural or directional, the simplest test is back-translation. This means taking the translation and rendering it back into the start language, then comparing the two start-language versions. When natural equivalence prevails, you can go from *Friday* to *viernes* then back to *Friday*, and it makes no difference which term is the start and which the translation. This is because the correspondence existed in some way prior to the act of translation. More to the point, the transfer of the Judeo-Christian seven-day week occurred several millennia before our act of translation, so the original directionality has now come to appear natural. That **naturalness is certainly an illusion** (in historical terms, all equivalents are probably the result of as much force and authority as is assumed in Kade's one-to-one technical terms). Yet the illusion has had a strong ideological pull on many translation theories. On the level of bad luck, you can go from "Friday the 13th" to "martes 13" and back again, and you can make people believe that the equivalence is somehow written into the nature of our cultural systems. The same kind of test might work for *Le juste prix*, and even for *Der Preis ist heiss*, if we define carefully the levels we are operating on. But the back-testing cannot be extended all the way. For example, what about the "lifelines" that become "jokers" and "wild-cards" but could become many other things as well? Can they also be justified as being in any way natural? For that matter, what should we say about the "Friday the 13th" that is recognized in Taiwan (I am told) not because it was always in the culture but because it traveled there in the title of a horror film? Some kinds of equivalence refer to what is done in a language prior to the intervention of the translator (hence the illusion of the natural); others refer to what transla-tors *can* do in the language (hence the directionality of the result).

"Directional" and "natural" are the terms I am using here to describe the different concepts elaborated by theories of translation; they are not words used by the theories themselves. They nevertheless help make some sense of a confusing terrain. As we have seen, most of the questions coming from structuralist linguistics concern strictly *natural* equivalence, or the search for it. When I mentioned Saussure's *sheep* and *mouton*, I talked about the words "translating each other." The same would hold for Polish milk and universal bad-luck days. For that linguistic paradigm, it should make no difference which of the terms is the start and which is the target. For the above definitions of translation, on the other hand, equivalence is something that results from a directional movement.

Reference to directionality was perhaps the most profound way in which the problem of structuralist linguistics was solved.

3.4 POLARITIES OF DIRECTIONAL EQUIVALENCE

Most theories of directional equivalence do not list solutions or linguistic levels (as in theo-ries based on natural equivalence) but instead separate different *kinds* of equivalence. They also talk about different kinds of translating, which amounts to much the same thing, since you translate quite differently depending on the level at which you want equivalence to work.

Many of the theories here are based on just two types of equivalence, sometimes presented as a straight dichotomy (you can translate one way *or* the other). That general approach goes as far back as **Cicero**, who conceptualized the one text as being translated from Greek into Latin in two different ways—**ut interpres** (like a literalist interpreter) or **ut orator** (like a public speaker) (Cicero 46CE/1996). That is, literally or freely. Note that the distinction need *not* map onto any profound difference between "natural" and "direc-tional" equivalence. If anything, the freer translation is likely to be the most "natural" in the target language, whereas the more literal translation is the one most likely to give recip-rocal directionality—but there is no guarantee. This is why I see the dichotomy as part of a directional theory of translation, since Cicero was not particularly concerned with anyone translating speeches from Latin back into Greek. The important point is that the naming of those two different ways necessarily assumes that some value remains constant between them; the results are different translations of the same thing. That was a fundamental conceptualization of equivalence, although without the term.

Dichotomies like Cicero's are found throughout Western translation theory. The German preacher and translator **Friedrich Schleiermacher** (1813/1963) argued that translations could be either **foreignizing** (*verfremdend*) or **domesticating** (*verdeutschend,* "Germanizing"). He famously described the two possible movements as follows: "Either the translator leaves the author in peace, as much as possible, and moves the reader toward that author, or the translator leaves the reader in peace, as much as possible, and moves the author toward that reader" (1813/1963: 63; my translation). Although Schleiermacher's preference was for the foreignizing option, whereas Cicero's was for the *ut orator* or domesticating method, both approaches recognize the possibility of a choice.

Perhaps the best-known of these theories was developed by the American linguist and Bible scholar **Eugene Nida**. This could seem paradoxical, since we have seen Nida's view of translation as incorporating naturalness. His examples, however, clearly show that the Bible can be translated to achieve either "**formal equivalence**" (following the words and textual patterns closely) or "**dynamic equivalence**" (trying to recreate the *function* the words might have had in their original situation). As we have seen, the term *Agnes Dei* can become the "lamb of God" that we know in English-language Christianity, but it might also become the "seal of God" for an Inuit culture that knows a lot about seals but does not have many lambs. The latter translation would be an extreme case of directional "dynamic equivalence"—there is no guarantee that seals will bring you back to lambs. On the other hand, the name "Bethlehem" means "House of Bread" in Hebrew, so it might be translated that way if we wanted to achieve dynamic equivalence on that level. In that case, our Bible translators traditionally opt for formal equivalence, even when they use dynamic equivalence elsewhere in the same text. (Of course, things are never quite that easy: the Arabic for Bethlehem, Beit Lahm, means "House of Meat"—so to whose name are we to be equivalent?)

Nida's definitions claim to be seeking a "natural" equivalent, which would be more on the dynamic side than the formal one. That is indeed his general ideological preference, since dynamic equivalence, the illusion of the natural, is well suited to evangelical purposes. At one stage Nida toyed with Chomsky's idea of "kernel phrases" as the *tertium comparationis*, the underlying third thing to which the start and target segments should both be equivalent. Yet Nida's practical applications remain remarkably directional. Nida was mostly talking about translating the Bible into the languages of cultures that are not traditionally Christian. What "natural" equivalent should one find for the name of Jesus or God in a language where they have never been mentioned? Most solutions actually concern a *directional* search for equivalence, not a natural one.

A similar kind of dichotomy is found in the English translation critic **Peter Newmark** (1988), who distinguished between "**semantic**" and "**communicative**" translation. The semantic kind of translation would look back to the formal values of the start text and retain them as much as possible; the communicative kind would look forward to the needs of the new addressee, adapting to their needs as much as necessary. Newmark's preferences tend to lie on the "semantic" side, especially with respect to what he terms "authoritative texts." In theory, however, translators can choose whether to render one aspect or another. There is no necessary assumption of just one "natural" equivalent, and the result is a generally directional theory.

These theoretical dichotomies are often presented as the ways translators work. They are obviously not on the same level as the lists of solution types we find in theories of natural equivalence. Here the categories generally name approaches to *the text as a whole*, as opposed to the many linguistic solutions that naturalistic theories locate at sentence level or below.

Large directional dichotomies can also be based on the way a translation *represents* its start text. The Czech theorist **Jiří Levý** (1963/2011) distinguished between "**illusory**" and "**anti-illusory**" translations. When you read an "illusory" translation, you are not aware it is a translation; it has been so well adapted to the target culture that it might as well be a text written anew. This is an ideal for many common conceptions: a translation is successful when you do not know it is a translation. An "anti-illusory" translation, on the other hand, retains some features of the start text, letting the receiver know it is a translation. This basic opposition has been reformulated by a number of others. The German theorist **Juliane House** (1997) refers to "**overt**" and "**covert**" translations, where "overt" means receivers are aware they are interacting with a translation, and "covert" means they are not. **Christiane Nord** (1997: 47–52) prefers the terms "**documentary**" and "**instrumental**," since the translation can either work as an explicit representation of the previous text (and thus as a "document") or re-enact the communicative function (as an "instrument"). The Israeli theorist **Gideon Toury** (1980, 1995/2012) talks about translations being "**adequate**" (to the start text) or "**acceptable**" (in terms of the norms of reception). The American theorist and translator **Lawrence Venuti** (1995), referring to Schleiermacher, identifies "**fluent**" translations as the domesticating kind he generally finds being done into English, and opposes them to "**resistant**" translations, which work to break that illusion. All these dichotomies model a choice made by the translator, a choice not necessarily determined by the text translated.

Polarities of directional equivalence

Many theories of directional equivalence are based on two opposed ways of translating, often allowing that there are possible modes between the two poles. The approaches are not always the same, and some of the theorists have very different preferences, but they are all thinking in terms of opposites. Here is a shortlist:

Cicero:	ut interpres	ut orator
Schleiermacher:	foreignizing	domesticating
Nida:	formal	dynamic
Newmark:	semantic	communicative
Levý:	anti-illusory	illusory
House:	overt	covert
Nord:	documentary	instrumental
Toury:	adequacy	acceptability
Venuti (1995):	resistant	fluent

All these terms work within the equivalence paradigm. In all cases, the two ways to translate can be seen as representing some aspect or function of the start text. So have translation theorists been saying the same thing over and over, down through the centuries? Not really. The relations between the poles have been thought about in many different ways. To see this, try to apply the oppositions to the simple examples we have used. If you take "martes 13," a formal-equivalence translation would be "Tuesday 13th" and a dynamic-equivalence translation would give "Friday the 13th." Now, which of those two translations is foreignizing? Which is domesticating? Which is moving the reader? Which is moving the author? It seems impossible to say—we need more information. Or rather, both translations could be domesticating in their way. If we wanted something foreignizing (anti-illusory, overt, documentary, adequate, resistant) we would have to consider something like "bad-luck *martes* 13th," "Tuesday 13th, bad-luck day," or even "Tuesday 13th, bad-luck day in Spanish-speaking countries." Is this kind of translation equivalent? Certainly not on the level of form (the last rendition adds a whole phrase). Could we claim equivalence in terms of function? Hardly. After all, a simple referential phrase has become a whole cultural explanation, at a place where the start text probably offers no explanation. Some would say that the explanation is not equivalent, since our version is long. Others might claim that this kind of expansion is taking implicit cultural knowledge and making it explicit, and since the cultural knowledge is the same, equivalence still reigns. Our version might then be a very good translation.

This is a point at which natural equivalence is threatened. Directionality becomes more important; we could use it to justify quite significant textual expansion or reduction. The equivalence paradigm nevertheless tends to baulk at this. How much explanation could we insert and still claim to be respecting equivalence? There is no clear agreement. The debate then concerns what is or is not a translation. And that is a question that the equivalence paradigm was never really designed to address—it merely assumed an answer.

3.5 ONLY TWO CATEGORIES?

Is there any reason why so many directional theories of equivalence have just two categories? Surely most translation problems can be solved in *more* than two ways? Naturalistic approaches tend to have many more than two categories (Vinay and Darbelnet listed seven main procedures; Koller gives five types; Reiss works with three). How should we explain the binarism on the directional side? Here are a few possibilities.

First, there may be something binary within equivalence-based translation itself. To grasp this, translate the following sentence into a language other than English (but not Dutch or German!):

(1)   The first word of this very sentence has three letters.

In French this would give:

(2)   Le premier mot de cette phrase a trois lettres.

Here the word-level equivalence is fine, but functional equivalence has been lost (since the first word now has two letters, not three). A true self-reference has become a false self-reference (cf. Burge 1978). So how *should* the English sentence be translated? We might try this:

(3)   Le premier mot de cette phrase a deux lettres.

This tells us that the first word of the *French* sentence has *two* letters. We have lost word-level equivalence with the English, but we have maintained the truth of the self-reference. Our translation would seem to have moved from anti-illusory to illusory, documentary to instrumental. In this example, are there only these two possibilities available—one kind of equivalence *or* the other? Think about it.

A second reason for having just two categories can be found in **Schleiermacher**, whom we have seen arguing that there are only two basic translation methods: you move either the author toward the reader, or the reader toward the author. Strangely, Schleiermacher claimed there could be no mixing of the two. This is because "just as they must belong to *one* country, so people must adhere to *one* language or another, or they will wander untethered in an unhappy middle" (1813/1963: 63; my translation). Translators, it seems, cannot have it both ways; they must decide to situate their texts in one country or the other.

These two reasons are both saying much the same thing. Translation has two sides, and thus two possible ways of achieving self-reference, and two possible positions from which the translator can speak. This might suggest that directional equivalence is a particularly good mode of thought for certain kinds of translation, and that those kinds, with just two basic sides, are particularly good for keeping people on one side or the other, in separate languages and countries. Or could that be the ultimate purpose of all translation?

Are the binarisms strictly necessary? The ideology of "one side or the other" is deeply anchored in Western nationalisms. The practical problems of translating, however, are rarely quite so simple. Consider the difficulties of translating someone's résumé or curriculum vitae. Do you adapt the normal form of résumés in the target culture? Or do you reproduce the form of the start text? The solution is usually a mix, since the first option means too much work, and the second option would disadvantage the person whose résumé it is. These days, however, many résumés are in a database that can be printed out in different formats and in different languages. The results are somehow equivalent to something; they certainly look like translations; but their production is not in accordance with any of the directional parameters listed above. In those cases, technology would seem to have returned us to a "natural" equivalence of a particularly artificial kind (see 7.3 below).

3.6 RELEVANCE THEORY

The German linguist and translation consultant **Ernst-August Gutt** (1991/2000) proposes a theory that addresses the main problems of directional equivalence. Gutt looks at theories of natural equivalence and says that, in principle, there is no limit to the kinds of equivalence they can establish. Each translation decision could need its own theory of equivalence. So all those theories are seriously flawed since, in principle, a theory should have fewer terms than the object it accounts for.

To overcome this difficulty, Gutt looks closely not at language or translations as such, but at the kinds of things people believe about translations. He distinguishes between different kinds of translation, using two binary steps:

■   As in House (see above), "**overt translations**" are marked and received as translations, whereas "**covert translations**" would be things like the adaptation of publicity for a new audience, which may as well not be a translation. Receivers of a covert translation need not have any special beliefs about its equivalence or non-equivalence.

■ Within the category of "overt translations," considered to be translation proper, there are two kinds: "**indirect translation**" covers all the kinds of translations that can be done without referring to the original context; "**direct translation**" would then be the kind that does refer to that context. In Gutt's terms, direct translation "creates a *presumption* of complete interpretative resemblance" (1991/2000: 196; italics in the original). When we receive a direct translation, we think we understand what receivers of the original understood, and that belief is not dependent on any comparison of the linguistic details.

Here the critique of natural equivalence (too many possible categories) brings us back to the two familiar categories ("direct" vs. "indirect"). And those two are very typical of directional equivalence. That alone could justify seeing Gutt as a theorist of equivalence.

What makes Gutt's approach especially interesting is the way he explains directional equivalence as a belief in "**interpretative resemblance**." He regards language as a very weak representation of meaning, no more than a set of "communicative clues" that receivers have to interpret. When he sets out to explain how such interpretation is carried out, Gutt draws on the concept of **implicature**, formulated by the philosopher **H. Paul Grice** (1975). The basic idea here is that we do not communicate by language alone, but by the relation between language and context. Consider the following example analyzed by Gutt:

(1)   *Text*: Mary: "The back door is open."
(2)   *Context*: If the back door is open, thieves can get in.
(3)   *Implicature*: We should close the back door.

If we know about the context, we can interpret the text as a suggestion or instruction, not just an observation. What is being said (the actual words) is not what is being meant (the **implicature** produced by these words interacting with a context). Grice explains implicatures as operating by breaking various maxims, here the maxim of "relevance." If we know about the context and the maxims, we can reach the implicature. If we do not, we will not understand what is being said. Note that Grice's maxims are *not* rules for producing good utterances; they are more like norms that are regularly broken in order to produce implicatures. The actual maxims might vary enormously from culture to culture. This variability is something that the linguists **Dan Sperber and Deidre Wilson** (1988) tend to sidestep when they reduce Gricean analysis to the one maxim: "be relevant." They thus produce "relevance theory," in fact saying that all meaning is produced by the relation between language and context. It is from relevance theory that Gutt develops his account of translation.

Grice's maxims

The following are Grice's maxims, the breaking of which creates implicatures:

■ *Maxim of Quantity*: Give no more and no less information to your audience than is needed for a full understanding of the intended message.

- *Maxim of Quality*: Do not misinform your audience; that is, say what you believe to be true and do not say something you do not believe to be true.
- *Maxim of Relevance*: Be relevant. Do not say something that is not relevant to the conversation.
- *Maxim of Manner*: Communicate your message in an orderly and clear manner without ambiguity and unnecessary wordiness.

These maxims may be culture-specific (they seem particularly English). However, the general idea that implicature comes from breaking maxims should not be culture-specific. Each culture is free to invent the maxims it wants, then break them.

Returning to the "back door" example, if we were going to translate text (1) we would have to know if the receiver of the translation has access to the context (2) and to the maxim being broken. If we can be sure on both counts, we might just translate the words of the text, producing something like formal equivalence. If not, we might prefer to translate the implicature, somehow rendering the "function." The notion of implicature can thus give two kinds of equivalence, in keeping with two kinds of translation. The fundamental dichotomy of directional equivalence persists.

Gutt, however, does not want those two kinds of equivalence to be on the same footing. He asks how Mary's utterance should be reported (or translated). There are at least two possibilities:

(4)   Report 1: "The back door is open."
(5)   Report 2: "We should close the back door."

Gutt points out that either of these reports will be successful if the receiver has access to the context; we can thus establish equivalence on either of those levels. What happens, though, when the new receiver does *not* have access to the original context? What if they do not know about possible thieves? What if they are more interested in the children being able to get in when they come home from school? If the reporter is working in this new context, only the second report (5), the one that renders the implicature, is likely to be successful. It will indicate that the back door should be closed, even if there are doubts about the reason. Gutt, however, prefers direct translation to allow interpretation in terms of the *start* context only. He would prefer the first report (4). For him, something along the lines of the second report (5) would have no reason to be a translation.

Gutt's application of relevance theory might be considered idiosyncratic on this point. It could be attributed to his particular concern with Bible translation. In insisting that interpretation should be in terms of the start context, Gutt effectively discounts much of the "dynamic equivalence" that Nida wanted to use to make Biblical texts speak to new audiences. Gutt insists not only that the original context is the one that counts, but also that this "makes the explication of implicatures both unnecessary and undesirable" (1991/2000: 175). In the end, "it is the audience's responsibility to make up for such differences" (ibid.). Make the receiver work! In terms of our example, the receiver of the second report (5) should perhaps be smart enough to think about the thieves. Only when there is a serious risk of misinterpretation should the translator inform the audience about contextual differences, perhaps by adding, "... because there might be thieves."

At this point, the equivalence paradigm has become quite different from the comparing of languages or the counting of words in phrases. The application of relevance theory shows equivalence to be something that operates more on the level of beliefs, of fictions, or of interpretative processes activated when people receive a translation.

3.7 EQUIVALENCE AS AN ILLUSION

Why not agree with Gutt that translations, when accepted as such, create a "presumption of complete interpretative resemblance"? That presumption could be all there ever was to equivalence. There is then no need to go further; no need actually to test the pieces of language according to any linguistic yardstick. Equivalence is always "presumed" equivalence, and nothing more.

Gutt's position here is close to Toury's (1980: 63–70, 1995/2012), where all translations manifest equivalence simply because they are assumed to be translations. Gutt's location of equivalence is also very much in tune with Pym (1992a/2010), except that Pym stresses that the belief in equivalence is historical, shared, and cost-effective in many situations: "each relation of equivalence is a transitory convention, a momentary link in [a] process of potentially endless exchange […] a fiction, a lie, a belief-structure necessary for the workings of [some] economies and the survival of [some] societies" (1992a/2010: 47).

Gutt, Toury, and Pym might agree that **equivalence is a belief structure**. Paradoxically, that kind of rough consensus also logically marks the end of equivalence as a central concept. If equivalence concerns no more than belief, linguists can venture into pragmatics, descriptive scholars can collect and analyze translation shifts, and historians might similarly shelve equivalence as an idea pertinent only to a particular conjuncture of social and technological factors. All those avenues take debate away from equivalence itself; they minimize the tussle between the natural and the directional, stifling the internal dynamics of the paradigm.

Equivalence might then appear to be dead, except for the occasional deconstructionist who has read little translation theory and needs a straw man to argue against. Then again, history has not finished.

3.8 THE VIRTUES OF DIRECTIONAL EQUIVALENCE

Since directional equivalence is part of the general equivalence paradigm, it shares many of the virtues listed for natural equivalence in the previous chapter. The following positive points might also be added:

1   Directional equivalence does not make grand ideological assumptions about what is natural, about the true nature of languages, or about translations being linguistically conservative (which tends to be the effect of natural equivalence). Its lighter ideological baggage means, for example, that it can be applied without contradiction to situations where there are hierarchical relations between languages.
2   This set of ideas generally casts its net wider than does natural equivalence, recognizing that translators have a broad range of renditions to choose from, and allowing

that the factors influencing their choices are not restricted to those of the start text. After all, if there are different equivalents to choose from, the selection criteria must come from somewhere close to the translator. To this extent, directional equivalence becomes compatible with the *Skopos* paradigm that we will meet in the next chapter.

3   Some theories of directional equivalence are clearly aware that translations create illusions and can be analyzed as such. This, however, may be a disadvantage for theorists who would prefer to see equivalence based on firm empirical criteria.

4   Directional equivalence solves the apparent "impossibility of translation" posited by structuralist linguistics. Equivalence becomes so possible that there are many ways of achieving it.

5   In posing its great polarities, directional equivalence sets the stage for discussions of translators' ethics. This is why many of the theorists mentioned here have expressed strong opinions about how one should translate.

6   In some cases, the same great polarities open a space where the translator has to decide between one kind of equivalence or another, and the theorist does not say which way the translator should go. In those cases (in Levý, House, or Toury, for example), the sub-paradigm opens up the way for empirical investigation. Instead of telling translators how to translate, theorists can try to find out how they actually *do* translate, in different cultures and in different historical periods. This leads into the descriptive paradigm (Chapter 5 below).

Do these virtues belong to directional equivalence itself or just to theories of directional equivalence? The question is legitimate, since I set out to categorize *theories* but the examples of directionality along the way refer to actual translations. So is directional equivalence something that happens in translations, or only in theories of translation? My answer is this: since equivalence is nothing but a belief-structure, it is always the result of theorization. That is, there is no substantial difference between the two sides of the question. The most virtue, though, should be in the theories that are the most lucid about directionality.

3.9 FREQUENTLY HAD ARGUMENTS

Some of the historical problems with the equivalence paradigm will be dealt with in the next few chapters, since there were other paradigms at work at the same time and it was from within them that many debates were generated. Let us nevertheless consider a few of the arguments that have concerned directional equivalence as such.

3.9.1 "Equivalence presupposes symmetry between languages"

Mary Snell-Hornby, we saw in the previous chapter, criticized the concept of equivalence as presenting "an illusion of symmetry between languages" (Snell-Hornby 1988: 22). We can now see that her criticism might be valid with respect to aspects of natural equivalence (those that are tied to an ideology of common "natural" usage), but it hardly holds at all for theories of directional equivalence. The theories of natural equivalence were basically analyzing languages. Directional theories, on the other hand, apply very much at the level of creative language use, in keeping with attempts to analyze *parole* rather than *langue*. As for the promotion of an "illusion," the tables turn as soon as we accept that much of what users believe about translations is indeed illusory. That is, the illusions come not from the theories, but from social usage.

3.9.2 "Theories of directional equivalence are unnecessarily binary"

We have seen that most of the directional theories operate on the basis of polarities. The French theorist and translator **Henri Meschonnic** (1973, 2003) argued that these opposi-tions (particularly Nida's distinction between formal and dynamic equivalence) depend on a more primary opposition between form and content, or on the separation of the **signifier** and the **signified** as parts of the Saussurean sign. Meschonnic considered that these separations are not valid, since texts function on both levels at the same time: they are worked by discourses marked by rhythm: "a way of thinking [*une pensée*] does something to language, and what it does is what is to be translated. And there, the opposition between *source* and *target* is no longer pertinent" (Meschonnic 1999: 22). This critique does not take us beyond equivalence. It simply stakes out a particularly demanding kind of constraint (the reproduction of discursive effects), well suited to the translation of some sacred, philo-sophical, and literary texts.

3.9.3 "Theories of equivalence make the start text superior"

This is a criticism in the spirit of **Vermeer** (1989a, 1989b/2012), from the *Skopos* approach that we will meet in the next chapter. If we ask what a translation is "equivalent to," the answer usually involves something in the start text. The text would be the deter-mining factor in the equivalence relation, and the equivalence paradigm thus tends to regard the start text as being superior to the translation. On the other hand, as soon as directional theories stress the *plurality* of possible equivalents, further criteria are required if the translator is to make a guided choice. The equivalence paradigm intimates but does not investigate those further criteria.

3.9.4 "Equivalence is not efficient; similarity is enough"

This is the general position of **Andrew Chesterman**, whom we cited at the beginning of this chapter. Should we be talking about similarity or equivalence? Chesterman claims that "[a]dequate similarity is enough—adequate for a given purpose, in a given context […] anything more would be an inefficient use of resources" (1996: 74). In other words, the equivalence paradigm makes translators work harder than they really have to. Then again, we have to ask exactly who perceives the equivalence (or the similarity). One of Chesterman's models ("divergent similarity," which I assimilated into directional equiva-lence) seems to operate in the eyes of the translator. The other model ("convergent similarity," our natural equivalence) is, for Chesterman, a relation established by anyone actually comparing the two texts. That comparison is a lot of work, hardly compatible with efficiency! In these terms, equivalence might be an assumption of similarity made by an end-user who has *no* direct access to the start text. For that user, equivalence has become a convenient fiction that allays suspicions of non-similarity. Since it would be too much work actually to check the validity of all the decisions made by the translator, we simply accept the translation as equivalent, as an act of trust. The illusion of equivalence should thus actually *reduce* cognitive effort at the point of text use. It may be quite efficient.

Theorists working within the equivalence paradigm will probably not win all these debates. They should nevertheless be able to hold their own, and can even find blind spots in the paradigms that came later.

SUMMARY

This chapter started by pointing out the rather strange way that a relation of similarity can depend on directionality (since a mother is not normally considered "like" her daughter). This relation introduces a series of theories about the general ways translators make decisions about how to translate. For example, you can choose the paths of formal or dynamic equivalence (in Nida's terminology). The history of translation theory gives many versions of this basic opposition, often making different recommendations about which of the poles is superior. At the end of the chapter I have related those options to Gutt's application of relevance theory. The text-user's "belief in interpretative resemblance" can be seen as a concept operative within the sub-paradigm of directional equivalence, since it depends heavily on directionality. At the same time, Gutt's approach fits in with a handful of theories that emphasize the social function of equivalence as a shared illusion, a social fiction that becomes cost-effective in the practice of cross-cultural communication. Although few theorists in this sub-paradigm would share that view (most believe they are describing linguistic facts), the idea of a functional illusion makes the concept of equivalence compatible with some of the other paradigms that we will meet in the next few chapters. Those newer paradigms will actually pick up threads from directional equivalence.

SOURCES AND FURTHER READING

The third edition of *The Translation Studies Reader* (Venuti 2012) includes fundamental texts by Jerome, Schleiermacher, and Nida. Munday (2012) mentions the polarities of directional equivalence in his chapter "Equivalence and Equivalent Effect." There are relatively few pedagogical texts presenting theories of directional equivalence, certainly as compared with the more linguistic theories of natural equivalence. Important theories like Kade's are also quite difficult to find. Key texts by Cicero, Schleiermacher, etc. are in the main anthologies. You might fruitfully tackle Gutt's *Translation and Relevance* (1991/2000), and the first chapter of Venuti's *The Translator's Invisibility* (1995) presents a rich mixture of argument and insinuation about the effects of equivalence. For an even more virulent debate, critical texts by Meschonnic are available in English (2003, 2011).

Suggested projects and activities

1 The Latin churchman and translator Hieronymus (Jerome) claimed he translated sense-for-sense, except in the case of the Bible, where he worked word-for-word because "there is mystery in the very order of the words" (Letter to Pammachius). What theories of equivalence can this be related to? Should we have different theories for different texts? Check to see what Hieronymus, in the Latin Vulgate, put for the Hebrew term 'almah in Isaiah 7:14. Compare this with other available equivalents.

2 The sentence "La primera palabra de esta misma frase tiene dos letras" could be rendered as "The first word of the sentence in Spanish has two letters." What kind of equivalence is this? Is the English sentence a translation or an explanation?

3 Can "The first word of this sentence has three letters" be translated into a language that has characters instead of letters, or does not have three-letter articles?

4 Compare different translations (in the same language) of the one paragraph. Do the differences indicate different kinds of equivalence?

5 For the following sentences, state which of Grice's maxims (see 3.6 above) are being broken and propose at least two different translations of each sentence.
Text: "Juliette is the sun" (see Appiah 1993/2012)
Context: The speaker loves Juliette.
Text: "Frequently had arguments"
Context: This book.
Text: "She was given a violin lesson for free, with no strings attached."
Context: A stand-up comic.

6 It has been suggested that Grice's maxims (see 3.6 above) are specific to English-language culture. For example, the "maxim of quantity" is coherent with the English recommendation to "keep it short and simple" (the KISS principle). A corresponding Italian principle might be "keep it long and complete" (KILC, cf. Katan 1999, 2000). Which of the maxims do you think might be operative in your culture? Remember that a maxim is operative when its transgression produces an implicature.

7 Find a poem that has been creatively translated into the students' first language. Now present the translation as if it were the start text, and the start as if it were the translation. Ask the class to evaluate the text that they now consider the translation. Will they find it inferior to what they believe the start text to be? Why?

8 The whole class translates a text into their first tongue. Then they see in what places they all agree on the one equivalent, and in what places there are many different equivalents (cf. the choice-network analysis proposed by Campbell 2001). Does it make sense to call some kinds of equivalence "natural" and others "directional"? Do the places with many equivalents correspond to what is hardest to translate?

9   Take the same start text as in Activity 7 above. Now, as in Chapter 2, use the automatic translation programs Babelfish and Google Translate to do back-translations of it several times (e.g. moving from English to German to English to German, for the one text). At what points does equivalence cease to be directional (i.e. when do we enter the ping-pong relation of natural equivalence, where we go back and forward between the same things)? Why do we reach those points? Is there more directionality in human translation or machine translation? Why?

10 Each student writes a short text about a topic they are closely related to (the most wonderful moment in their life, or the moment they were most frightened), in their mother tongue. Other students then translate those texts (into *their* mother tongue, if the class group is mixed). The first students receive their translations back and are asked to evaluate them. How do they feel about being translated? Do theories of equivalence have any relation to their feelings? Usually, no matter how exact the translation, the experience will be felt to be most real in the start text. What might this say about the nature of equivalence? (My thanks to Andrew Chesterman for this task.)

11 As an extension of Activity 10, the translation is revised by a third student and by the author of the start text. Who will make the most changes to the translation? Why? What does this say about the nature of equivalence?

12 As suggested in the chapter on natural equivalence, consider the terms your language uses for websites (e.g. "site," "webpage," "browser," "navigate," "surf"). How did those terms come into your language? If they evolved from situations of one-to-none equivalence (see 3.2 above), were they borrowed from a foreign language or generated from within your language. Do the terms indicate a global hierarchy of languages? Which strategy does your culture prefer? Which strategy *should* it prefer?

13 For philosophers: Do the terms "natural equivalence" and "directional equivalence" constitute yet another binary polarity (as in 3.4)? Have we failed to rise above Western tradition?

CHAPTER 4

Purposes

This chapter looks at a group of theories that have been opposed to the equivalence paradigm. These theories propose that a translation is designed to achieve a purpose. If that purpose is to repeat the function of the start text, as is the case in Reiss's theory of text types, then there should actually be little difference between the two paradigms: the relation between start-text function and target-text function is still one of equivalence. However, as soon as a theory accepts that the target-side purpose can be *different* from the start-side function, we are dealing with a new paradigm. For Vermeer, the target-side purpose (which he calls *Skopos*) is the dominant factor in a translation project. Vermeer thus claimed to have "dethroned" the start text and have gone beyond equivalence. This approach accepts that the one text can be translated in different ways in order to carry out different functions. The translator thus needs information about the specific goals each translation is supposed to achieve, and this requires extra-textual information of some kind, usually from the client. In this way, the linguistic frame of the equivalence paradigm becomes much wider, bringing in a series of professional relationships. Several different theories address this extended interpersonal frame. Holz-Mänttäri focuses on the translator's status as an expert in cross-cultural communication. Hönig and Kussmaul consider how much information the receiver of the translation really needs. The chapter closes with a view of translation that concerns not so much texts but *projects*, understood as sets of materials and information. Gouadec proposes numerous categories for the way translation projects should be organized on the basis of information from the client. Like all the theories covered in this chapter, he picks up many factors that were overlooked by theories of equivalence.

The main points covered in this chapter are:

- The *Skopos* theory developed by Hans Vermeer breaks with the equivalence paradigm by giving priority to the target-side purpose to be fulfilled by the translation.

- For *Skopos* theory, equivalence characterizes a situation where the functions of the start text and the translation are supposed to be the same, and is considered a special case.

- This theory allows that the one text can be translated in different ways to achieve different purposes.

- Holz-Mänttäri's concept of "translatorial action" sees the translator as an expert in cross-cultural communication who can do much more than translate.

- Hönig and Kussmaul's "principle of the necessary degree of precision" (the "good enough" theory) states that the translator should give the details that the reader needs, which may be more than those in the start text, or less.

- Gouadec's approach to project analysis is similarly based on purpose as defined by the client, but it assumes that complete information in the pre-translation phase will resolve most translation problems.

4.1 *SKOPOS* AS THE KEY TO A NEW PARADIGM

A paradigm shift in translation theory can be dated from 1984, at least as a symbolic point. That year saw the publication of two books in German: *Grundlegung einer allgemeinen Translationstheorie* (Foundation for a General Theory of Translation) by Katharina Reiss (also written Reiß) and Hans Vermeer, and *Translatorisches Handeln* (Translatorial Action) by Justa Holz-Mänttäri. Both books, in different ways, directly challenged the idea that a translation has to be equivalent to a start text.

Those books are not exactly world-famous; they were very slow to become known outside of German. General texts on translation theory do nevertheless carry frequent references to **Skopos theory**, the theory of *Skopos*, a Greek word for "purpose" (it could also be translated as "aim," "goal," or "intended function"). The basic idea is that the translator should work in order to achieve the *Skopos*, the communicative purpose of the translation, rather than just follow the start text. This "*Skopos* rule" appears to mean that the translator's decisions should be made, in the last instance, in accordance with the reasons why someone asked the translator to do the translation. Yet it could also mean that the dominant factor is what the end-user wants the translation for. Then again, the determining factor might be what the translator *thinks* the purpose should be. For the general paradigm, all these interpretations are possible and have proved mildly revolutionary, since none of them is on the side of the author. The theories thus invite the translator to look in a new direction.

Vermeer's *Skopos* rule

Vermeer formulates the *Skopos* rules as follows:

> An action is determined by its goal [*Zweck*] (it is a function of its goal [*Zweck*]).
> (Reiss and Vermeer 1984: 100)

This would be a general principle of action theory. What it means for the translator is described in the following terms:

> The dominant factor of each translation is its purpose [*Zweck*].
> (Reiss and Vermeer 1984: 96)

Note that both these formulations use the normal German term *Zweck* ("goal," "aim," "purpose") rather than the technical neologism *Skopos*. Why the Greek term is necessary remains unclear.

A more elaborate explanation can be found in Vermeer:

> Each text is produced for a given purpose and should serve this purpose. The *Skopos* rule thus reads as follows: translate/interpret/speak/write in a way that enables your text/translation to function in the situation in which it is used and with the people who want to use it and precisely in the way they want it to function.
>
> (Vermeer 1989a: 20; translation from Nord 1997: 29)

The important point here is the *Skopos* rule does not actually say *how* a text should be translated. It simply tells the translator where to look for indications about the way to translate. In each case, you have to find out or construct what the intended purpose is. Vermeer is clear on this point:

> What the *Skopos* states is that one must translate, consciously and consistently, in accordance with some principle respecting the target text. The theory does not state what the principle is: this must be determined separately in each specific case.
>
> (Vermeer 1989b/2012: 198)

The novelty of the approach thus lies in what it does *not* say. For this paradigm, the translator's choices need *not* be dominated by the start text, unless of course equivalence happens to be stipulated as essential for the purpose. A legal agreement, for example, may be adapted to target-side textual norms if and when it is to be governed by the laws operative in that culture, or it may be rendered with the start-text form if and when the translation is more for purposes of understanding, or again, it may be translated almost word-for-word if, for instance, it is to be cited as evidence in court. The start text would be the same in all cases. What is different is the *purpose* the translation has to serve. One text, several possible translations, and the key factor determining each actual translation is the purpose, the *Skopos*.

The idea is simple enough. It has led theorists into considerations of what purposes are, how they are defined in relation to clients (a dimension wholly absent from the equivalence paradigm), and how they turn translations from texts into projects. This paradigm shift, however, was complicated by several factors.

First, the *Skopos* idea was presented by Hans Vermeer in a book of which he was the co-author (although he had announced the idea as early as 1978). The other co-author, Katharina Reiss, was working within a less radical paradigm, based on text types, in the same book.

Second, Reiss and Vermeer were in Heidelberg; Holz-Mänttäri was working in Tampere, Finland, where her work was published. So the two books published in 1984 came from distant contexts and have different approaches.

Third, Vermeer made sure his term (*Skopos*) become the company logo. The German-language scholars who followed the general paradigm have nevertheless been quite free in selecting from the ideas of Reiss and Holz-Mänttäri, as well as from Vermeer.

So there is a rather more complicated story to tell.

Some key terms

- **Skopos**: The purpose or aim of the translation; the function it is supposed to carry out in the situation of reception.
- **Skopos theory**: Here, the set of propositions based on the idea that the target-side *Skopos* or purpose has priority in the translator's decisions. This theory is only one part of the purpose paradigm, alongside other theories that also talk about purposes as functions, without giving priority to the target side.
- **Brief**: The instructions the client gives to the translator; *Auftrag* in German; also called "commission" in English. In actual translation practice, the normal terms would be "instructions" or "job description."
- **Translatorial**: Adjective to describe qualities of *translators*, as opposed to the adjective "translational," used to describe qualities of translations.
- **Translatorial action**: All the actions carried out by a translator, one of which may be translating.
- **Translatory**: Here, adjective to describe the translation *process*.

4.2 REISS, VERMEER, AND THE ORIGINS OF THE *SKOPOS* APPROACH

As we have noted, the equivalence paradigm was prominently represented in German by **Werner Koller**'s textbook *Einführung in die Übersetzungswissenschaft* (Introduction to Translation Science, 1979 with many later reprints). Koller had formulated a complex concept of equivalence based on different kinds of meaning. That amounted to saying that the way you translate (the kinds of equivalence you seek) depends on the **function** of the text or fragment you are translating. If the text you are working on mainly refers to things in the world, you should make sure those references are exact. If a poem is functioning primarily on the level of form, then you should primarily seek equivalence on the level of form, and so on. For Koller, and for most people at the time, *the way you translate depends on the kind of text you are translating*. That paradigm was pluralist, functionalist, and start-oriented. That view seems happily at home within the equivalence paradigm.

Katharina Reiss was another theorist working more or less within the equivalence paradigm. Her theory had actually been published earlier than Koller and was quite compatible with his concept of equivalence. In her 1971 book *Möglichkeiten und Grenzen der Übersetzungskritik* (translated into English in 2000 as *Translation Criticism: Potential and Limitations*), Reiss had proposed that different text types require different kinds of translation solutions. She recognized three basic text types: **expressive, appellative** ("appeal-focused," or "calling"), and **representational** (or "content-focused"), with each text classified according to which of these functions is dominant. These were actually based on the three linguistic persons (related to language functions by Bühler in 1934/1982). The "expressive-focused" text is oriented by the first person ("I") and would cover such things as personal letters and many literary genres. The "appeal-focused" text would involve genres like publicity, which have to have an effect on the second person ("you"), the receiver, and should be rendered so as to have such effects. The "content-focused" text would then be anything that refers to the external world, to third persons ("he," "she," "it," "they") and thus requires a mode of translation where the references are exact. In 1976 Reiss revised her typology. The term "appellative" became "**operative**," which is easier to understand in English. The basic idea remained the same: *the communicative function of a text tells you what kinds of solutions to use when translating it.*

Reiss's text types and corresponding translation methods

Table 4.1 lists the initial and revised terms for Reiss's three basic text types, and the aims that the translator should have when rendering each type.

Table 4.1 Reiss's correlations of text types and translation methods (adapted from Nord 2002/2003)

Text types 1971	Text types 1976	Translation method
Content-focused	Informative text	Correctness of contents, acceptability of form
Form-focused	Expressive text	Correctness of contents, corresponding form
Appeal-focused	Operative text	Effect has priority over content and form

Reiss's work was actually more sophisticated than the triadic models, since she recognized mixed genres and considered the implications of communication media (for example, when a novel becomes a film, we would expect the translation strategies to change). The model is quite easily extended by recognizing further language functions. Drawing on **Roman Jakobson** (1960) we could add the "metalinguistic," "phatic," and "poetic" functions, in fact adding a vertical axis to Bühler's three-person model. The basic idea nevertheless remains unchanged: whatever the function of the start text is, the translator should try to have it work in the translation.

　　This is where misunderstandings arise. Reiss's position has been called "functionalist," which is fair enough. Her main idea, after all, is that the way we translate depends on the function of the text we are translating. Many other theorists have picked up that idea, and the banner of "**functionalism**" has been used as a general term for this approach. **Christiane Nord** (1988/1991), for example, gives an extensive description of how texts should be analyzed prior to translation, so that translators can then ascertain the function of those texts with exactitude (in very Germanic fashion, Nord's analysis comprises some 76 questions that students should be taught to answer before translating). The analysis, says Nord, should first be of the instructions for the target text, then of the start text, in order to locate the correspondences and differences between the two. Nord is also aware that in professional translation process these analyses become largely automatic: no one really ever asks all 76 questions. On the level of theory, Nord certainly recognizes that translations can have functions different from their start texts, yet the main weight of her actual analyses has tended to fall on the start side. In her comments on her own co-translating of Biblical texts, for example, Nord (2001) first isolates the "intended function" of problematic start-text passages and then considers how that function can be reproduced or modified in order to emphasize "otherness" with respect to current readerships (which in this case is the "intended function" of the translation). **Mary Snell-Hornby** placed a similar "functionalism" at the heart of her influential "integrated approach" (1988). The basic message underlying these theorists was that one should translate the functions of texts, not the words or sentences on the page. Of course, that message can be traced back as far as Cicero, at least, since it is essential to the very concept of equivalence. "Functionalism" should have been nothing new.

What is strange is that both Nord and Snell-Hornby *opposed* their functionalism to the equivalence paradigm, especially as represented by Koller (cf. Nord 1988/1991: 23, 25–26; Snell-Hornby 1988: 22). In hindsight, that was rather ungenerous. These writers somehow equated equivalence with literalism, whereas the concept of equivalence had been developed precisely so that the "dynamic" categories could be distinguished from literalism. Nida's approach, and certainly Koller's, could also legitimately be called "functionalist." In fact, all the functionalist models of equivalence remain entirely compatible with Reiss's insistence on text types. And "functionalism," as we shall see in the following chapters, was a term that could also be extended to many of the theorists pursuing descriptive approaches. If "function" was the only game in town, the German-language theorists were having a debate about very little.

Consider a chestnut example like Adolf Hitler's ***Mein Kampf***. What is the function of this text? In some parts it is certainly expressive, manifesting a strong first-person character, as befits an autobiography. In other aspects, it gives a vision of history, and is thus referential. Finally, its overall function is undoubtedly to convert readers to the cause of National Socialism, so it should also be classified as "appelative," as a "call to action." How should we translate the text? The mixing of functions is not the real problem (functionalism never promised pure categories, beyond its carefully selected examples). If we analyze the start text carefully, if we refer back to what we know about the author's intentions and the effects on the first readers, we should probably translate *Mein Kampf* in such a way as to convert even more readers to National Socialism. That could be the outcome of straight start-text functionalism. However, many publishers and perhaps most translators would feel unhappy about that kind of goal. In most contemporary situations it would make better political sense to translate the text as a historical document, adding footnotes and references to historical events that happened after the text was written. The translator might decide to tone down the most rabble-rousing prose. Alternatively, we might make the exclamations even more outrageously strident, to defuse the "call to action" by making it unbelievable. A few well-selected translation solutions could potentially direct readers down one path or the other.

Start-text functionalism cannot really discuss the reasons why a translator might want to change the function of the text. But Vermeer's concept of *Skopos* can. For Vermeer, the translator of *Mein Kampf* would have to give priority not to how the original German text functioned, but to **the effect the text is supposed to have on the target reader**. Those two functions could be quite different, and in this particular case they probably *should* be very different. Even in instances of what Vermeer calls "functional constancy" (*Funktionskonstanz*), where the *Skopos* requires the start-text function to be maintained, significant changes may be required. In fact, maintenance of start-text function (one kind of equivalence) is probably the principle that requires the most textual shifts. The first right-wing translators of Hitler into English wanted to have him accepted by the new readership, and thus toned down the rhetoric and tried to make Mr. Hitler sound like a quite rational politician (cf. Baumgarten 2009).

Vermeer's concept of giving priority to the *Skopos* thus radicalized a functionalism that was already there, shifting its focus from the start to the target. It brought in pragmatic factors like attention to **the role of clients**, to the importance of the translator having **clear instructions** prior to translating, and to the general principle that the **one text can be translated in different ways**, to suit different purposes. Those were all good ideas. They were not particularly troubling in themselves, given that they called on common sense and a dash of existentialist liberalism (each translator has to decide for themselves). So why such a hoo-hah?

The problem could have been this. As long as you are analyzing text-based equivalence, you are doing **linguistics** of one kind or another. But if you have to choose between one *purpose* and another (e.g. different reasons for translating *Mein Kampf*), linguistics will not be enough. You are engaged in applied sociology, marketing, the ethics of communication, and a gamut of theoretical considerations that are only loosely held under the term "cultural studies." Theories of equivalence could be formulated in linguistic terms, and translators could thus be trained in faculties of language and linguistics. The more radical versions of target-side functionalism, on the other hand, justified the creation of a new academic discipline. They could remove translator training from the clutches of traditional language departments. Translation theory thus surreptitiously became a debate about **academic power**. "Equivalence" was on one side; "functionalism" on the other; and they were opposed, even when, as theories, they were basically compatible.

4.3 HOLZ-MÄNTTÄRI AND THE TRANSLATOR'S EXPERTISE

While all of this was happening, Justa Holz-Mänttäri was in Finland, busy rewriting the entire translation process from the perspective of **action theory**, which was also of some importance to Vermeer. To do this, she felt the need to change the terms commonly used to describe what translators do: a "text" became a *Botschaftsträger* (message-bearer); translators, who were called upon to do many things beyond translating, had their general profession described as *Texter* (on the model of a "reader," who reads; so a "texter" is someone who "texts," well before SMS gave the term a different meaning). Coupled with impressive syntactic density, such neologisms make Holz-Mänttäri a monument to why translators say they cannot understand translation theory.

Holz-Mänttäri's guiding ideas are not difficult to grasp. She starts from a functionalist view not just of texts but also of society (drawing on Malinowski's theory of different social institutions fulfilling comparable social functions). Within this frame, functions are manifested in actions, each of which is guided by its aim. The communication of messages is an action like any other, ruled by the function the message is to fulfill. Different social groups, however, are experts in carrying out different kinds of actions. When a message has to cross into another culture, the people sending that message will require help from an **expert in cross-cultural communication**. That expert should be the translator, who may be called on to do many different things, including giving advice on the other culture or writing a new text on the basis of information provided by the client.

Holz-Mänttäri's theory fitted in well with target-side functionalism. Taken individually, most of her ideas would seem unlikely to upset anyone. The idea of actions achieving aims was a mainstay of pragmatics and many kinds of sociology; it was working in the same way as Vermeer's *Skopos* rule. Holz-Mänttäri's arguments against the simple determinism of "when X in the source, then Y in the translation" amounted to a non-mechanical view that was common fare within the equivalence paradigm. What did rankle, however, was the idea that a translator could actually write a new text and still be called a translator. That was stretching definitions of the term "translator." Nonetheless, if you look at the terms closely, Holz-Mänttäri and others were talking about "**translatorial action**," the range of actions carried out by translators (and other "texters"); her interest was not limited to the physical facts of translations. We thus find hierarchies like Figure 4.1, where "translatorial action" (the adjective "translatorial" refers to the person, the "translator") is categorized as "mediated cross-cultural communication." The action would be properly "translational" (the adjective refers to the thing, the translation) when it is with respect to a start text. You can also see that attempting to repeat the same function as the start text is just one possible aim of translating; translators can legitimately attempt to carry out new functions.

Seen in this way, both Holz-Mänttäri and Vermeer were producing critiques of traditional equivalence-based definitions of translation. They were also challenging the traditional role of linguistics in the training of translators. At the same time, they were quite possibly reacting to changes in the translation profession, where translators are increasingly being called on to do more than translate (terminology, post-editing, reviewing, desktop publishing, and project management, and then there are logical career moves into international marketing and public relations). The theorists were perhaps allowing the profession to erupt into theory.

That did not mean, however, that translators could do whatever they liked.

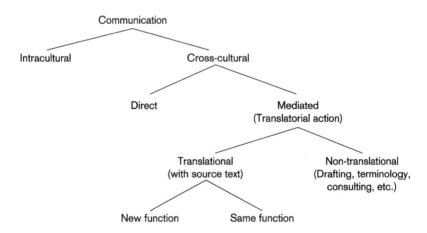

Figure 4.1   Translatorial action as a form of mediated cross-cultural communication (adapted from Nord 1997: 18)

4.4 PURPOSE-BASED "GOOD ENOUGH" THEORY

An important consequence of the purpose paradigm is that the translator can give *more* information than is in the start text if necessary, and *less* information if so required. That possibility was partly recognized within the equivalence paradigm, but never fully condoned. Nida, for example, talked about "addition" as something a translator could do with a text, but he immediately explained that "there has been no actual adding to the semantic content of the message, for these additions consist essentially in making explicit what is implicit in the source-language text" (1964: 230–1). Similarly, what Nida calls "subtraction" apparently "does not substantially lessen the information carried by the communication" (1964: 233). The equivalence paradigm generally does not legitimize cases of outright addition or omission, where the translator need not point to something in the start text as the reason for what is in the target text. In fact, while an author like **Vázquez-Ayora** could certainly discuss the category of "paraphrase" as something that translators are occasionally called upon to do, he issues repeated warnings that such uses of reduction do not really belong to the domain of translation: "To translate does not mean to explain or comment on a text, or to write it as we see fit" (1977: 288; my translation). Somewhere beneath this general refusal to allow additions or omissions we might find the Biblical prohibitions of modifying the sacred text (cf. Deut. 4:2; 12:32; Rev. 22:18–19). More generally, an age of strong authorship tends to respect the integrity of all texts, and for as long as the start text remains the measure and justification of translation solutions, the question of exactly how much the translator can add or take away need never be formulated as such. On the other hand, in an age where many texts are relatively authorless (brochures, webpages, and instructions do not usually carry the name of any one author), there seems to be greater translatorial liberty.

One answer to the problem was formulated by **Hans Hönig** and **Paul Kussmaul**, theorists who were influenced by *Skopos* theory in the 1980s. They formulated the "**principle of the necessary degree of precision**," which proposes that the appropriate amount of information is determined by the required function of the translation (1982/1996). That seems to be just another formulation of the *Skopos* rule. Its illustration, however, is a little more challenging.

Hönig and Kussmaul discuss the question of how to render culture-specific terms like "Bachelor's" or "Master's" degrees, which tend to occur in relatively authorless texts like a curriculum vitae. They recognize that the translator cannot tell the reader *everything* about studies and degrees in the foreign institution, nor is it fair simply to leave the reader totally unaware of the way basic terms and structures differ. As Hönig puts it in a later text (1997: 11), "there has to be a cut-off point where translators can safely say: 'This is all my readers have to know in this context'."

Where that point lies depends on the specific function of the translation, so there is not really any further general principle to be announced. What remains of interest is the way this is explained. Here is Hönig's 1997 account of an example that has incited debate (cf. Hönig and Kussmaul 1982/1996: 53):

> The principle of the necessary degree of precision is by no means limited to culture-specific terms, and indeed not to the meaning of words alone, but it can best be illustrated by this type of translation problem. For instance, the term "public school" implies such a large amount of culture-specific knowledge that it is impossible to render its

meaning "completely" in a translation. Within a functionalist approach, however, the function of a word in its specific context determines to what degree the cultural meaning should be made explicit. In a sentence such as [my emphasis]:

(2a) In Parliament he fought for equality, but he sent his son to *Eton*.

The translation will have to be different from translating the identical term "Eton" in the sentence:

(3a) When his father died his mother could not afford to send him to *Eton* any more.

The following translations would be sufficiently detailed:

(2b) Im Parlament kämpfte er für Chancengleichheit, aber seinen eigenen Sohn schickte er auf eine der englischen Eliteschulen.

(... one of the English elite schools)

(3b) Als sein Vater starb, konnte seine Mutter es sich nicht mehr leisten, ihn auf eine der teuren Privatschulen zu schicken.

(... one of the expensive private schools).

Of course, there is more factual knowledge implied in the terms "Eton" or "public school" than expressed in the translation, but the translation mentions everything that is important within the context of the sentence, in other words, the translation is semantically precise enough.

Here the translator has made certain assumptions about the readers' knowledge of English institutions, and has given information accordingly. To that extent, the solutions are determined by the target-side situation, and thus by the assumed purpose of the translation, as the *Skopos* rule would have it. There is no question of the translation being exact or perfect; there is no need for excessive work to go into any kind of strategic analysis or componential semantics; the rendition is simply "good enough" for the situation concerned. The translator has assumed that "this is all my readers have to know," and no more need be said.

Note that in the above citation Hönig does not really speak about the relation between the translation and the reader. He actually refers to "the function of a word in its specific context," and this is later glossed as "the context of the sentence." Further, the two different translations of the term "Eton" are not really presented as adding or taking away anything. When all is said and done, those translations are *making explicit* a few semantic values that English-language readers of the source text are assumed to activate. Despite the best principles of target-side functionalism, the actual practice suggests that we are not too far removed from the basic principles of equivalence, in this case directional and dynamic.

At this point I return to one of the basic problems of the purpose paradigm. If the nature of the start text can determine one kind of function (as it seems to do in Hönig's example), are we always sure there are no other purposes to be respected?

4.5 WHO REALLY DECIDES?

Despite doubts about how radically new some of the functionalist approaches were, Hans Vermeer saw his *Skopos* rule as "dethroning" the start text. For him, the translator's decisions could no longer be based solely on what was in the text. Once you accept that principle, a whole new dimension opens up. Suddenly there are numerous social actors involved: the paying client, the person actually giving the job (perhaps a translation company or agency), the translator, editors, and hopefully a final reader or user of the translation.

German-language functionalist theories are full of diagrams connecting all those agents and describing their possible roles. Together, all these factors somehow converge in the one *Skopos* or purpose, the thing that the translation is supposed to achieve. We might say, for example, that a child-like suicide note is undoubtedly an expressive text (as Reiss's text typology might classify it), but when rendering it in a courtroom situation the translator should work with absolute philological exactitude, since the new purpose is to decide if the note was really written by the child (an authentic example, taken from Mayoral 2003). In this case, the function of the text is quite different from that of the translation, and the change responds to a new purpose.

That kind of analysis works well for as long as everyone agrees on the purpose of the translation. However, what happens when there is no clear agreement? Imagine, for example, that a neo-Nazi party has asked you to do a new "dynamic" equivalence translation of *Mein Kampf*, or the defense attorney insists that the suicide note be translated in a way that arouses no suspicion of forgery. How should the translator decide in such situations?

If you read the functionalist theories closely, you find remarkably little agreement on this question. The start text may have been dethroned, for some, so who is the new king?

For Holz-Mänttäri, **the properly trained translator is the expert** in solving problems concerning translation, and so should be left to decide on such issues. Authors and clients, on the other hand, tend to be experts in their own respective fields, and so should be left to decide about such things as field-specific terminology and the desired effect on the reader. Holz-Mänttäri thus presents a world of complementary expertise, full of mutual respect, and with a prominent and well-defined place for the properly trained translator. The translator is sovereign in properly translational matters.

Vermeer's position is more difficult to pin down. We have seen him describe the translation process as making a text "function in the situation in which it is used and with the people who want to use it and precisely in the way they want it to function" (1989a: 20). This appears to make the end-user king. Yet we also find Vermeer describing the translator as a respected expert (1989a: 40), a professional who "acts translatorially" (1989a: 42) and whose ethical responsibility is to fulfill the goal of the translation as well as possible (1989a: 77). So who decides what that goal is? The answer must lie somewhere in the following: "The highest responsibility of the translator is to transmit the intended information in the optimal manner" (1989a: 68, my translation). But then, who decides what information is really intended, and who determines what "optimal" means here? On the second question, at least, Vermeer does give a clear answer: "optimal" is "in the eyes of the translator" (1989a: 68). So here, as in Holz-Mänttäri, the well-trained translator ultimately decides.

Here we come up against one of the shortcomings of the whole paradigm. For some decisions, the theorists seem to say, we cannot really help translators, who must ultimately act in their own name in each specific situation. As in basic existentialism, this places huge responsibilities on the shoulders of translators, along with considerable liberties. According to Margret Ammann (1994), the old categories of equivalence and eternal binary choices had sought to *repress* **the translator's individuality**, whereas Vermeer's *Skopos* theory would emphasize precisely that individuality, at once **liberating** and **empowering** the translator.

Other theorists, however, have seemed less anxious to travel down that road. Reiss has never renounced the priority of text functions, and Hönig and Kussmaul's seminal principle, as we have seen, was far from ignoring the start text. In Nord and Snell-Hornby, on the other hand, we find more emphasis on the **client's instructions**. For example, Nord states that the *Skopos* remains "subject to the initiator's decision and not to the discretion of the translator" (1988/1991: 9); she consequently defines a "translation mistake" as a failure to comply with the client's instructions (1997: 75); and she later insists that "the translation purpose is defined by the translation brief, which (implicitly or explicitly) describes the situation for which the target text is needed" (2001: 201). For her, the *client* clearly has the final say, not the translator. So who are we to believe?

Much depends here on the words you use to describe the instructions that the translator receives (or does not receive) from the client. In English translation, Vermeer prefers the term "**commission**," which might call up the image of a portrait painter getting very broad indications but basically being left to tackle a creative task. When editing Nord (1997), I opted for the client's "**brief**," which conjures up a defense attorney who receives information from the client but ultimately decides how to argue the case. The French theorist Daniel Gouadec prefers "**job description**," in which as many technical details as possible are agreed upon in advance, as if the translator were helping the client to build a house. This is one of the many points on which translation theory has had to rely on metaphors, selecting comparisons in accordance with the assumptions of the theorist. The metaphors say a lot about who has the power (the "agency") to make decisions.

Christiane Nord has sought to add a prescriptive dimension to these relations. She claims that the translator has ethical obligations not only to texts (the traditional focus of "fidelity") but also to people: to senders, clients, and receivers, all of whom merit the translator's "**loyalty**" (Nord 1997: 123ff.). Nord sees this interpersonal loyalty as a general relationship of solidarity that should override any interpersonal conflicts: "If the client asks for a translation that entails being disloyal to either the author or the target readership or both, the translator should argue this point with the client or perhaps even refuse to produce the translation" (2001: 200). Interestingly enough, when she herself was criticized as the co-translator of New Testament documents (cf. Nord 2001), Nord's response was not particularly in terms of loyalty (why should she not have been loyal to the translation critics?) but in terms of *marked* functionality as a question of being honest. If the translators' preface says the purpose of the translation is to work in a certain way, then, says Nord, the translation cannot be criticized for working in that way. If you do what you promise to do, that is the purpose. Note that in this case the *Skopos* principle is not protected by the relatively hierarchical power structures of the translation classroom; Nord cannot use it to tell students to think beyond the surface of the text. In this more exposed situation, Nord ultimately claims that translators have the right and responsibility to do what they see fit. At that point, she would rejoin the sovereign translator of Holz-Mänttäri and Vermeer.

4.6 THE VIRTUES OF THE PURPOSE PARADIGM

Let me now pull together these various strands. The following would be principles to which most of the above theorists would agree:

1   The translator's decisions are ultimately governed by the purpose of the translation.

2   The purpose of what translators do ("translatorial action") can be to produce equivalence to various aspects of the start text, or to engage in rewriting, or to give advice, or anything in between.
3   The one text can be translated in different ways to suit different purposes.
4   A key factor in defining the purpose of the translation is what instructions are given by the client or negotiated with the client.
5   In the last analysis, the purpose of the translation is defined by the individual translator, working in relation with the other social actors involved.

This general approach has several strong points that distinguish it from the equivalence paradigm:

1   It recognizes that the translator works in a professional situation, with complex obligations to people as well as to texts.
2   It frees the translator from theories that would try to formulate linguistic rules governing every decision.
3   It forces us to see translation as involving many factors, rather than as work on just one text.
4   It can address ethical issues in terms of free choice.

These are all good things. In its day, this approach was exciting, even revolutionary, apparently putting paid to the equivalence paradigm.

4.7 FREQUENTLY HAD ARGUMENTS

Although there have been several broad critiques of *Skopos* theory, few of them have received serious answers. When Vermeer responded to a series of objections (most accessibly in Vermeer 1989b/2012), he did so at a straw-man level. One might argue, for example, that not all actions have aims (since we never know the complete outcome of an action prior to undertaking it), and Vermeer answers, quite correctly, that we nevertheless *orient* our actions in terms of intended aims, and that all actions have aims by definition (since that is the way he defines "action"). The debates have tended to stay there, without scaling many philosophical heights.

The following are some of the arguments that might be picked.

4.7.1 "We translate words, not functions"

All the theorists in this paradigm stress that we should translate what texts are supposed to do, their intended function, not the actual words on the page. Even when they disagree on who is "intending" the function, they all agree that the function has priority over the words. The British critic **Peter Newmark** (1988: 37) retorted that words are "all that is there, on the page," so words are all that we can translate. This debate should serve to indicate that the sense or functions that we translate are always as *constructed* by us on the basis of the information available, and much of that information is packaged in words. "Intentions," no matter whom they belong to, are not immediately available. Newmark was right, but so what?

4.7.2 "Purposes are identified in the text"

A slightly more sophisticated version of Newmark's critique argues that there is no function or intention that is not expressed in words, so it is impossible to do without some kind of linguistic analysis of the start text. In this line, **Kirsten Malmkjær** (1997: 70) picks up **Hönig's "Eton" illustrations** and claims that, in Hönig's own analysis, "what is necessary depends far less on the function of a translation than on the linguistic context in which a problematic expression occurs." For example, if the main verb of a sentence is "afford" (as in "his mother could not afford to send him to Eton"), then the term "Eton," no matter what the language, is likely to be invested with the value "expensive," so there is really no need to spell this out for the foreign reader, and no reason for claiming "function" to be a new paradigm. This is a valid comment on Hönig and Kussmaul's general approach, but it cannot be applied to cases where the one start text can be translated in several different ways (as in the case of the child's suicide note mentioned above).

4.7.3 "The concept of purpose (or *Skopos*) is an idealism"

This is a more philosophical version of the same critique. If textual meaning is considered to be unstable and always open to interpretation, the same can be said of any assumed purposes or functions. Although the *Skopos* approach undoes the assumed stability of the start text, the same critique can be applied to its own key terms. There is no reason why greater stability should ensue from a shift of focus from the start to the target. As Chesterman has remarked (2010: 224), the explanatory power of the *Skopos* rule is weak "because it relies on an optimal set of working conditions with optimally competent translators."

4.7.4 "The *Skopos* theory is unfalsifiable"

This is a rather simple piece of reasoning. If every translation is dominated by its purpose, then the purpose is what is achieved by every translation. To separate the two, we would have to look at "bad" translations where purposes are somehow *not* achieved, thus complicating the notion of what a translation is. However, if the purpose is ultimately defined by the translator, as Vermeer would suggest, then how can we consistently accuse translators of not fulfilling the purpose that they themselves have defined? Some appeal might be made to a principle of internal contradiction (one part of the translation goes one way, the other goes the other, so it is bad …). But who said a translation only has to have one sole purpose? The longer one continues that line of argument, the less the *Skopos* rule seems to be saying.

4.7.5 "The theory does not address equivalence as a default norm"

This argument posits that, in our societies, the dominant concept of translation requires that the translator aims to achieve as much equivalence as possible, on whatever level, unless there are special-case indications to the contrary. The analysis of purpose would then concern those special cases, and the linguistic analysis of equivalence can carry on regardless (my thanks for Basil Hatim for stating this position, although it could also be derived from Gutt's isolation of "direct translations," which would be those to which the default norm applies). A counter-argument might be that there are now many forms of translation, including dialogue interpreting and fansubbing, where the default norm is now non-operative, to the extent that the profession has changed so much that equivalence itself has become the special case. No empirical studies, to my knowledge, have tested these claims.

4.7.6 "Purpose analysis is mostly not cost-effective"

This kind of criticism focuses on the extreme rigor with which these theories are formulated, asking if translators really have to do so much theoretical work. We might think here of Nord's 76 questions to be asked of the start text (and potentially another 76 of the target text as well). Translators, it might be argued, mostly cut corners by adhering to the historical norms of their profession, without extensive thought about specific purposes. They are instinctively working in "good enough" mode anyway, with or without the theoretical back-up. The reply to this might be that a lot of translations would be much better if they were done in terms of specific purposes rather than by following endemic norms. That reply, however, would change the nature of the theory, taking it from a descriptive stance to an overtly prescriptive positioning. In fact, the critique brings out the very ambivalent status of the whole paradigm, which has a strong pedagogical purpose beneath a thin veil of descriptivism.

4.7.7 "The well-trained translator is a self-serving notion"

As I have noted, the descriptive illusion is maintained by focusing only on the "good" translator, or on what translators do when they are properly trained experts. This enables the descriptive position to be prescriptive at the same time, particularly when one realizes that these theories have been used to modify training curricula, thus effectively helping to produce the "good" translators that they themselves define as "good." The ultimate risk is that we may be institutionalizing no more than the theorists' opinions.

4.7.8 "The theory cannot resolve cases of conflicting purposes"

This is admitted to when the theory allows that individual translators have to make their own choices in many cases. What some might see as a failure to develop a guideline ethics thus becomes a moment of liberation and empowerment.

4.7.9 "The theory contradicts ethics of truth and accuracy"

Newmark (1997: 75) reduces Vermeer to the notion that "the end justifies the means," described as "a kind of brutalism that excludes factors of quality or accuracy." In thus opposing what he saw as "the ideal of the commercial *skopos*," Newmark affirmed his belief that "translation is a noble, truth-seeking activity, and that it should normally be accurate" (1997: 77). In taking that stance, Newmark was certainly traditionalist and willfully unsophisticated, not to say technically wrong (Vermeer defined quality in terms of target-text function, and he allowed that there should be as much accuracy as required—although he did indeed say that "the end justifies the means," in Reiss and Vermeer 1984: 101). Newmark nevertheless quite probably expressed the beliefs of most people who employ translators, not to mention the professional ethics of a good many translators themselves.

Further arguments can be found in Chesterman (2010). As should be clear, the paradigm shift from equivalence to purpose has been anything but smooth. Many of those debates are still working themselves out, and some will be continued in our next chapters.

4.8 AN EXTENSION INTO PROJECT ANALYSIS

I close this chapter with a brief look at an approach that extends the notion of purpose in a very practical way. The French translator-trainer **Daniel Gouadec** (2007) has virtually no intellectual association with the German-language theorists that we have been considering; his thought has developed from the training of technical translators. In broad terms, Gouadec sees translation as concerning large-scale projects that involve not only clients and companies but also teams of translators, terminologists, and other communication specialists. He argues that special attention should be paid to clients' instructions, which he terms "**job specifications**." If the specifications are as complete as possible, the translator will know exactly how to translate. And if the specifications are not complete enough, the translator should seek further details.

Table 4.2 is a version of what a job description might entail. Trainees are taught to ask the client for information on all the categories.

The first column of Table 4.2 reminds us that clients can provide much more than the start text: in-house glossaries, parallel texts (texts in the target language on the same subject matter), previous translations done in the same field, and perhaps the telephone number or email of an expert in the field. The client might express surprise that a translator could need all that. But the material is often the best source of information

Table 4.2 Material and information in a job description for translators (cf. Gouadec 2007: 15)

Material	Function information	Task information
Source text	Desired function of translation	Deadlines (for delivery of raw
Source images, appendices, etc.	Readership profile	translation, of revised translation)
Specialized glossaries	Quality required (for information, for publication, revisions, terminology)	Format of translation (which translation memory)
Parallel texts		
Previous translations	Who revises?	Costing basis (by word, character, page, hour, day)
Contacts with experts or consultants		Estimated cost
		Terms of payment
		Signed contract

for any translator in search of appropriate terminology and phraseology. Rather than guess or search the web, translators can reduce risk by using the material that their client already has.

The second column is very close to what the German theorists would call *Skopos*, the desired function of the translation. The third column concerns agreements on delivery arrangements and financial matters. Those are all aspects overlooked by most other approaches, yet rarely overlooked by professional translators.

For Gouadec, if all the elements of the translation project can be located and defined in this elaborate "**pre-translation**" phase, through discussion and negotiation with the client, the actual translating will present relatively few problems. In fact, Gouadec goes a little further. For him, there remain many decisions for which translators are probably more competent than their clients, particularly concerning such things as forms of address (polite or formal second person, for example). Translators should decide on these "optional" elements, but then present a list of proposed decisions to the client for approval. Pre-translation thus does as much as possible to remove all possible sources of doubt. It effectively establishes the equivalents prior to doing the job.

If we compare Gouadec's approach with German-language *Skopos* theory, several significant differences emerge. Most obviously, Gouadec sees the translator as a language technician able to follow explicit instructions as **part of a team**. Holz-Mänttäri and Vermeer, on the other hand, tend to see the translator as an expert individual trained to make decisions and to be responsible for them. Their ideal translator would be a consultant on cross-cultural communication, able to advise clients about how to present themselves in a different culture.

In terms of the theories we have surveyed so far, we might say Gouadec does everything possible to establish agreement (possibly on equivalents) and thus reduce the areas in which translators have to decide for themselves. Plurality is his enemy. For German-language *Skopos* theory, however, the variety of possible purposes is a liberation from equivalence, and thus presents an ethical confrontation with uncertainty. They took the idea of translation purposes in one direction, whereas Gouadec (and most of the profession with him) has taken it in another.

SUMMARY

This chapter has presented a paradigm that is based on a simple idea: a translation need not be equivalent to its start text. The various theories in the paradigm differ with respect to the degrees to which translations can break with equivalence, but they all focus on the target-side purpose that the translation is supposed to achieve. In theory, the one start text can be translated in different ways to achieve different purposes. This means the translator needs information about the purpose, and that information should ideally be in the instructions provided by the client. The translator is thus placed in a social situation where they have to negotiate with all the parties involved. For Vermeer, the translator is the one who ultimately decides the purpose (*Skopos*) of the translation. For Holz-Mänttäri, the translator is the expert in cross-cultural communication, which means that translators may rewrite or give advice, as well as translate. For Nord, the ethical component of these relationships is "loyalty" to people rather than the "fidelity" that would characterize a relationship to a text in the equivalence paradigm. This general view of the translator's situation can be extended to include the work of Gouadec, who emphasizes the way technical translators work in teams, and who argues that complete information from the client in the pre-translation phase will determine most of the translator's decisions.

SOURCES AND FURTHER READING

The third edition of *The Translation Studies Reader* (2012) has a synoptic text by Vermeer (Reiss was in earlier editions). Munday (2012) has a chapter on "functional theories," which includes the main ideas of the paradigm alongside the analyses of source texts. The best introduction is still Christiane Nord's *Translating as a Purposeful Activity* (1997), which contains the main citations, diagrams, and criticisms. Nord, however, tends to privilege the client's wishes more than the translator's freedom and she remains close to pedagogical considerations. Vermeer and Nord are to be preferred to some of the accounts that have not benefited from extensive readings of the German texts. Reiss and Vermeer (1984) was translated and published in English in 2013, and further translations from Vermeer are due to appear, although Holz-Mänttäri (1984) has not been translated. Reiss's text-type theory of 1971 has been translated into English as *Translation Criticism: Potential and Limitations* (2000). Gouadec's checklists are in *Translation as a Profession* (2007).

Suggested projects and activities

1   Find or invent a short text with "Eton" in it, preferably with photographs, language errors, and a few historical inaccuracies. Get different groups to translate the text according to different instructions (for a left-wing history, as a coffee-table book, or to attract students, for example). Compare the different solutions used, especially with respect to the term "Eton." If there are no differences, what does this say about *Skopos* theory?

2   This is an activity in five parts, not all of which work every time:

(a) In groups, select texts from three very different genres (say, contracts, advertising, or poetry, but also mixed genres like self-descriptions from Internet dating services). Translate fragments of them in order to respect the different genres.

(b) Once you have completed Task A, find or invent names for the different translation solutions you have used. You might like to use the terms proposed by Vinay and Darbelnet, but any classification will do.

(c) Once you have completed Tasks A and B, try to apply the solution types you have used for one text to the other two, and vice versa. For example, you might try to translate a contract using the same kind of solutions you use to translate an advertisement, or you could translate an instruction manual using the solution types you have used for a novel.

(d) Once you have completed Tasks A, B, and C, try to imagine as many different situations as possible for which all the texts could be translated. Is it really true that the one text can be translated in many significantly different ways? Are there really so many different reception situations?

(e) On the basis of this exercise, do you find that the main difference is the nature of the texts or the different purposes for which the translations are carried out?

3 Find or invent transcriptions of mediated medical encounters (e.g. a conversation between a doctor and a patient via an interpreter) and delete the interpreter's renditions. Students do written translations in the place of the deleted renditions. They then act out the scenes, producing oral translations. Now compare the written translations with the students' spoken ones, and if possible with what the interpreter actually did. Which translations are the most literal? Which are the closest to functions? Why?

4 Translate the two sentences: a) "In Parliament he fought for equality, but he sent his son to Eton," and b) "When his father died his mother could not afford to send him to Eton any more." Now consider Newmark's argument that "to translate 'Eton College' as 'one of (!) the English elite schools' or as 'one of the expensive private schools' suggests that the translator is unaware of Eton's importance as a British institution, and underrates or fails to enlighten the likely readership" (1997: 76). In what circumstances would you consider Newmark's criticism to be correct? Would it make you change your translation?

5 For the same two sentences, consider Malmkjær's argument that "the presence in the [second] sentence of 'could not afford' effortlessly activates the EXPENSIVE sense of 'Eton' for the English reader. It would of course be possible for a German reader to attach the appropriate senses to 'Eton' by means of conscious inference and possibly some research, even if the place/ school name had been left to fend for itself in the [target text]" (1997: 71). Can a similar argument be made for the first sentence (consider the function of "but")? Does this mean that linguistic analysis alone can identify text functions? Does it mean that cultural terms sometimes require no special translation solution, since syntax tells the story?

6 Find three published translations (websites will do). Imagine you are the client who ordered the translations and write appropriate job specifications.

7 For philosophers: If all translations are dominated by their purpose, how can we define a bad translation?

8 Ask some professional translators about the kinds of instructions they actually receive from their clients. Which metaphor (order, commission, brief, job specification, etc.) best describes that communication, if indeed there is any communication? If you find that professional translators receive no such instructions, is the theory therefore wrong, or should we change professional practice?

9 Vermeer proposed that translators should be trained to become "intercultural management assistants" or "consultants" (1998: 62). Is this a realistic aim? Or should translators be trained to become competent technicians able to carry out orders (as in Gouadec)? What happens when you only have a two-year training program and something has to be sacrificed? Could these different roles develop at different stages of a translator's professional career?

CHAPTER 5

Descriptions

Simple description should require no grand theory. Some of the most significant concepts in European translation theory have nevertheless come from a broad "descriptive paradigm." This paradigm can be traced back to the Russian Formalists at the beginning of the twentieth century, informed by the idea that scientific methods can be applied to cultural products. That idea then connected with translation theorists in three broad regions. The first link was with the work done in Prague, Bratislava and, more loosely connected, Leipzig. The second link was with the "Tel Aviv school" (Even-Zohar, Toury, and the development of Descriptive Translation Studies). And the third link was through the Netherlands and Flanders. When literary scholars from those three areas met and discussed their projects, Translation Studies started to take shape as an academic discipline. That history is important—the descriptive paradigm did not come from the same roots as the others mentioned in this book. This chapter focuses on the main theoretical concepts derived from descriptive studies: translation shifts, systems and polysystems, "assumed translations," target-side priority, norms, universals, laws of translation, and insights from process studies. In hindsight, descriptions have turned out to be anything but simple.

The main points in this chapter are:

- Rather than prescribe what a translation *should* be like, descriptive approaches try to say what translations *are* like or *could be* like.
- Translation shifts are patterned differences between translations and their start texts. They can be analyzed top-down or bottom-up.
- Translations play a role in the development of cultural systems.
- The innovative or conservative position of translations within a cultural system depends on the system's relation with other systems.
- Translations can be studied as facts of a target culture, as opposed to the start-culture context that is predominant in the equivalence paradigm.
- Translators' performances are regulated by collective "norms," based on informal consensus about what is to be expected from a translator.
- Some proposed "universals of translation" describe the ways in which translations tend to differ from non-translations.

- Some tentative "laws of translation" describe how translations tend to correlate with relations between cultures.
- Comparative descriptions of the cognitive processes of novice and experienced translators can indicate what translators should be trained in.

5.1 WHAT HAPPENED TO EQUIVALENCE?

Equivalence went out of style. *Skopos* theory made it unfashionable by arguing that since "functional constancy" (the closest thing they had to equivalence) is no more than one of many possible things a translator can achieve, translation usually requires transformations of a rather more radical kind. For those theorists, equivalence became quite a small thing, a special case. At almost the same time, other theorists were dismantling equivalence in precisely the opposite way. For this second group, for what Gideon Toury would eventually assemble as "Descriptive Translation Studies," **equivalence was a feature of *all* translations**, simply because the texts were thought to be translations, no matter what their linguistic or aesthetic quality (cf. Toury 1980: 63–70). That changed everything. If equivalence was suddenly everywhere in translations, or almost, it could no longer be used to support any linguistics that would help people create it. Translation theory was thereby moved to a realm that was relatively unprotected by any parent discipline; it founded its own discipline. More than pure theory, however, the descriptive approach emphasized the need to do research, mostly of the kind done in structuralist literary studies. These theories were out of touch with the growing number of training institutions; they were in an institutional context quite different from *Skopos* theory.

5.2 THEORETICAL CONCEPTS WITHIN THE DESCRIPTIVE PARADIGM

The name "**Descriptive Translation Studies**" (with the capitals) was never fully consecrated until Toury's book *Descriptive Translation Studies – and beyond* (1995/2012). It has since become a flag of convenience for a loose flotilla of scholars. Around that name there is now a rather large body of thought and research. On the surface, it appears to be a paradigm in which scholars set out to **describe** what translations actually are, rather than just **prescribe** what they should be like. Those terms, though, are simplifications. If the aim were merely to describe, there would be little need for any grand theory. And yet what we find here is a host of theoretical concepts: systems, shifts, norms, universals, and laws, to name the most prominent, plus an ongoing debate about how to define "translation" itself. Despite the emphasis on description, this remains very much a space for theorizing.

In the following sections I will briefly describe the main concepts of the paradigm.

A shortlist of concepts in the descriptive paradigm

Here are some of the scholars who helped develop the descriptive paradigm. Many other names could be listed and most names should be associated with more than one idea:

1 The relations between source and target texts can be described in terms of "translation shifts" (Levý, Miko, Popovič).
2 The innovative or conservative position of translations within a cultural system depends on the relative prestige attached to the start culture, and correlates with the type of translation solutions used (Even-Zohar, Holmes, Toury).
3 Translation Studies should be an empirical descriptive discipline with a hierarchical organization and a structured research program (Holmes, Toury).
4 When selecting texts to study, translations should be considered facts of the target culture (Toury).
5 To understand not just translations but all kinds of "rewriting," we have to consider the social contexts, especially patronage (Lefevere).

5.2.1 Translation shifts and their analysis

The most obvious way to analyze translations is to compare start and target texts as sets of structures. You note where the structures are different. You then have specific structures (the differences) that belong to the field of translation. That idea is as simple to understand as it is difficult to apply.

The structural differences between translations and their start texts can be described as **"translation shifts."** For **Catford**, shifts are "departures from formal correspondence" (1965: 73): if formal correspondence is what we find between "Friday the 13th" and "viernes y 13," then any other rendition will be a shift of some kind. The range of possible shifts might thus include anything detected by anyone within the equivalence paradigm. A shift might come from the translator's decision to render function rather than form, to translate a semantic value on a different linguistic level, to create the correspondence at a different place in the text, or perhaps to select different genre conventions. Much research can be carried out in this way: compare the texts, collect the differences, then organize the shifts.

There are at least two ways of approaching this task: **bottom-up analysis** starts from the smaller units (usually terms, phrases, or sentences) and works up to the larger ones (text, context, genre, culture); **top-down analysis** goes the other way, starting with the larger factors (especially constructs like the position of translations within a sociocultural system) and working down to the smaller ones. In principle, it should make no difference which end you start at: all roads lead to Rome, and there are always dialectics of loops and jumps between levels. However, the difference between bottom-up and top-down approaches has a lot to do with the role of theory.

5.2.1.1 Bottom-up shift analysis

The complexity of bottom-up analysis is seen in the model developed by **Kitty van Leuven-Zwart** (1989, 1990), where shifts are categorized on many levels (cf. Hermans 1999: 58–63). The model is rarely used, and for good reason.

In van Leuven-Zwart, the basic textual units entering into comparison are called **"transemes."** For example, the two units might be the English "she sat up suddenly" and the Spanish "se enderezó," which basically means that she sat up. What these two transemes have in common would be the "architranseme." Once you have identified that, you start to look for shifts, which can then be categorized in much the same way as Vinay and Darbelnet proposed. For example, you might note that the two phrases occupy corresponding positions in the texts but the English has a value (suddenness) that seems absent in the Spanish. So you write down "absence of aspect of action," and call it a shift. Eventually you will have a notebook full of such shifts, which hopefully form patterns that say something about the translation. What could be wrong with that?

Since this "sit up" example is presented as being relatively uncomplicated, it is worth looking into the difficulties it might involve. To follow the discussion, you might first translate "she sat up suddenly" into your favorite languages-other-than-English:

■   For a start, can we be sure that the value of "suddenly" is not in the Spanish? The verb "enderezó" is in the preterite, which in Spanish has a value in opposition to the past imperfect ("enderezaba"), a tense that does not exist as such in English. Both languages can say "she was in the process of sitting up," but English does not have a specific tense for such drawn-out actions; Spanish does. One could thus argue, in pure structuralist mode, that the selection of the Spanish preterite in itself represents the value "suddenness." The shift would then be from the English adverbial to the Spanish tense.

■   Alternatively (although possibly for similar reasons), we might check large corpora of general English and Spanish and note that the English verb "sit" is associated with adverbials and phrasal particles far more often than is the case for the Spanish verb "enderezarse" (none the least because "sit up" and "sit down" have no formal equivalents in Romance languages). In that case, the translator might have omitted the value "suddenly" (which could be expressed as "de repente," for example) because it would be an unusual collocation in Spanish. Comparative frequencies might thus justify the translator's decision, without denying the underlying logic of structures.

■   More worryingly, if we try to apply this type of analysis to our "Friday the 13th" example, how can we be sure that the non-shift involves the form or the function? In a context framed by superstition, surely "martes 13" (Tuesday the 13th) would be the expected translation, the normal one, the non-shift? What right do we have to pick one rendition and call it the "proper" or "expected" translation, and thereby relegate all other renditions to the category of "shifts"?

■   Finally, there are many cases where formal correspondence itself implies some kind of shift. For example, the American English term *democracy* certainly corresponds formally to the East German term *Demokratie* (as in the Deutsche Demokratische Republik), but with a shift of ideological content (cf. Chesterman and Arrojo 2000). So why should formal correspondence itself not represent a shift?

In all these ways, bottom-up shift analysis presupposes far too quickly that meanings are clear and stable (i.e. not subject to interpretation), and that there is thus one common core (the "architranseme") in relation to which all the rest would represent "shifts." On that score, the approach seems no different from the equivalence paradigm. Even without questioning the way in which transemes are identified, there must remain doubt about the identification of the shift and its causation. The bottom-up accumulation of shifts tends to be methodologically murky, and the long lists of differences only rarely congeal into firm findings. This approach can produce much doubt and even more data. At the end of the day, it requires orientation from a few reductive theories. That is one of the reasons why the descriptive paradigm is full of theories.

5.2.1.2 Top-down shift analysis

The descriptive work in central Europe tended to be much more theoretical than any bottom-up description. In Leipzig, **Otto Kade** (1968) explicitly argued that a bottom-up approach ("induction") had to be accompanied by top-down analysis (a "hypothetico-deductive" approach) if theoretical results were to be achieved. In Bratislava and Nitra, the analysis of "**shifts of expression**" (cf. Popovič 1968/1970; Miko 1970) did not assume any simple desire to maintain equivalence. Shifts could thus be approached top-down, starting from major hypotheses about why they might exist.

Anton Popovič, for instance, claimed there were "two stylistic norms in the translator's work: the norm of the original and the norm of the translation" (1968/1970: 82). This seems obvious. Yet consider the consequence: as soon as the two "**stylistic norms**" are announced, the multiplicity of shifts is already theorized in terms of causation. This approach connects with the study of literary style, where the two interacting "norms" would be the voices of author and translator. On another level, shifts could be patterned differently because of historical factors (the nature of the receiving system, patronage, new text purposes, different translation concepts). Or again, some shifts might result from the translation process itself (these would later be dubbed "universals"). On all those levels, the top-down approach seeks **causal factors** (the reasons for the shifts) that are quite different from those of the equivalence paradigm. These descriptive approaches could obviously join forces with the bottom-up analyses carried out by linguists, but their theoretical frame was fundamentally different. In effect, despite the misnomer "descriptive," these were theories about the possible causes (personal, institutional, historical) of why people translate differently.

As an example of top-down analysis, consider **James S Holmes's** analysis of **translations of verse** (Holmes 1970). In some cultures (notably in French), foreign verse forms can consistently be rendered in prose. So the problem is solved: translators know what to do (translate into prose), and readers know what to expect. That would be one huge kind of shift, and it has little to do with any linguistic equivalence. In other situations, however, alternative shifts may be appropriate. Holmes models no fewer than five options (the form of the translation might be prose, mimetic, analogical, organic, or extraneous), with a degree of complexity that can only come from a dialectic of top-down hypothesis meeting some degree of bottom-up testing.

A model of options for the translation of verse (from Holmes 1970)

1 *Verse as prose*: All foreign verse is rendered as prose, as has been the norm in translations into French.
2 *Mimetic form*: The translator chooses a form in the target language that is as close as possible as the one used in the text. For example, an English sonnet can be rendered as a Spanish sonnet, even though the metric systems will not correspond. Often this involves introducing a new form, as when English *terza rima* was modeled on the Italian verse form.

3 *Analogical form*: The translator identifies the function of the form in the start-language tradition, then finds the corresponding function in the target-language tradition: "Since the *Iliad* and *Gerusalemme liberata* are epics, the argument of this school goes, an English translation should be in a verse form appropriate to the epic in English: blank verse or the heroic couplet" (Holmes 1970: 95). This option might be an application of the equivalence paradigm at a high textual level. It is to be distinguished from the blanket "verse to prose" option to the degree that it requires identification of the way the specific form functions in the start culture.

4 *Organic or content-derivative form*: The translator refuses to look solely at the form of the start text (as is done in the above options) and instead focuses on the content, "allowing it to take on its own unique poetic shape as the translation develops" (Holmes 1970: 96).

5 *Extraneous form*: The translator adopts a form that is unconnected with the form or content of the start text, and that is not dictated by any norm for translations. In other words, anything can happen.

For Holmes, these options are appropriate to **different historical situations**. Mimetic form tends to be found "in a period when genre concepts are weak, literary norms are being called into question, and the target culture as a whole stands open to outside impulses" (Holmes 1970: 98). This might be the case of German in the first half of the nineteenth century. On the other hand, "the analogical form is the choice to be expected in a period that is in-turned and exclusive" (Holmes 1970: 97), such as the neoclassical eighteenth century in France. As for the use of "organic" form, Holmes sees it as being "fundamentally pessimistic regarding the possibilities of cross-cultural transference" (1970: 98) and he associates it with twentieth-century Modernism. "Extraneous" form has "a tenacious life as a kind of underground, minority form […] resorted to particularly by metapoets who lean in the direction of the imitation" (1970: 99).

Holmes thus suggests that translators' decisions are culture-bound, give or take a few unruly "metapoets." When asked how any decision should be made, the descriptivist will usually say, "it depends on the situation." But then, how many different things can a decision actually depend on? Is there any way to model the huge range of variables in "the translator's situation"? Descriptivists have made use of at least three concepts that are of some help here: systems, norms, and target-focus.

5.2.2 Systems

As we have seen, Holmes classifies the options and gives them a logical symmetry, largely thanks to distinctions between form, function, and content. What he does is **systematic** (ordered, thorough, complete), but not necessarily **systemic**. Systems are something else.

A language is systemic. You can see this by stopping in mid-sentence and considering the *restricted* set of what words can follow. The language system limits the choices. The same is true of the translator as a language producer, since the target language imposes limited sets of choices at each point. However, does the same kind of systemic restriction concern how to translate a verse form? The translator can certainly select one of Holmes's five options, and that choice might have meaning in terms of the overall history of verse forms, but is it a decision like those where we are obliged to select a certain kind of verb or adverbial? Is it properly systemic? To a certain extent, yes: all receiving cultures have literary genres, and they mostly maintain structural relations between themselves. Then again, no: those sets of genres need bear no resemblance at all to the five alternatives outlined by Holmes. The target culture is one thing; the sets of theoretical alternatives are something quite different. In this case, the kind of choice outlined by Holmes surely cannot be considered a psychological reality. If the translator was working into German at the beginning of the nineteenth century, all kinds of social and cultural factors not only made the use of mimetic form appropriate, but also made Holmes's alternatives relatively unthinkable. Germanic culture, without a state, was prepared to draw on other cultures in order to develop. Translations of Homer brought hexameters into German, and translations of Shakespeare brought in blank verse. A literary translator in that cultural environment would then see "mimetic form" as the *normal* way to go about translation. The translator might even see it as the true or correct way in which all translations should be done, in all sociocultural environments. Prescriptive theorizing could result ("All translations should use mimetic form!"); some structural oppositions might be proclaimed in theory ("German mimetic form is better than French translations into prose!"); but the choices are not made within an abstract system comprising purely translational options.

As **Toury** would later clarify, the kind of system elaborated by Holmes belongs to the level of the theorist (the options *theoretically* available), which is to be distinguished from the alternatives actually available to the translator at the time of translating, which are in turn quite different from what the translator actually does. Toury distinguishes between three levels of analysis: "all that translation [...] CAN involve," "what it DOES involve, under various sets of circumstances," and "what it is LIKELY to involve, under one or another array of specified conditions" (1995/2012: 9)

Three levels of analysis in Descriptive Translation Studies

Delabastita (2008: 234) relates Toury's three levels of analysis to the notion of norms:

1 Level of system: theoretical possibilities ("can be")	For each translation problem or source text, it is possible to envisage a whole range of possible or theoretical solutions or target texts [as does Holmes].
2 Level of norms: culture-bound constraints ("should be")	On the intermediate level of norms, some of these possible relationships will be recommended or even required as being the only ones that can generate "genuine" translations, whereas others will be dismissed or even simply ignored.
3 Level of performance: empirical discursive practice ("is")	We can then observe which relationships have actually materialized in a given cultural setting. By definition, these empirical relationships constitute a subset of the possible relationships; their degree of frequency in a given cultural situation is a crucial indication that certain norms have been at work.

The top-down thinking is clear (although you could work upwards at the same time). Note, though, that the term "system" is used here only in the sense of "theoretical possibilities." The problem then becomes: Are the levels of "should be" and "is" properly systemic in any strong sense?

When **Holmes** tries to explain why an option is associated with a particular period, he cites a range of phenomena: "genre concepts," "literary norms," "cultural openness/closure," "pessimism/optimism about cross-cultural transfer." Those are all things in the target culture. Holmes mentions them in a fairly off-hand way; they seem to be quite separate, isolated phenomena. However, it is possible to see such things as being bound together, as aspects of the one culture. In other theorists, cultural systems can impose quite strong logics. Lotman and Uspenski (1971/1979: 82), for example, talk about entire cultures being "expression-oriented" or "content-oriented" (along with various more complex classifications). The stronger the logic by which the system is presumed to operate, the more that system can be seen as determining the nature of translations.

When the Israeli scholar **Itamar Even-Zohar** analyzes the relation between translations and cultures, he uses the term "**polysystems**." This "poly-" means "many" or "plural," indicating that a culture is a system made up of many other systems (linguistic, literary, economic, political, military, culinary, etc.). For Even-Zohar, translated literature can be seen as a sub-system occupying a position within the literature that hosts it. The translations can become a key element in the literature (and thus "innovative" or "central"); they may be secondary or unimportant ("conservative" or "peripheral"); or they can occupy positions in between. In these terms, translation is a way one polysystem "interferes" with another, where the verb "to interfere" is not pejorative. Even-Zohar proposes that translations play an innovative or central role when

> (a) a polysystem has not yet been crystallized, that is to say, when a literature is "young," in the process of being established; (b) when a literature is either "peripheral" (within a large group of correlated literatures) or "weak," or both; and (c) when there are turning points, crises, or literary vacuums in a literature.
>
> (1978: 23)

Even-Zohar's approach goes well beyond Holmes's attempt to explain translations. The view of systems as dynamic and plural allows him to ask what translations actually *do* within target cultures, and how they evolve from relations between cultures. Even-Zohar's general finding is nevertheless rather negative: "the 'normal' position assumed by translated literature tends to be the secondary [peripheral] one" (1978: 25), that is, that translations tend to have a conservative, reinforcing effect rather than a revolutionary, innovative one. That kind of finding is not popular with those who would see translations as a hidden and maligned cause of change. Even-Zohar nevertheless stresses that translation is essential for *any* cultural system (since no culture is entirely independent) and that translational processes occur within polysystems as well as between them.

The term "system" varies in meaning and importance from theorist to theorist. In each case, you have to read the descriptions closely, paying particular attention to the verbs and the agents of the verbs (who is supposed to be doing what). In strong systems theory, the systems themselves do things, as if they were people. In other approaches, people do things within systems of constraints. That is a big difference, bearing on human liberty, determinist history, and the role and nature of translations.

Like "system," "**function**" becomes a slippery term here. For descriptive studies, the "function" of a translation is its **position within a system**. When Even-Zohar says a translation is relatively "**central**" or "**peripheral**," he effectively means that its *function* is either to change or to reinforce the receiving language, culture, or literature. The function is what the text does in the system. For the purpose paradigm, on the other hand, the "function" of a translation is generally conflated into the *Skopos*, the action that the translation is supposed to enable, just as the function of a text is assumed to be the action in which the text is used (to teach, to express, to sell, etc.). Although both paradigms would claim to be "functionalist," the term "function" means one thing in systems theory and something else in relation to action theory. There must be common ground between the two usages, yet few theorists have sought it. One attempt might be **André Lefevere**'s view of systems (1992), which includes factors very close to the translator (patrons, editors, publishers). Another attempt has been the use of **network theory** to study the same relations sociologically (see 8.5 below). A third avenue would be the concept of **translation culture** (Prunč1997), understood as interrelations between all participants in the production of translations. The broadest and most basic bridge has nevertheless been the concept of translation norms.

5.3 NORMS

In his three-level schema (the one I have reproduced above), after the level of what "can be" **Toury** opens a space for what "should be," which he describes in terms of "norms." Norms are positioned somewhere between abstract possibilities (such as Holmes's alternatives) and what translators actually do (the kinds of considerations that *Skopos* theory deals with). For Toury, norms are

> the translation of general values or ideas shared by a community [...] into performance "instructions" appropriate for and applicable to concrete situations. These "instructions" specify what is prescribed and forbidden, as well as what is tolerated and permitted in a certain behavioural dimension.
>
> (1995/2012: 63)

The term "performance instructions" might suggest that a norm is the same thing as a client's job description. It could also misleadingly be associated with a set of rules or official regulations. In the descriptive paradigm, however, the term *norm* usually operates at a wider, more social level. For example, in the nineteenth century the norm for translating foreign verse into French was to render it into prose. There was no official rule stating that this *had* to be done, but there was an informal collective agreement. When translators approached the foreign text, they would accept that their work was not to imitate what the text looked or sounded like. When publishers hired translators, they *expected* them to render verse as prose. And when readers approached a literary translation, they would similarly accept that foreign poetry had to be in prose. Of course, the norm was not respected by all translators; norms are not laws that everyone has to follow. Norms are more like common standard practices in terms of which other types of practice are marked.

Now, why did the "verse into prose" norm exist? On several different levels, it embodied the idea that French culture was superior to others. In Toury's terms, it conveyed at least that much of the society's "general values and ideas." Given this assumed superiority, there was no reason to accept any foreign influence on the French genre system. In Even-Zohar's terms, the perceived prestige of the target system allocated translation a peripheral role and hence a conservative range of acceptable forms. Further, if we follow Toury, there would be some kind of social (though not juridical) penalization involved whenever a translator did not adhere to the norm. For instance, a text that differed radically from the established genres might be considered peculiar, ugly, or simply not worth buying. In every culture, the nature of a good translation is determined by such norms, since "bad translations" are penalized in some way. In avant-garde systems, the norm becomes to break existing norms.

The concept of norms covers many related but different things. Toury (1995/2012: 82) makes a basic distinction between "**preliminary norms**," which concern the selection of the text and the mode of translation (direct/indirect, etc.), and "**operational norms**," which would concern the decisions made when translating. However, as the "verse into prose" example shows, norms also have social and epistemological dimensions. They concern what translators think they are supposed to do, what clients think translators ought to do, what text-users think a translation should be like, and what kind of translations are considered reprehensible or laudable within the system. **Chesterman** (1997) organizes these various aspects by distinguishing between "**professional norms**," which would cover everything related to the translation process, and "**expectancy norms**," which are what people expect of the translation product. If translators in a given society usually add explanatory footnotes, that might be a professional norm. If readers are frustrated when such notes do not appear, or if the notes are in an unusual place, then that frustration will be in relation to expectancy norms. Ideally, the different types of norms reinforce one another, so that translators tend to do what clients and readers expect of them. In times of cultural change, the types of norms might be thrown out of kilter, and considerable tension can result.

The concept of norms has been important for relations between descriptive research and the other paradigms of translation theory. If the concept is applied seriously, you should probably give up the idea of defining what a good translation is supposed to be (although it is still possible to say what a good or bad social effect might look like, and thus evaluate the way norms work). In fact, the very notion of what a translation is becomes very relative. This **relativism** would be a major point of compatibility with the *Skopos* paradigm. However, relativism runs counter to much of the linguistic work done in the equivalence paradigm. When a linguist analyzes a text to see how it should be translated, the basic assumption is not only that the answers will come from the nature of that text, but more importantly that the nature of translation is a very clear thing; there is not much relativism involved. In the *Skopos* paradigm, the answers will come from the situation in which the translation is carried out, to the extent that it matters little whether a text is a translation or a liberal rewrite. In the descriptive paradigm, however, questions about the borders between translations and non-translations can be answered in terms of norms, which in turn express values from the wider system within which the translator is working. In this sense, the theory of norms positions translation somewhere between the relative certainty of equivalence and the relative indifference of *Skopos* theory.

Such comparisons of paradigms were made in the 1980s, when the various approaches were starting to congeal into a discipline called Translation Studies. Scholars working in the descriptive paradigm, usually with a background in literary studies, criticized the "prescriptive" work done in the equivalence paradigm. How could a theory set out to tell someone how to translate, when the very notion of translation varied so much from culture to culture? The call for descriptions was thus initially a negation of the **prescription** associated with the equivalence paradigm. Similarly, whereas the equivalence paradigm invited analysis to start from the *start* text, the descriptive paradigm tended to favor the *target* text and its position in the *target* system. Toury (1995/2012) explicitly recommends **beginning analysis from the translation** rather than from the start text; he thus creates space for research that takes no account of the start text at all. For example, you can simply compare different translations, or compare translations with non-translations within the target system. That kind of opposition helped to make Toury the *enfant terrible* of his day.

The concept of norms nevertheless allows a kind of prescriptivism to be introduced into descriptive studies, almost through the back door. Even if the role of theory is not to tell translators how to translate, a descriptive approach can identify the norms by which a translation may be considered good by people in a certain place and time. This has allowed for a certain application of descriptive studies in the **training of translators and interpreters**. Toury (1992) has suggested, for example, that trainees be asked to render the same text according to different norms (e.g. translate as one might have done in nineteenth-century Germany, or under conditions of censorship). The trainee will thus become aware that there are many different ways to translate, each with certain advantages and disadvantages. Of course, the same kind of exercise can be recommended within the purpose-based paradigm: translate the one text in different ways in order to achieve different purposes. Another kind of compatibility is proposed by Chesterman (1999), who suggests that the study of norms will enable teachers and learners to predict the **relative success of one translation approach or another**. No teacher can tell any student there is only one way to translate (since many norms are available), but empirical research can make it possible to predict success or failure when dominant norms are broken.

In all these ways, the concept of norms has helped bridge some of the gaps between descriptivism and prescriptivism.

The concept of norms has thus helped bring several approaches closer together, at the same time as the empirical discovery of norms has increased our historical understanding of the way translations operate. The fundamental concept, however, is not clear-cut. Consider, for example, the way the German sociologist **Niklas Luhmann** (1985: 33) describes legal norms as "**counterfactual expectations**," in the sense that they do not take account of the way people *actually* behave. When these expectations are defeated (we find that there are criminals), the legal norms do *not* adapt accordingly (criminals must still be punished, no matter how many criminals there are). Many expectancy norms concerning translations could be of this counterfactual kind. For example, no matter how often we find that translations are domesticating, users of translations might still insist that they should *not* be. If some norms are working like this, then the bottom-up counting of facts and frequencies will never connect with the social pronouncements of what is acceptable or unacceptable. This is another reason why a descriptive approach requires theoretical concepts.

Whenever theorists tell us about norms, we should ask exactly how they have discovered those norms. If bottom-up, the empirical patterns may not all have equal status as psychological or social facts. And if top-down, then we should ask where the theorist found the categories of analysis, and why.

5.4 "ASSUMED" TRANSLATIONS

Here is a theoretical problem that cuts to the heart of empirical methodologies. If you set out to discover the diversity of translation norms, can you pretend to be sure from the outset what is meant by the term "translation"? If you can, exactly what criteria should you use for collecting a set of things called "translations"? And if not, how can you avoid imposing your own translation norms on other cultures and periods? This is one of the classical aporias that tend to worry Western researchers.

Toury's initial solution has been to leave the defining to the people we study. For him, translations are taken to be "all utterances in a (target) culture which are presented or regarded as translations, on any grounds whatever" (Toury 1995/2012: 27). In other words, we wait to see what each culture and each period has to say about what is or is not a translation. This is the operative concept of "assumed translations," which simply means that **a translation is a translation only for as long as someone assumes it is one**. A **pseudotranslation** (a non-translation that is presented as a translation) might then be held to be a translation only for as long as the trick works, and it becomes a non-translation for those aware of the false pretense.

That solution remains fraught with logical difficulties. For example, if each language has different words for "translation," how do we know those words are translations of each other? In order to select the words, we would surely need our own concept of translation. The debate over that issue has been one of the most recondite activities in Translation Studies (cf. Gutt 1991/2000; Toury 1995; Hermans 1997, 1999; Halverson 2007; Pym 1998, 2007a). For some, the problem is basically without solution, since if we use our normal terms to describe another culture's term "we naturally translate that other term according to our concept of translation, and into our concept of translation; and in domesticating it, we inevitably reduce it" (Hermans 1997: 19). Alternatively, one might recognize that much of the damage has already been done: the Western translation form has travelled across the globe, to the extent that there is considerable common ground when discussing its status in different host cultures. On this second view, the descriptivist theorizing of translation would itself have travelled along similar paths.

What makes a translation a translation?

Descriptivists try to be as explicit as possible about their procedures. They cannot simply accept that "everyone knows what a translation is." This is where the paradigm enters a clearly theoretical mode. For example, Toury (1995/2012) posits that we will recognize an "assumed translation" because three things are held to be true about it:

1 *The source text postulate*: "there is another text, in another culture/language, which has both chronological and logical priority over [the translation]. Not only has such an assumed text presumably *preceded* the one taken to be its translation, but it is also assumed to have served as a *point of departure* and as a *basis* for the latter" (1995/2012: 29; italics in the text).
2 *The transfer postulate*: "the process whereby the assumed translation came into being involved the transfer from the assumed source text of certain features that the two now share" (1995/2012: 29).

3 *The relationship postulate*: "there are tangible relationships which tie [the assumed translation] to its assumed original" (1995/2012: 30). Thanks to these relationships we can talk about translations being more or less literal, functional, adaptive, and so on.

Compare these three features with a brief summary of what Stecconi (2004) considers necessary if semiosis is to be counted as translation:

1 *Similarity*: A translation is like a previous text.
2 *Difference*: A translation is different from that previous text, if only because it is in a different language or variety of language.
3 *Mediation*: There is a translator between the two sides, mediating between them.

Chesterman (2006) finds these three features in the words that many languages have for "translation," although he claims that modern Indo-European languages give more weight to the "similarity" dimension. He suggests this may be why so much is made of "equivalence" in European theories.

Pym (2004a) proposes that two "maxims" operate when translations are received as translations:

1 *The maxim of translational quantity* holds that a translation represents an anterior text quantitatively: if a start text is longer, the translation is assumed to become longer too, within some kind of reason.
2 *The maxim of first-person displacement* holds that the discursive first person of the text ("I") is the same first person as the anterior text, even when the two texts have been produced by different subjects.

The first maxim is broken when the receiver thinks the translation is too short or too long; the second is broken when the receiver thinks the first person of the text is the translator. In both cases, the breaking of the maxim produces meanings from the limits of translation.

There are many similar attempts to define translation in a formal but relativistic way, particularly as a version of reported speech (Bigelow 1978; Folkart 1991). Almost all this conceptual work is overlooked by theories of "cultural translation."

5.5 TARGET-SIDE PRIORITY

As we have seen, **Toury** upset linguistics-based studies of translation not only by opposing prescriptivism, but more profoundly by insisting that translations should be studied in terms of their *target* contexts. This led to an extreme position: in Toury's words, "translations should be regarded as facts of target cultures" (1995: 139; cf. 1995/2012: 23). This should be understood as part of a research methodology; it does not mean that translations somehow never have start texts. Toury's argument is that the factors needed to describe the specificity of translations can be found within the target system. This is based on the assumption that translators first serve the culture into which they are translating, either in order to reinforce its norms or to fill perceived "gaps."

The principle of target-side priority has been contested. The researchers working on literary translation at **Göttingen** in the 1990s generally preferred a **"transfer" model**, which explicitly traced movements *between* cultures. Others have objected to the separation of the two cultures, arguing that translators tend to work in an "**intercultural**" space in the overlap of cultures (cf. Pym 1998). More generally, as with the problem of defining translations, the binary opposition of start and target has been increasingly criticized from indeterminist perspectives, as we shall see later.

5.6 UNIVERSALS OF TRANSLATION

If translations can be studied scientifically, then the aim of such study could be like that of all science. We thus find various proclamations that the aim of research is to discover "universals" or "laws" of translation. That is an area for research, rather than for translation theory as such. But what the terms "universals" and "laws" mean is by no means clear, and that is where theorization has been necessary.

A "universal of translation" would be **a feature that is found in translations and not in other kinds of text**. Yet it should not be too obvious or tautological: it should not simply ensue from the way someone decides to define what a translation is. For example, if we say "a translation presupposes a previous text," the proposition might be interesting as part of a universal definition but it is rather too obvious to be a universal in the sense we are discussing here. The term "universal" is generally used to refer not to the semiotic functions of translations (the relations people assume or activate when they approach a translation) but to linguistic features that can actually be measured.

A universalist proposition might be something like "translations tend to be longer than their start texts." Many people believe this to be true, but could it be true of all translations? There is a minor problem with the different ways in which text length can be measured in different languages, but that can be solved (for example, we might do an experiment where a text is rendered from language A into language B, then back into A, and so on, hypothesizing that the texts will become longer with each translation). In many cases there will be some expansion, at least in the first few moves. But the "universal" will probably not hold for all genres and languages. For example, it seems not to hold for technical reports rendered from Spanish into English, basically because experienced translators tend to eliminate many of the Spanish circumstantials. It could hardly hold for translated subtitles, which generally have to be shorter than the spoken language they render. And it could scarcely describe simultaneous or consecutive interpreting, which are nevertheless modes of translation. Further, even if the proposition were found to be true for all languages, genres, and modes, could this kind of research tell us why that might be so? The search for universals is not an easy affair.

The early research on potential universals was mostly carried out by scholars associated with the Tel Aviv school in the 1980s. Here are some of the proposed universals:

5.6.1 Lexical simplification

Lexical simplification can be defined as "the process and/or result of making do with *less* [different] words" (Blum-Kulka and Levenston 1983: 119). This means that translations tend to have a narrower range of lexical items than do non-translations, and they tend to have a higher proportion of high-frequency lexical items. The language is usually flatter, less structured, less ambiguous, less specific to a given text, more habitual, and so on (cf. Toury 1995/2012).

5.6.2 Explicitation

Explicitation was defined by Blum-Kulka (1986/2004) as a particular kind of simplification due to the greater "redundancy" of translations. The hypothesis is as follows:

> The process of interpretations performed by the translator on the source text might lead to a TL [target language] text which is more redundant than the source text. This redundancy can be expressed by a rise in the level of cohesive explicitness in the TL text. This argument may be stated as "*the explicitation hypothesis*", which postulates an observed cohesive explicitness from SL [source language] to TL texts regardless of the increase traceable to differences between the two linguistic and textual systems involved. It follows that explicitation is viewed here as inherent in the process of translation.
>
> (1986/2004: 292)

In practice, this means that translations tend to use more syntactic markers than do non-translations. In one of the clearest examples, Olohan and Baker (2000) find that the optional English reporting *that* (as in "She said [that] she would come") is more frequent in a corpus of English translations than in a comparable corpus of English non-translations. Translations might thus be more explicit than non-translations.

5.6.3 Adaptation

Adaptation is the tendency for translations to adapt to the target language and culture. Zellermayer (1987) found that translations from English into Hebrew were consistently more informal and spoken in character than the translations going the other way. This was attributed to the more oral nature of Hebrew written texts in general.

5.6.4 Equalizing

Equalizing is the term used by Shlesinger (1989) for the way simultaneous interpreting reduces both extremes of the oral-literate continuum (where texts at one end have many of the qualities of spoken language, while those at the other have all the qualities of written language):

Simultaneous interpretation exerts an equalizing effect on the position of a text on the oral-literate continuum; i.e., it diminishes the orality of markedly oral texts and the literateness of markedly literate ones. Thus, the range of the oral-literate continuum is reduced in simultaneous interpreting.

(Shlesinger 1989: 2–3; see Pym 2007b)

The mediation process would bring the features towards a mid-point. Shlesinger found the tendency to equalizing to be more powerful than the evidence of Zellermayer's "adaptation" and Blum-Kulka's "explicitation." Although formulated only for interpreting, the hypothesis might also hold for written translations.

5.6.5 Unique items

Unique items are the basis for a hypothesis formulated by the Finnish researcher Sonja Tirkkonen-Condit (2004), well beyond the Tel Aviv school. The claim is that linguistic elements found in the target language but not in the start language tend *not* to appear in translations. Or better, such "unique items" are less frequent in translations than in non-translations, since "they do not readily suggest themselves as translation equivalents" (2004: 177–8). This has been tested on linguistic structures in Finnish and Swedish, but it might also apply to something like the structure "to be done" in English (as in "they are to be married"). The hypothesis is compatible with the general thrust of simplification, although not reducible to it.

The study of translation universals has developed significantly thanks to **corpus studies** (for the frequencies of elements) and **think-aloud protocols, Translog, screen recording**, and **eye tracking** (for the translation processes). However, although there is now a body of research, we are not in a position to proclaim that any of the above hypotheses holds in all cases. Explicitation, for example, has been shown to prevail in a number of studies, but translations also exhibit **implicitation** (the reverse of explicitation), and in some cases there is more implicitation than explicitation (Kamenická 2007).

On the level of theory, the issue of universals becomes more nebulous the more you look at it. It is not clear, for example, if simplification, explicitation, and equalizing are separate things or just different manifestations of the same underlying phenomenon. It is not obvious whether a universal has to be true in all cases studied, or just generally true when a lot of translations are put into one corpus and a lot of non-translations are put into another. No one is sure if the tendencies discovered are really specific to translation, whether they occur with similar frequencies in all interlingual mediation, whether they can also be found in processes of "retelling" within the one language, or whether the frequencies of linguistic items have any automatic correspondence with social or psychological importance. In all, the notion of universals is a very long way from the conceptual clarity with which the concept is used in Chomsky's linguistics. Here, it seems, researchers are merely counting things on the surface level of language. This means they have no way of saying why a potential universal should be universal.

I note that many of the more empirical studies on universals have been on non-literary texts, in contradistinction to the early history of the descriptive paradigm. Perhaps for this reason, the researchers tend to forget about the radical options available to translators throughout history: researchers collect texts and translations from a newspaper, or from contemporary European languages, in the belief that the samples will eventually represent all languages and all translation practices. They thus overlook schemata like Holmes's five options for the rendition of form. "Simplification" could be a necessary consequence of strategies adopted in a "mimetic form" approach; something like "adaptation" could appear to be universal in a situation where "analogical form" is the norm, and so on. That is, the apparent universals could be dependent on specific kinds of social contexts. Alternatively, something like "explicitation" might be found to hold throughout all of Holmes's large-scale historical contexts.

5.7 LAWS

Universals are linguistic features supposedly specific to translations. Laws, on the other hand, are principles stating *why* such features should be found in translations. The universals locate the linguistic tendencies, and the laws relate those tendencies to something in the society, culture, or psychology of the translator.

The need to consider causes is obvious from the theoretical shortcomings of searches for universals. Work based on "**comparable corpora**," in particular, can compare translations done into English with non-translations originally written in English. This method is certainly economical (no need to learn languages), but it is fundamentally unable to say *why* shifts occur. In the study on the high frequency of optional reporting *that* in translations in English, the researchers suggest the phenomenon has a psychological cause, "subconscious explicitation" (Olohan and Baker 2000). However, since the corresponding connectors in the *start* languages must have been overwhelmingly non-optional (English is special in this regard), the cause might also have been straight interference. Or it could be the effect of "equalizing," removing the orality of implicit *that*. On the level of universals, it is impossible to say, and the categories are poorly distinguished anyway (Pym 2008). On the level of laws, however, one might hazard a guess.

The term "laws" is associated with **Even-Zohar** (1986 and elsewhere) and especially with **Toury** (1995/2012), from within the same Tel Aviv school where the early notions of universals were developed. A law of translation would ideally be one of the principles underlying the way translation norms come about, which should in turn explain linguistic universals.

Such laws would be like what Even-Zohar (1978) proposes when he says translations tend to play an innovative cultural role when the target system feels itself to be inferior. You could see this "innovative" function as a certain set of translation norms: translators might use Holmes's "mimetic" form; they would adopt foreignizing options and import elements. On the linguistic level, they might use less simplification, explicitation, adaptation, and equalizing than would be the case otherwise. The law then proposes that what happens when translating is related to a certain context of production, here involving a relation of asymmetric prestige. Note, however, that the relation between the norms and the context is not one of automatic correspondence. These are "laws of tendency," a term that can be understood in two senses: 1) in the long run, factors on the two levels tend to correlate to a significant degree, and 2) the more the prestige is asymmetric on the context level, the more the translations will have an innovative role.

Toury proposes two laws of translation. The first is a general "**law of growing standardization**" (1995/2012: 303ff.), which brings together many of the proposed universals.

Toury proposes that, when compared with their start texts, translations are simpler, flatter, less structured, less ambiguous, less specific to a given text, and more habitual. The explanatory part is then as follows:

> the more peripheral [the status of the translation], the more translation will accommodate itself to established models and repertoires.
>
> (Toury 1995/2012: 307)

This could mean that the apparent "universals" are especially present when translations are not particularly important or active within a culture. And that should beg the question of how "universal" a universal can be.

Toury also proposes a "**law of interference**" (1995/2012: 310–15). This basically says that translators tend to bring across structures that are in the start text, even when those structures are not normal in the target language. Surely nothing to get excited about? Toury nevertheless makes two interesting claims about tendencies. He posits, first, that **interferences tend to be on the macrostructural level** (text organization, paragraphing, etc.) rather than on the smaller levels of the sentence or the phrase. That is, translators tend to transform the small things but copy the big things. Toury then hypothesizes that "tolerance of interference […] tends to increase when translation is carried out from a 'major' or highly prestigious language/culture" (1995/2012: 314). This is a new formulation of the law first proposed by Even-Zohar. We might think, for example, that English-language cultures feel themselves to be superior, so they tolerate no interference from any other culture. We might then look at a few translations of French cultural theory, where there are all kinds of telltale syntactic interferences such as sentences beginning "For X is always already…" or high proportions of cleft sentences. Since the source culture ("French theory") is held to be prestigious, the interferences are tolerated. This makes sense: you only imitate people you admire.

Research on these laws has not evolved with the same enthusiasm as the investigation of universals. This might be because causation is complex in any sociocultural field. Toury recognizes this difficulty: "There seems to be no single factor which cannot be enhanced, mitigated, maybe even offset by the presence of another" (2004: 15). This amounts to saying that contexts are multiple and irreducible; there can be no simple laws.

The relative lack of interest in laws might also suggest a certain stagnation in this kind of theory. For many scholars with a literary background, the writing of history is probably enough of a goal. The interest in high-level abstractions has tended to come from quite a different mode of description, closer to Cognitive Science.

5.8 PROCESS STUDIES

Process studies have been important in Interpreting Studies since the 1970s, when neuroscientists and psychologists helped explain how conference interpreters perform their magic (cf. Pöchhacker 2004). Descriptive Translation Studies then met with process studies from the 1980s, particularly in Scandinavia, resulting in an intriguing body of data gathered through think-aloud protocols, keystroke logging, screen recording, and eye tracking. We now know something about what goes on in interpreters and translators' brains, beyond merely comparing the inputs and outputs.

Of particular interest is the growing body of data that compares novices with experienced translators. In principle, the differences should enable us to say how one becomes a professional, and thus what we should be training novices in. The findings suggest that the more experienced translators tend to do the following (here I adapt and simplify Englund Dimitrova 2005: 14–15):

1 Use more paraphrase and less literalism as coping strategies (Kussmaul 1995; Lörscher 1991; Jensen 1999).
2 Process larger translation units (Toury 1986; Lörscher 1991; Tirkkonen-Condit 1992).
3 Spend longer reviewing their work at the post-drafting phase but make fewer changes when reviewing (Jensen and Jakobsen 2000; Jakobsen 2002; Englund Dimitrova 2005).
4 Read texts faster and spend proportionally more time looking at the target text than at the start text (Jakobsen and Jensen 2008).
5 Use top-down processing and refer more to the translation purpose (Fraser 1996; Künzli 2001, 2004; Tirkkonen-Condit 1992).
6 Rely more on their memory and less on looking things up (Tirkkonen-Condit 1989).
7 Express more principles and personal theories (Tirkkonen-Condit 1989, 1997; Jääskeläinen 1999).
8 Incorporate the client into their uncertainty-management processes (Künzli 2004).
9 Automatize some complex tasks but also shift between automatized routine tasks and conscious problem-solving (Krings 1988; Jääskeläinen and Tirkkonen-Condit 1991; Englund Dimitrova 2005).
10 Display more realism, confidence and critical attitudes in their decision-making (Künzli 2004).

This set of propositions might appear to have been derived bottom-up, from the disinterested analysis of data. All empirical research, though, starts from hypotheses, which are formulated in terms of theories. Taken together, these results sound rather like the main tenets of *Skopos* theory (greater independence of the professional, with less literalism and more awareness of contexts and clients). That narrative is also reinforced by the way "professionals" are defined and selected in the various research projects. It could be that the empirical research that was *not* carried out within the purpose paradigm (because of the idealist nature of those theories) has actually been done in this cognitivist niche of the descriptive paradigm. That said, empirical research, by its very nature, retains a capacity to question grand theories. It can even question its own general consensus: Jensen (1999) reports that experienced translators tend to use a "knowledge-telling" mode of production, rather than the "knowledge-transforming" mode that would seem more in tune with target-side functionalism: they would engage in less problem-solving, goal-setting, and re-analyzing behavior than do young professional translators. In other words, despite the pedagogical theories, they go fast and do things as simply as possible. As the researchers always conclude, more research is needed.

5.9 FREQUENTLY HAD ARGUMENTS

I will now bring together a few general aspects of the descriptive paradigm. The following points would be considered positive:

1   The historical variety of translation has been revealed.
2   The paradigm has played a central role in the development of Translation Studies as an academic discipline.
3   It has created knowledge that is useful for all aspects of Translation Studies, including the pedagogical prescriptive approaches it originally opposed.
4   It breaks with many of the prescriptive pronouncements of the equivalence paradigm, albeit while creating its own illusions of objectivity.

The counterweight to these positive points is a series of arguments about the failings of the paradigm.

5.9.1 "Descriptions do not help train translators"

The usual argument is that translation theory should help people learn about translation, and for this we need prescriptions (for good translations), not descriptions (of just any old translations). Various scholars have responded to this. Toury (1992) points out the usefulness of descriptions in the training situation, since an instructor can always present alternative ways of translating, none of which is ever perfect (in Toury's words, "everything has its price"). We have seen above how Chesterman (1999) also argues that empirical research should reinforce training, since it can predict the success or failure of certain solutions.

5.9.2 "The target side cannot explain all relations"

This is a common critique even within the descriptive paradigm. By no means everyone would agree with Toury that "translations should be regarded as facts of target cultures." The target-side focus certainly cannot explain how translations work in postcolonial frames, where the distinctions between cultures are blurred, or wherever power asymmetries are so great that the start side is actively sending translations to the target culture. Many researchers retain the importance of the start side, and many more are prepared to question whether there are just two cultures at stake. For that matter, consider the role of cross-cultural relations in the explanatory parts of Toury's laws. If translations are ultimately explained by how prestigious one culture is in the eyes of another, they cannot be facts of one culture only.

5.9.3 "The models concern texts and systems, not people"

This is a general critique that might be made of virtually all scientific approaches to cultural products in the twentieth century. Still, Toury's abstract concepts of norms and laws are offset by his interest in how translators become translators (1995/2012: 277–94), and recent moves within descriptivist projects have incorporated sociological models, particularly **Bourdieu**'s concept of "habitus" (Simeoni 1998; Hermans 1999). This would meet up with calls for a more humanized "Translator Studies" (Chesterman 2009).

5.9.4 "The focus on norms promotes conservative positions"

This argument supposes that descriptions of norms can only help to reproduce those norms, without attempting to improve translation practices. The basic response is clear enough: you have to understand a situation before you can start improving it (as if there were disinterested understanding). A slightly better response is that norms can be taught as a series of viable alternatives (as in Toury and Chesterman), so the discovery of norms becomes a way to empower translators by enhancing their repertoires of solutions. As for the apparent promotion of conservatism, Toury actually proposes that we train students to *break* norms, as he himself has done within Translation Studies.

5.9.5 "The definition of 'assumed translations' is circular"

This is an argument for theorists who drink beer. As we have seen, Toury initially refuses to define what a "translation" is, saying that the definition is made by the people who produce and use translations. I noted that this raises the technical problem of how the different terms for "translation" are assumed to be translations of each other. In the end, the researcher needs criteria for the selection of those terms, and those criteria must effectively constitute a theoretical definition of translation. So who is doing the assuming and/or the defining? Surely the theorist-researcher, in the first place. Yet many researchers in this paradigm do not want to take responsibility for their definitions. They pretend that everything comes from the object of study. This leads to a more serious critique.

5.9.6 "Descriptivist theory is unaware of its own historical position"

This argument sees the descriptive paradigm as an exercise in positivism. The paradigm would require belief in a neutral, transparent, objective knowledge about translation, and progress would be the accumulation of that knowledge. A great deal of conceptual armor is built around that belief. However, the armor has cracks at several points: the problem of defining translations, the problem of how to use descriptions of norms, and the possibility that the various levels of description are themselves translations of a kind (check the way Toury uses the term "translation" to describe norms). At all these points, some attention is required to the role of the person doing the describing. The descriptive paradigm has not been able to rise to that challenge. The role of subjectivity in the constitution of knowledge is better handled by theories of uncertainty, and the wider senses of "translation" would be better developed by theories of "cultural translation." We will meet both those paradigms below.

5.10 THE FUTURE OF THE DESCRIPTIVE PARADIGM

Where does the descriptive paradigm go from here? There have been calls for a "**sociological turn**," for an alliance with a discipline better equipped to handle contextual variables. **Theo Hermans** (1999) closes his account of the descriptive paradigm by pointing to the sociologies of **Bourdieu** and **Luhmann**. And so one turns that corner, to find what?

The great modernist sociologies are based on the same structuralism that shaped the descriptive paradigm itself, albeit sometimes with scope for self-reflexivity (the sociologist can do the sociology of sociologists). Further, these sociologies are overwhelmingly of single societies only, of systems in the "one side or the other" sense that has reigned within the descriptive paradigm. They fit in so well with the target-side orientation of descriptive approaches that they risk bringing in little that is new. Indeed, some of the descriptive literary studies of the 1970s and 1980s were already doing systemic sociology of a kind.

A great deal of research has been carried out within the descriptive frame. There are countless studies on literary translations, linguistic analyses of shifts, a growing body of research that integrates various social actors, wlth their agency and power relations, plus all the empirical work using corpora, think-aloud protocols, keystroke recording, and eye tracking. We could add the empirical work done on the cognitive dimensions of conference interpreting and more recently the social and political dimensions of community inter-preting. Along the way, we have a good deal of work on translation and gender, translation and postcolonialism, translation and censorship, translation and minorities, translation and languages of limited diffusion, and so on, all of which could be placed more or less within the descriptive frame. And any new phenomenon that merits attention, like translation in the interactive Web or the work of volunteer translators, is likely to be approached in straight descriptive terms. And yet, relatively few these numerous descriptive ventures come up with any major new statement on the level of translation theory. True, encounters with feminism, in particular, have **questioned the subservient status of the translator**, likening assumed inferiority to the position of women within patriarchy (cf. Delisle 1993; Simon 1996; von Flotow 1997). Feminism is also the probable origin of claims that **translators should become more visible** in their texts and societies (Venuti 1995, 2012). Yet on both those counts, and in much of the rest, the concepts come from other disciplines and are *applied* to translation, making translation theory an importer rather than producer of ideas.

In this respect, the potential of the descriptive paradigm, which once paradoxically housed the most powerful theorizing of translation, has not been realized. Other modes of thought have taken the lead.

SUMMARY

This chapter has sketched out a set of descriptive theories that oppose the equivalence paradigm in that they aim to be non-prescriptive, their prime focus is on "shifts" rather than types of equivalence, and they do not undertake extensive analysis of the start text. They tend to be like purpose-based *Skopos* approaches in that they emphasize the target-culture context and the *function* of translations. They nevertheless differ from purpose-based approaches in that they see functions in terms of the positions occupied by translations within the target *systems*, rather than with respect to a client or a job descrip-tion. Descriptive theories also tend to concern what translations are *usually* like in a partic-ular context, rather than the ways in which particular translations might differ. They are thus able to talk about the "norms" that guide the way translations are produced and received. The paradigm is relativistic in that it is very aware that what is considered a good translation in one historical context may not be rated so highly in a different context. The research based on those concepts has done much to reveal the diversity of translation practices in different historical periods, different cultures, and different types of communication. It has been accompanied by theorizing of possible universals and laws of translation, although the paradigm has not seemed able to maintain a strong relation between the discovery of diversity and the development of new concepts.

SOURCES AND FURTHER READING

The third edition of *The Translation Studies Reader* (Venuti 2012) has texts by Toury, Even-Zohar, and Lefevere, with the first two relegated to the section "1960s–1970s." Munday (2012) deals with the paradigm in his chapters on "Discourse and Register" and "Systems Theories." A historical account of the systems-approach is Hermans' *Translation in Systems* (1999). The early conference proceedings (Holmes *et al.* 1970, 1978) are full of ad hoc insight into the development of the paradigm. The same could be said of the seminal collection *The Manipulation of Literature* (Hermans 1985), which is rather more profound than its title. Anyone undertaking empirical research on translations should have tackled Toury's *Descriptive Translation Studies – and beyond* (1995/2012), although it is not an easy read. Numerous papers on various aspects of methodology are available online at the sites of Itamar Even-Zohar (http://www.tau.ac.il/~itamarez/) and Gideon Toury (http://www.tau.ac.il/~toury/). A more entertaining approach to literary translation is André Lefevere's *Translation, Rewriting, and the Manipulation of Literary Fame* (1992). For insights on the various sociocultural aspects of descriptive studies, see the selection of José Lambert's articles in *Functional Approaches to Culture and Translation* (Delabastita *et al.* 2006). For a critical account of systems and norms, see Pym (1998). A broad update on recent work in the descriptive paradigm can be gleaned from the volume *Beyond Descriptive Translation Studies* (Pym *et al.* 2008).

Suggested projects and activities

1   Consider all the language situations you participate in on a typical day, not only with newspapers, television, and websites but also in shops, banks, and public services. How much of this linguistic material must have been trans-lated in one way or another? (Consider news events that have happened outside of your languages.) How much of that material is actually marked as translational? Why (not)?

2   Where do translators and interpreters work in your town or city? What laws or policies orient their work?

3   Look up translations of John 1 ("In the beginning was the Word, and the Word was with God, and the Word was God") in as many languages as you can (cf. Nord 2001). Which translations make sense, and which do not? Could the differences be described in terms of shifts? Are there different norms at work?

4   Find out about the Mexican interpreter La Malinche (also called Doña Marina). What systems was she operating within? What was her relation with the systems? What norms would have regulated her work? Are these systems and norms different depending on whether her story is told by feminists or by

Mexican nationalists? (The same exercise can be done for any number of high-profile translators, preferably working in situations of conflict.)

5 Find a code of ethics for translators. Could any of the principles be described as norms? If so, what kind of norms are they? How would they relate to an empirical study of what translators actually do? (For a critical analysis of codes of ethics, see Pym 1992a/2010; Chesterman 1997.)

6 Find an authoritative history of your favorite national literature (e.g. French literature, Russian literature). Are translations part of the history (cf. Rosa 2003)? Are they mentioned in a separate chapter? In the index? Should they be? Would the inclusion of translations make any sense in the case of minor literatures in major languages (e.g. Australian literature)? Can periods of great change, such as the Italian Renaissance, really be written without reference to translations?

7 Select one page of a literary text and a professional translation of it. Try to divide the texts into paired segments (one start-text unit corresponds to one target-text unit) and identify the translation shifts. Are the shifts easily categorized? Can they all be described in terms of equivalence? For how many of the shifts could we say there are social or political factors involved? Should we talk about "shifts" or "variations," or perhaps "deviations," or even "errors"?

8 Find out about The Poems of Ossian (1773). Could this text be described as a translation? If not, what is it? Should it be analyzed within the field of Translation Studies?

9 Use a concordancer (or even the Readability tools in Word) to analyze the frequency of linguistic features in two different translations of the same text. Do the quantitative differences indicate some kind of different norms?

10 Use the same tools to compare a translation with its start text. Do your findings support any of the proposed universals?

11 Listen to translators talking about their work, as they are translating, when they are discussing a translation they have done, or when they are disagreeing, perhaps on one of the many Internet discussion lists for translators. What terms indicate the existence of norms? If you can identify a norm, can you also identify the punishment for non-compliance (in theory, norms are defined by the existence of sanctions)?

CHAPTER 6

Uncertainty

This chapter deals with a few theories that can be difficult to understand. The basic idea is that you can never be entirely sure of the meanings you translate, and yet you translate nevertheless. In the first part of the chapter we find there are two groups of theories dealing with this problem: some express uncertainty about translations, since alternative renditions are always possible, while others express uncertainty about *all* meanings, not just in translations. A reading from Plato's dialogue *Cratylus* (c.400BCE/1977) should help explain the difference. Then come a few ideas about how translation is possible even when we are uncertain. The last part of the chapter presents deconstruction, where uncertainty becomes a basis for regarding translation as transformation.

The main points in this chapter are:

- There are reasons for doubting any cause–effect relationship between start and target texts.
- The same reasons can be extended to uncertainty about communicating meanings in general.
- Some theories do not question the meaningfulness of texts (they are "determinist" with respect to language), but they do not accept that start texts fully cause translations (they are "indeterminist" with respect to translations).
- Other theories are more completely indeterminist because they question all meanings.
- There are several ways to explain how translation is still possible in a world of uncertainty: illumination, consensus-oriented dialogue, hermeneutics, social constructivism, game theory, and non-linear logic in general.
- Deconstruction is an indeterminist approach that accepts that all translation involves transformation.

6.1 WHY UNCERTAINTY?

The equivalence paradigm had its heyday in the 1960s and 1970s. So why did it decline? On the basis of our last two chapters, it would seem that equivalence was undermined by two new kinds of theory: *Skopos* theory and descriptivism. That, however, would only be partly correct. As we have seen, the newer paradigms did not do away with equivalence: they just made it narrower (in *Skopos* theory) or wider (in Toury's Descriptive Translation Studies).

The basic tenets of equivalence still underlie much of the work done on translation today. It is still the dominant paradigm in most linguistic approaches, especially in terminology and phraseology. Indeed, the concept of equivalence operates in new sectors like software localization, where many source and target phrases mostly have to match in both function and approximate length (see 7.5.4 below). Equivalence is by no means dead. But it has certainly been questioned.

There are at least two underlying reasons for the increasing dissatisfaction with equivalence:

1 **Instability of the "source"**: Descriptive research has shown that what translators do varies according to their cultural and historical position. For example, in the pre-print age, texts were often manuscripts that were constantly being copied, modified, and rewritten, as well as translated, making translation just another step in an endless sequence of transformations (in this, medieval texts were rather like our websites and software programs today). They were not stable points of departure to which any translation could be considered equivalent. So the concept of equivalence was not something that medieval translators argued about. Similar doubts about equivalence occur in our own technocratic age, where the success of a text tends to be measured in terms of the user pushing the right button or clicking on the right link, rather than by comparison with any anterior text.

2 **Epistemological skepticism**: Alongside the growing awareness of variability, the intellectual climate of the humanities was changing quite dramatically from the 1970s. Various forms of structuralism had assumed that scientific study could produce stable scientific knowledge in a world of relations between objects. However, philosophers had long been questioning that certainty. The relations between things could not be separated from relations within language, and language could not be assumed to be transparent to those things. In literary studies and cultural philosophy, structuralism gave way to post-structuralism and deconstruction. Those movements asked serious questions about equivalence. If a piece of language was supposed to be equivalent to some other piece of language, who had the right to say so? How could you ever be certain you had located the thing in common? What was equivalent to what, exactly, for whom, and with what authority? Those questions concern **epistemology** (the study of the ways knowledge is produced), and they are asked from a position of skepticism (whatever knowledge is produced, we are not entirely sure about it). A challenge to equivalence thus came from **epistemological skepticism**: the knowledge provided by equivalence might not be wrong, but we are not entirely sure about it.

So there are at least two reasons for questioning equivalence: technological changes affecting the stability of start texts, and a general intellectual climate of skepticism. In this chapter I will be concerned with the various ways epistemological skepticism has affected translation theory. We will see that there is more than one current at work: some theories express doubts about how translations represent their sources, while others are skeptical about *all* meanings. To grasp these theories in at least part of their complexity, we will meet a few ideas that go beyond traditional translation theory.

Some key terms

- **Epistemology**: The study of the ways knowledge is produced, in this case the construction of meanings on the basis of the text to be translated and the purpose to be achieved.
- **Skepticism**: The general attitude of having doubts about something.
- **Epistemological skepticism**: The general attitude of having doubts about how we obtain knowledge.
- **Determinism**: The belief that an event is caused by a previous event or set of events that we can know about. For example, you might believe that a translation is caused ("determined") by what is in the start text, or by the instructions received from the client.
- **Indeterminism**: The belief that not all events are wholly caused ("determined") by previous events. If the one text can cause many different translations, then none of the translations can be wholly "determined" by that text. Indeterminism would generally allow for some free will or agency on the part of the translator.
- **Indeterminacy**: Here, an instance of indeterminism believed to occur in a particular phenomenon. A belief in general indeterminism might make us believe in the particular indeterminacy of translation.
- **Determinist theory**: Here, a theory that assumes that, in a communication act, what is understood is determined by what is said or meant. Applied to translation, we would say that the correct translation is the one that corresponds to the author's ideas, intentions, message, or words.
- **Indeterminist theory**: Here, a theory that does *not* assume determinacy. An indeterminist theory would accept that translation does not involve a transfer of ideas, intentions, meanings, or words. Most indeterminist theories accept that a translation is based on an active interpretation of previous texts.

6.2 THE UNCERTAINTY PRINCIPLE

If you are told that "Friday the 13th" is equivalent to "martes 13" (Tuesday the 13th), you might accept the fact. Most professional translators would probably say the two are equivalent just because they are equivalent. The translators would perhaps then refer to some kind of **authority**, perhaps a dictionary, a bilingual friend, or probably themselves. Alternatively, you might remain skeptical, no matter what the authority. "**Skepticism**" means you are unsure about something. But there are several ways of having doubts. You might sit there and stare at the unknown word and get nervous about how little you really know, or you might ask more questions about the word. Even if you believe you will never be certain, you can still try to obtain knowledge. You could send translators mad by asking precisely what situations the equivalence holds in, or when the equivalence started to be produced, or why some formal difference persists, or how long the difference will remain (surely we should get the Spanish to adopt English superstitions about Friday, or vice versa?). Those questions will not help our translators at all. But they do lead to awareness of the authorities that the whole equivalence paradigm ultimately rests upon.

If we adopt this active kind of skepticism, we need not be asking annoying questions just for the fun of it. Even if we believe the questions can *never* be answered in any final way, or that we will ever reach any final truth, we might still consider it our duty to express doubt about all those authorities (teachers, dictionaries, experts, translators) that stop others from asking questions.

The kind of skepticism that most concerns the humanities derives from the **observer effect**: each observation is affected by the position of the observer. Something happens— let us say a car accident—and each observer's account will be different. Each person was standing in a different position; they have different backgrounds and thus different inter-ests in the accident. The element of uncertainty is simple enough in such cases, as is the epistemological skepticism of someone trying to investigate the accident. We can never trust any one observation absolutely. You might say that the thing observed—the car accident—never fully causes (explains, justifies, or accounts for) the person's actual obser-vation. Here we will say that the accident never fully **determines** the observations. **Indeterminism** is the general belief that events and observations are related in this way. Similarly, we could say that a text never fully determines (causes, explains, justifies, or accounts for) what a receiver understands of it. Each receiver brings a set of conceptual frames to the text, and the reception process is an interaction between the text and those frames. The same would hold for translation: no text fully determines a translation of that text, if only because translations rely on observations and interpretations.

The idea of indeterminism does not suit theories of equivalence. If we say that two texts are equivalent, we assume there is a stable understanding of both texts, at least to the extent that they can be judged to have the same function or value. Indeterminism, as part of the general uncertainty principle, means that stable understanding can never be simply assumed.

6.2.1 Quine's principle of the indeterminacy of translation

In the late 1950s the American philosopher **Willard Van Orman Quine** set out to find to what extent indeterminacy could affect language. To do this, he proposed a thought experiment involving translation. Here is a summary:

Imagine a "jungle linguist" who arrives in a village where people speak a completely unknown language. The linguist sets out to describe the language. They witness an event: a rabbit runs past, a native points to the rabbit and exclaims, "Gavagai!" The linguist writes down "*gavagai* = rabbit". An equivalent translation is thus produced.

Now, asks Quine, how can we be sure that *gavagai* really means "rabbit"? It could mean, "Look there, a rabbit!," or perhaps, "A rabbit with long legs," or even, "There is a flea on the rabbit's left ear," and so on. Quine argues that numerous interpretations are possible, and that no amount of questioning will ever produce absolute certainty that *gavagai* means "rabbit." Even if the linguist spends years with the tribe learning their language, there will always remain the possibility that each speaker's use of the word carries unseen individual values.

Quine actually argues that there are degrees of certainty for different kinds of proposi-tions. As far as translation is concerned, however, the message is that **indeterminacy will**

never completely go away. Quine posits that the one source (*gavagai*) can give rise to many different renditions ("rabbit," "flea on rabbit," etc.), all of which may be legitimate and yet "stand to each other in no plausible sort of equivalence relation however loose" (1960: 27). Whatever relation there may be between the translations, it is not certain, and that idealized, impossible certainty was what Quine associated with "equivalence." But if not equivalence, what is the relation?

In a later formulation of this indeterminacy principle (1969), Quine claims that **different translators will produce different translations**, all of which can be correct, and none of the translators will agree with the others' renditions. If the previous example of the jungle linguist seemed abstract and far-fetched (after all, there are no untouched tribes left in the world, and ethnolinguists have far more subtle modes of conducting fieldwork), the claim that different translators translate differently sounds familiar enough. And the claim that translators disagree with each others' translations seems uncomfortably close to home, especially when there is an element of authority or prestige at stake.

Indeterminacy accounts for those differences, disagreements, and uncertainties; the concept of equivalence does not. That is one good reason for incorporating indeterminacy into a theory of translation. Indeterminacy, however, is not a term used in many translation theories, at least not beyond Quine and the tradition of analytical philosophy. For the most part, its nagging doubts have worked their way into translation theory through a variety of intermediary disciplines and movements. Here I sketch a few of the connections.

Quine's principle of the indeterminacy of translation

Manuals for translating one language into another can be set up in divergent ways, all compatible with the totality of speech disposition, yet incompatible with one another. In countless places they will diverge in giving, as their respective translations of a sentence of one language, sentences of the other language which stand to each other in no plausible sort of equivalence however loose.

(Quine 1960: 27)

6.2.2 Indeterminism in theories of language

The basic idea of indeterminacy might be considered obvious. The American linguist **Noam Chomsky** regarded Quine's principle as simply saying that "theories are underdetermined by evidence," in the sense that a phenomenon can be accounted for by more than one theory (since a theory is ultimately like an observation, or like a reading, or like a translation). This, says Chomsky, is "true and uninteresting" (1980: 14, 16). That is, **so what?** In Chomsky's own field there is little doubt that different grammars can be written to describe the same language, and all of them will be adequate to some degree and yet different from each other. In literary theory, texts are accounted for by a succession of paradigms (philology, New Criticism, structuralism, Marxism, deconstruction, psychoanalysis, gender studies, etc.), none of which can be said to be wrong. In fact, in all the sciences, both natural and human, the twentieth century saw a general divergence between the production of theories and the gathering of evidence; in all fields of inquiry, you can come up with a new

theory on the basis of old facts (or do a new translation of an old text). The study of translation is obviously no different in this respect (which, by the way, is how this book can address
many different paradigms, all of them correct). Indeterminacy is the very basis for a plurality
of theories.

Now, **indeterminacy can be seen in all communication**, across the board. Although
its workings are clearer when illustrated between languages, it also applies *within*
languages. Whatever we say will be only one of many possible variations on what we think
we mean, and what others make of our words will be only one of many possible interpretations. Indeterminism says we cannot be sure of communicating anything, at least not in any
exact sense. We cannot assume there is a meaning that is encoded on one side and then
decoded on the other. The opposite of indeterminism might then be a theory that assumes
"**codes**," or "**transmission**," or "**meaning transfer**," or a "**conduit**" (all those metaphors
have been used) that is somehow able to guarantee equivalence.

The general idea of indeterminacy can be used to divide translation theories into those
that assume the possibility of exact communication of some kind (**determinist**: what X
means is what Y understands) and those that do not (**indeterminist**: we can never be sure
that the two share the same meaning). All students in the humanities should spend a few
sleepless nights worrying that they will never be fully understood, and a few more nights
concerned that they will never fully understand anyone else; then some five minutes
accepting that they do not understand themselves either. Students of translation should
probably invest some supplementary afternoons in existential preoccupation, since indeterminacy is even more of a problem when different languages and cultures are involved.

As we shall soon see, most indeterminist theories of translation simplify the division
between themselves and the determinist theories, especially when it comes to equivalence.
They make it look like there are just two camps, us and them, and a revolutionary battle
to be fought, dethroning the illusions of equivalence. The problem, though, is that the
indeterminist troops are far from united. More specifically, **many determinist theories
of language become indeterminist when applied to translation**. Things are complicated. Let us look at a few classical examples, since the problem has been around for
a very long time.

6.3 DETERMINIST VIEWS OF LANGUAGE WITH INDETERMINIST THEORIES OF TRANSLATION

Here I approach translation from the perspective of an ancient story about language.
Plato's dialogue *Cratylus* is based on two characters who hold opposed views about the
way words have meanings. They present their views, and Socrates asks them questions.
The character Hermogenes argues that words are just arbitrary labels for things (i.e. encod-
ings). The character Cratylus, on the other hand, argues that each thing has its proper word
(i.e. the shape of the word fits the thing, as in onomatopoeia):

> Cratylus says that everything has a right name of its own, which comes by nature, and
> that a name is not whatever people call a thing by agreement, just as a piece of their
> own voice applied to the thing, but that there is a kind of inherent correctness in
> names, which is the same for all people, both Greeks and non-Greeks.
>
> (383A, trans. Fowler c.400BCE/1977)

Hermogenes' position would seem the more correct. Give or take a few onomatopoeias, **words would seem to have an arbitrary relation to their referents**. That is what **Saussure** posited as one of the very foundations of systemic linguistics. It is also a way of explaining why words vary enormously from language to language, and thus why translation is necessary.

We nevertheless find Socrates spending a lot of time defending Cratylus's position. He argues that the Greek words actually do tell us something about the nature of things. For example, the word for truth, *aletheia*, is decomposed into *theia*, meaning "divine," and *ale*, meaning "wandering." Truth, it seems, is a "divine wandering" (421 B). That whole section of the dialogue is a farrago of insightful and playful etymology, brilliant enough to make one half-believe the theory. It reaches the level of syllables and rhythms, which are found to be particularly suited to what they express. Name-givers would use them the way painters use different colors. For example, the sound O is the chief element of the word *gogguloon* (meaning "round") (427 C), and we might add that the mouth makes more or less the same shape when we say *round, rund, rond, redondo*, etc., which are perhaps correct names. The theory even assumes some kind of infallibility. Socrates states that if a word cannot be analyzed in this way (the word *pyr*, for "fire," is an example), it "is probably foreign; for it is difficult to connect it with the Greek language" (409 E). That fails to explain why Greek alone should have all the good names, but let us proceed.

In the second part of the dialogue, Socrates starts to pull apart this same theory. Some of the weak points should be clear already. If the words are to be understood in terms of semantics within Greek, how could their correctness be for all people "both Greeks and non-Greeks"? Further, within the Greek language, Socrates finds words for "intellect" or "memory" that do *not* reflect movement. They would thus contradict the wonderful "divine wandering" theory found in the word *aletheia* ("truth") (437 B). These, apparently, are names that have been badly given. If it is possible to give a name badly, and yet those names are used, then there must be some degree of social convention in the names for things. Language is to some extent arbitrary.

If we look at these two theories, which one would be the less deterministic? Hermogenes' position is actually saying that the assigning of words to things or concepts is arbitrary, and thus *undetermined* by anything except convention. That theory makes translation easy: if you know the conventions, you just decode and encode. In fact, it makes equivalence quite possible. This means that **an indeterminist theory of naming can produce an equivalence-based theory of translation**. Think about it.

On the other hand, Cratylus's theory, which is highly deterministic (the nature of the thing determines the correct name), would make equivalence virtually impossible, and perhaps translation as well. How could we translate *aletheia* as *truth* if the Greek term really means "divine wandering"? This deterministic view says that Greek can only properly be understood in terms of Greek. So **no full equivalence is possible** beyond that language. Welcome to the paradoxes of theory.

6.3.1 Cratylistic determinacy in translation

Cratylus is not about translation, but it does illustrate a paradox to be found in many contemporary theories of translation. Indeed, the paradox of a **determinist theory of**

expression underlying an indeterminist theory of translation is so widespread that we might label all these theories "Cratylistic." Here are a few examples.

As mentioned in the chapter on equivalence (2.2), **Wilhelm von Humboldt** saw different languages as building different views of the world. The idea can be found in a number of approaches. For example, the Russian linguist **Roman Jakobson** (1959/2012: 142) claimed that Germans see death as a man (*der Tot*, masculine gender) whereas the Russians see it as a woman (смерть, feminine gender) because the languages attribute those genders. Similarly, says Jakobson, "the Russian painter Repin was baffled as to why Sin had been depicted as a woman by German artists: he did not realize that 'sin' is feminine in German (*die Sünde),* but masculine in Russian (грех)" (1959/2012: 130). So our languages would shape the way we perceive the world. The masculine sins of Russian cannot really be a full equivalent of the feminine sins of German, and their rewards in death are similarly non-equivalent. Does each language really determine the way these things are seen?

The **"world-view" theory** would be a modern version of Cratylistic determinism. For Cratylus, the nature of the thing determines its correct name; for linguistic relativism, **the nature of the language system determines perception of the thing**. Either way, there is a strong deterministic link between expression and concept. In fact, strict "world-view" linguistics would be deterministic in an even stronger sense, since they see each piece of knowledge as being determined by the entire language, not just by a few creative name-givers. In its extreme form, this systemic determinism means that knowledge cannot be conveyed beyond the language in which it is formulated. Translation could at best give us a suggestion of what we are missing.

Modernist aesthetics, which in Europe would date from the late nineteenth century, has followed similar paths. In the work of art, we are told, form and content are inseparable. Each set of words, or of sounds, has meaning precisely because of what they are and the way they have been put together: "that which is to be communicated is the poem itself," said the poet **T. S. Eliot** (1933/1975: 80): the poem would not convey any "meaning" that existed prior to the poem. This whole tradition has been traced back to Cratylus by Genette (1976). For most of the thinkers concerned, translation cannot be governed by equivalence, at least not on any aesthetic level.

The clearest formulation of this tradition is perhaps in the Italian theorist **Benedetto Croce** (1902/1922: 73) when he describes

> the *relative* possibility of translations; not as reproductions of the same original expressions (which it would be vain to attempt) but as productions of *similar* expressions more or less nearly resembling the originals. The translation called good is an approximation which has original value as work of art and can stand by itself.

Croce significantly describes the "**similarity**" or "approximation" as a "**family likeness**." The metaphor was to become rather better known through **Wittgenstein** (e.g. 1958: 32), who talked about "family likenesses" (Anscombe translates it as "family resemblances") to describe the relations between the elements of semantic sets. From there, the metaphor has been used within the equivalence paradigm to describe different ways translations relate to their start texts (see 3.1 and 3.9.4 above). It has also served in the descriptivist paradigm to portray the way translations are different yet belong to the same set (cf. Toury 1980; Halverson 1998). However, for the Modernist aesthetic, where form cannot be separated from content, the sense of "family likeness" was more radically *negative*: a likeness was the best that translation *should* hope to achieve, since there could be no absolute equivalence. Translations are all very well, but they will never replace originals. That is one way determinist theories of language, or of expression in general, have sought to retain the possibility of translation, by weakening the concept. It is a way that actually meets up with some forms of directional equivalence. Yet there are other ways as well.

6.3.2 Using Cratylistic determinacy as a way of translating

The German philosopher **Martin Heidegger** used something like Cratylistic method as a way of developing thought. For instance, he saw the Greek word for truth, *aletheia*, as configuring *Unverborgenheit* ("unhiddenness," "disclosedness") (1927/1953: 33, 219), based on its particles *a-* (absence of) and *-lethe* (deception). This is clearly quite unlike the "divine wandering" that Cratylus found by analyzing the word as *ale-theia*. Heidegger generally postulates that words convey knowledge within their own language, and that etymology conceals that knowledge. He nevertheless exploits the differences between languages in order to develop knowledge, and this is where we find his main reflections on translation. To take one of his more elaborate examples, the Latin philosophical term *ratio* would have as its normal equivalent the German term *Grund* (ground, or reason, or cause). That equivalent, however, suppresses many other possible interpretations. *Ratio* could also be rendered as *Vernunft* (reason), or indeed as *Ursache* (cause). In Latin, we are told, *ratio* also means "reckoning," "calculation," and it works as a translation of the Greek term *logos*. "*Grund* is the translation of *ratio*," says Heidegger,

> but this statement is a commonplace, and will remain as such for as long as we do not think about what translation actually means in this and similar cases. Translation is one thing with respect to a business letter, and something quite different with respect to a poem. The letter is translatable; the poem is not.
>
> (1957: 163; my translation, here and throughout)

Given his implicit disdain of anything as banal as a business letter, Heidegger's attention is devoted to precisely what is **"not translatable," the "remainders," the non-equivalents** that are somehow covered over by the "commonplaces" of official equivalence. Rather than valuing family likenesses, Heidegger values the productive conflict of differences.

Heidegger's use of translation in this example cannot really be attributed to indeterminism in Quine's sense, since there is no epistemic doubt about the intentions of any speaker. The differences have more to do with history, with a mode of historical knowledge that is stronger than any individual:

> A word will have multiple references, therefore, not primarily because in talking and writing we mean different things by it at different times. The multiplicity of referents is historical in a more fundamental sense: it stems from the fact that in the speaking of language we ourselves, in accordance with the destiny of all beings' Being, are at different times differently "meant" or "spoken."
>
> (1957: 161)

We do not speak a language, **the language speaks us**. We become vehicles for the words and concepts that have been handed down to us across the centuries; the ideas of our cultural ancestors pass through us. This idea is like what biological evolutionists say about us being vehicles for the transmission of genes, rather than the genes being ways in which we transmit ourselves. In this context, Heidegger insists that a translation (*Übersetzung*) is not just an interpretation of a previous text but also **a handing-down, a question of legacy** (*Überlieferung*) (1957: 164). Heidegger gives the past more value than the present, and the task of translation—like that of philosophy itself—would be to recuperate lost or suppressed knowledge.

Similar themes are at work in the German Jewish thinker **Walter Benjamin**. His 1923 essay "The Task of the Translator" plays with the idea of a future "true" or "pure" language (*reine Sprache*), of which the current languages would be partial representations, each containing its own piece of truth. Here is Rendall's translation:

> All suprahistorical kinship of languages consists […] in the fact that in each of them as a whole, one and the same thing is intended; this cannot be attained by any one of them alone, however, but only by the totality of their mutually complementary intentions: pure language. Whereas all the particular elements of different languages—words, sentences, structures—are mutually exclusive, these languages complement each other in their intentions. […] In *Brot* ["bread" in German] and *pain* ["bread" in French], what is meant is the same, but the mode of meaning differs. It is because of the mode of meaning that the two words signify something different to a German or a Frenchman, that they are not regarded as interchangeable and in fact ultimately exclude one another; however, with respect to their intended object, taken absolutely, they signify one and the same thing.
>
> (Benjamin 1923/2012: 78)

From this it follows that the texts we find in different languages are parts of what the pure language could express. They are like "**fragments of a broken vessel**," as Benjamin puts it, and to translate them into each other reveals their fragmentary nature. Much has been written on Benjamin's essay, particularly about how and when the "broken fragments" are supposed to connect with each other (see, for example, Jakobs 1975; de Man 1986; Benjamin 1989; Gentzler 1993/2001; Bhabha 1994/2004; Vermeer 1996; Rendall 1997). What interests me here, though, is the way Benjamin effectively **turns the indeterminacy of translation from a problem into a virtue**. Although there is apparently no way that the words *Brot* and *pain* can be full equivalents in the here and now, the attempt to translate them into each other must produce knowledge not only about the thing they signify, but also about the different modes of signification. Translation creates knowledge about the differences between languages. Benjamin makes the interesting claim that **translations themselves are untranslatable**, "not because they are difficult or heavy with meaning, but because meaning adheres to them too lightly, with all too great fleetingness" (my translation from Benjamin 1923/1977: 61; cf. Rendall 1997: 199–200). The act of translation would be like quickly opening a window on differential signification, then seeing that window close as the subjectivity of the translator disappears and history moves on. This is not quite like Cratylus finding the "correct" names in Greek (as indeed Heidegger tends to). Translation would be more like the space created by the debates in *Cratylus* itself, a space of critical and sometimes playful exchange. If there is a "family likeness," as

Croce put it, it is not because the start *text* is the parent, nor is it because one of the contemporary terms is better than any other. It has more to do with the way the passage from one term to the other, the brief jump across languages, enables a glimpse of similarities and differences that are otherwise hidden. Translators would have their own special hermeneutics.

What this means for actual translating is far from clear. Within the tradition that dates from German Romanticism, Benjamin might be seeking quite literalist translations, but there is no guarantee. Benjamin's essay was the preface to his renditions from Baudelaire's *Les Fleurs du mal*, which are not at all literalist translations—they privilege prosody over reference. And then, the only bread in Baudelaire comes from Christian tradition ("bread and wine" in the poem *La Bénédiction* and "to earn one's daily bread" in *La Muse vénale*), and that common Christian tradition, more than the intimacy of different kinds of bread, gives French and German shared expressions (yes, equivalents) at both points. Despite that, Benjamins only uses the German term for bread, *Brot*, in an evocation of "one's daily bread," in a poem where Baudelaire makes no reference at all to bread—Benjamin needed the rhyme. Benjamin's theoretical text has clearly been much more successful than his example (see 8.1 below).

All these theories, like Cratylus, posit a strong, almost mystical relation between expression and meaning. They thus do away with the idea of encoding something in one language and decoding it in the other. As we have seen, some of these theories would deny the possibility of translation altogether, while others accept it as a mode of transformation, or similarity, or knowledge-production, or insight, somehow beyond the boundaries of equivalence.

6.4 THEORIES OF HOW TO LIVE WITH UNCERTAINTY

These theories of indeterminacy are not of the kind where we can say "so what?", as Chomsky might have said to Quine. The theories question the possibility of translation, and thus the very thing we are supposed to be studying. The same threat explains why equivalence theory originally had to oppose much of structuralist linguistics. Following Saussure, structuralists were saying that meaning was formed within an entire language system, and that translation was not possible in any strong sense. Now we see they had some support from Modernist aesthetics and twentieth-century philosophy—nobody except translators liked translation, apparently. And yet, the fact of translation as a social practice, its existence as something that people use and trust, would suggest that the theories were overstating the case.

Is it possible to accept indeterminism and still recognize the viability of translation? Let me suggest a few theories that can propose some kind of compatibility.

6.4.1 Theories of illumination

The first theory comes from the fourth/fifth-century theologian **Augustine of Hippo** (Aurelius Augustinus). In *De catechizandis rudibus* (2.3.1–6) Augustine offers an intriguing analogy to explain why translations can be different and yet talk about the same thing. Here the process of communication goes from ideas to "traces" or "vestiges" (*uestigia*), and only then to language. Augustine argues that language conveys thought very imperfectly:

> the idea erupts in my mind like a rapid illumination, whereas my speech is long and delayed and not at all like the idea, and while I speak, the thought has hidden in its secret place. The idea has left no more than a few vestiges imprinted in my memory, and these vestiges linger throughout the slowness of my words. From those vestiges we construe sounds, and we speak Latin, or Greek, or Hebrew, or any other language. But the vestiges are not Latin, nor Greek, nor Hebrew, nor of any other community. They are formed in the mind, just as a facial expression is formed in the body.
>
> (c.400/1969; my translation)

The indeterminacy of language is clear enough. Ideas come as light, and language is like no more than a weak trace of that light, as when you close your eyes immediately after seeing a bright object. Yet Augustine does not abandon communication altogether. What is communicated is here anterior to language, and thus potentially available to all. Our words will have sense for someone who has experienced the same light. Thus our texts do not communicate messages as such; they help receivers to recall the **illuminations** that they have previously found for themselves.

Parts of this theory live on in the **translation of religious texts**. The legend of the Septuagint, the translation of the Hebrew Bible into Greek, says that 72 translators worked in isolated cells and all produced identical translations, in clear defiance of anything like Quine's problem with *gavagai*. How was it possible for them to overcome linguistic indeterminacy? Presumably because they were not just any old translators: they were rabbis, with faith, and divine spirit oriented their words. Others have also seen faith as some kind of guarantee against indeterminacy. **Luther** stated that "no false Christian or sectarian mind can translate faithfully" (1530/2002: 94; my translation), and in the preface to most versions of the Bible you will find some passage saying that the translators were "united in their faith." These translators all claim to be able to overcome indeterminacy through a shared experience that is somehow prior to language. **Revelation** or **faith** would be pre-linguistic experience of which words need be no more than vestiges.

Augustine's idea need not be restricted to religious messages. Contemporary **theories of education** stress that we learn through experience, by actually doing things and discovering knowledge for ourselves, rather than by understanding someone else's words. Further, contemporary theories of reading see the text's schemata as interacting with the reader's schemata, such that meaning is actively created from the experience that readers bring to the text. And again, relevance theory of the kind **Ernst-August Gutt** (1991/2000) applies to translation can accept that language is hugely indeterminate (meaning is created by breaking maxims) and yet "context" provides mystical access to intention. All these ideas can be seen as handling indeterminacy in a rather Augustinian way. The **real communication lies in shared experience**, and this can overcome the indeterminacy of language.

A possible extension of this view might be found in recent call for translations that work as experiences in themselves, rather than as representations of anterior experiences (cf. "involvement" in Pym 2012: 122–3 and "event" in Venuti 2013: 184–6).

6.4.2 Theories of consensus

A second way of living with indeterminacy emphasizes the role of **dialogue** and **consensus**. The seventeenth-century philosopher **John Locke** had a transmissionist model of communication, based on encoding and decoding:

> When a Man speaks to another, it is, that he may be understood; and the end of Speech is, that those Sounds, as Marks, may make known his Ideas to the Hearer.
>
> (1690/1841: 281, section 3.2.1)

This formulation is so fundamental that the corresponding view of language is sometimes called "Lockean." However, if you read Locke's text you find examples like the following:

> I was at meeting of very learned and ingenious Physicians, where by chance there arose a Question, whether any Liquor passed through the Filaments of the Nerves. The Debate having been managed a good while, by a variety of arguments on both sides, I (who had been used to suspect, that the greatest part of Disputes were more about the signification of words, than a real difference in the Conception of Things) desired, That before they went any farther on this dispute, they would first examine, and establish amongst them, what the word Liquor signified. [...] They were pleased to comply with my Motion, and upon Examination found, that the signification of that Word, was not so settled and certain, as they had all imagined; but that each of them made it a sign of a different complex Idea. This made them perceive, that the Main of their Dispute was about the signification of that Term; and that they differed very little in their Opinions, concerning some fluid and subtle Matter, passing through the Conduits of the Nerves; though it was not so easy to agree whether it be called Liquor, or no, a thing which when each considered, they thought it not worth the contending about.
>
> (1690/1841: 343, section 3.9.16 "On the imperfection of words")

Here we find that language is not fully determined by its referent, nor by concepts (the word "Liquor" only produces confusion). However, that indeterminacy is overcome through dialogue, through the opening up of individual narratives. The point of indeterminacy is ultimately avoided or considered "not the worth." A similar argument was formulated by the philosopher **Jerrold Katz** (1978: 234), who argued with respect to **Quine** that if two different translations are both correct, then their differences are not worth bothering about. The important point is that language enables us to keep talking about language, and it is through those exchanges that understandings are reached.

Seen in this way, a Lockean theory need not exclude initial indeterminacy. It might even teach us how to live with it. Keep the dialogues going, and consensus might ensue. Does that solution help translators? Few intermediaries are allowed time to conduct long dialogues about language. Brislin (1981: 213) proposed that **conference interpreters** should be allowed to stop debates when there are misunderstandings based on words, but not many job profiles actually give them that power.

6.4.3 Hermeneutics

Benjamin and Heidegger were writing in the tradition of German Post-Romanticism. One line of that tradition has been particularly concerned with the idea that texts are not immediately meaningful and need to be **actively interpreted**. This general field is known as **hermeneutics**, from the Greek *hermeneu*, meaning "to interpret," or indeed "to translate." The nineteenth-century development of hermeneutics was closely linked to ways of making historical sense of the Bible, especially in view of the growing scientific knowledge that contested literalist readings. The way you mentally construe a text informs the way you translate it, so it is not surprising to find thinkers like Schleiermacher concerned with both hermeneutics and translation. A long tradition of scholars have claimed that every translation is based on an interpretation.

In the twentieth century, hermeneutics became more general in its application, especially in **Husserl, Heidegger**, and **Hans Georg Gadamer**. Although these thinkers have relatively little to say about translation, their insistence on the active nature of interpretation has become part of the general intellectual climate. Gadamer (1960/1972) gives positive value to the interpreter's subjective involvement in the text, described as a necessary kind of "**prejudice**" (*Vorwurf*). Instead of trying to be scientific and objective about the text to translate, translators should seek to recognize the ways they are personally positioned with respect to the text, and what particular desires and aims they have in carrying out their task. Subjective prejudice need not be a bad thing; here it becomes a source of **motivation and involvement**, about which the translator should be as aware as possible.

What hermeneutics has to say

Chau (1984) summarizes "what insights the translator can gain from hermeneutics":

1 There is no truly "objective" understanding.
2 "Prejudices" are unavoidable and can be positive.
3 There is no final or definitive reading.
4 The translator cannot but change the meaning of the source text.
5 No translation can represent its source text fully.
6 Understanding is not always explicable.

The development of hermeneutics connected with the "**philosophy of dialogue**," a set of ideas about the way human relationships should be formed. Writings by **Buber, Marcel**, and **Levinas** argue that the relation between the self and the "other" (the person you are communicating with) should be open, dialogic, and respectful of difference. Applying this to translation, **Arnaud Laygues** (2006) insists that the translator should not ask "What does this *text* mean?" as the classical hermeneutic tradition would have us ask, but **"What does this *person* mean?"** The uncertainty remains, but here the doubts about things become an ongoing dialogue with a person. The problem of indeterminacy is humanized. We are no more certain of what a text means than we are of the people around us, and yet we keep interacting with people, without trying to make those people sound like ourselves. The practical message is that we should keep interacting, without domesticating the text. Of course, the notion of extended dialogue runs into the same problems I have just mentioned with respect to Locke.

The view of translation as interpersonal dialogue underlies much of the work of the French translator **Antoine Berman** (1984/1992, 1985/1999, 1995). In his study of German Romantic and hermeneutic approaches to translation, Berman (1984/1992) insists that the ethical translator should *not* adapt the foreign text to the target culture but should maintain its foreignness. If we try to "make sense" of the foreign text, we turn it into *our* sense, *our* culture, which can only lead to **ethnocentric translation**. For Berman, "the ethical act consists in recognizing and receiving the Other as Other" (1985/1999: 74; my translation). This particular approach meets up with the "foreignizing" side of the dichotomies we met in our discussion of directional equivalence (3.4 above).

Perhaps the best-known theorist in the hermeneutic tradition is **Paul Ricœur**, who has written with subtlety on how relations between the self and the other construct identity. Writing on translation, Ricœur (2004) is keenly aware that there is no encoding-decoding at stake, and that great texts will always retain their untranslatable secrets. His findings sound provocative: "one must conclude," writes Ricœur, "that misunderstanding is allowed, that translation is theoretically impossible, and that bilinguals must be schizophrenic" (2004: 29). If you look closely, though, Ricœur's dichotomies are close to those of natural equivalence, where structuralist theories had long ago posited that translation was impossible simply because the theories could not explain it.

6.4.4 Constructivism

Hermeneutics started from the problems of interpreting texts, in a situation usually involving just one reader or translator. However, some compatible ideas have come from quite different areas of the sciences, where the problem is not so much how an individual makes sense of a text but how social groups make sense of the world.

The fundamental idea of constructivism is that our knowledge of the world is not simply given or passively perceived. Long-standing experiments in the **psychology of perception** show that we actively "construct" what we see and know of the world. We have all seen the picture of the vase that is also an image of two faces, depending on how your brain wants to construct the image. Any interpretative process is a constant inter-action between both the objective (the world beyond the person) and the subjective (the person's own mental frames). These tenets are compatible with the uncertainty principle. Constructivism could be seen as a general epistemology, and it has informed areas of psychology, sociology, and philosophy. Its fiefdom, though, is in the psychology of educa-tion, particularly in the American tradition, and it is from there that it reaches translation theory.

What does constructivism have to do with translation? The American theorist **Donald Kiraly** (2000) argues that constructivism should be opposed to the entire "transmissionist" paradigm of encoding and decoding. According to **"transmissionism,"** knowledge would be something that can be moved from one passive receptacle to another, like water being dished out into buckets. Some knowledge goes into a text and is then channeled to another text (some talk about the "conduit" metaphor, where meaning flows through a kind of tube from one language to another). Translation would be a mode of transmission. For Kiraly, the same transmissionism is at the base of the way many translators are trained. A teacher, like a text, possesses knowledge that can then be poured into the minds of passive students, who are lined up like so many empty vessels. Constructivism says that knowledge does not work that way. Translators actively construct both the start text and the translation, just as students actively participate in their learning process. Kiraly's main concern is to apply constructivism to **translator education**. His ideas connect with a string of movements like learner-centered education, autonomous learning, and action research. His views are compatible with indeterminism, and they incorporate a view of translation based on that principle.

The correlative, of course, is that the equivalence paradigm is made to appear transmissionist. For Kiraly, the way equivalence assumes stable knowledge would reinforce a **teacher-centered mode of transfer**. He thus presents a choice between two enormous paradigms: transmissionism (equivalence) or constructivism (active creation), and there is no doubt that constructivism is better.

This opposition is too simple. In the first place, transmissionism would only apply to what I have called "natural" equivalence; "directional" theories, on the other hand, stress that the translator actively produces equivalence. Second, Kiraly's own position does not exclude the values of knowledge through **practical experience, discussion**, and **consensual understanding**. His classroom methodology is explicitly based on practice, on students finding their own illumination, and on group work, on students getting together to talk about what they are doing. In this, Kiraly correctly identifies his approach as "*social* **constructivism**." Here there is no drastic uncertainty that would destroy all attempts at communication. Social constructivism might teach us to live with indeterminacy.

6.4.5 Game theory

Uncertainty can also be modeled in terms of someone translating, in the way I did in the introduction to this book. A text can be rendered in many different ways, and from the perspective of indeterminacy there can be **no absolute rule for deciding between those various translations**. Someone might claim that "the translation has to have exactly the same cultural function," but that is not universally true. Not only are there many cases in which translations are more determined by the *form* of the start text (think of lip synchronization in film dubbing), but different people will see the text "function" quite differently. So translators will decide, and their decisions are only partly determined by the text.

This means that most of the translator's decisions cannot be called wholly "right" or wholly "wrong." When confronted with something like the German "Der Preis ist heiss" (The Price is Hot) as a translation of "The Price is Right," you might say "**Yes, but . . .**," and then add doubts about taste or fidelity ("hot" does not mean "right," however loose). Alternatively, you might greet the translation with "**No, but . . .**," followed by expressions of personal appreciation. For Pym (1992b), these judgments are **non-binary**, since they involve more than "right" vs. "wrong" (i.e. more than two terms). This is the general form of problems that concern translation rather than something else (like referents or authoritative terminology). Translation is indeterminate. As translators proceed, they encounter numerous points where their rendition could be one of several possible translations, and the decision to opt for one of the possibilities depends on more than what is in the text (as I said in the introduction, the translator often has to theorize in order to decide).

Imagine that a text comprises a set of points requiring the translator to make major decisions. Many of those points have something to do with each other. A decision made at one point may have consequences for decisions at other points. The Czech translation theorist **Jiři Levý** (1967/2004) explained this using the example of the Brecht play *Der gute Mensch von Sezuan*. The title of the play is sometimes rendered as *The Good Woman of Sezuan*, since the main character is a woman. But the German word *Mensch* can mean "man," "person," "guy" (it has a colloquial register), or "soul" (which is the genderless option that mostly wins out). This ambiguity becomes functional in the play, since the main character is a woman who pretends to be a man. According to Levý, the way the translator chooses to render *Mensch* in the title will have repercussions for the way similar terms are rendered throughout the text. **One decision becomes a determinant for others**. The result is that translating is determined not just by the start text, but by the patterns of the translator's own decisions. Levý thus saw translating as being akin to playing a game with finite information (like chess). His aim was to apply **game theory** to the translator's decision-making process.

Indeterminism should probably take us further than Levý's example. Is translating a text really like playing chess? On the chessboard, every move has some consequence for all future moves. In translating, though, no more than a handful of textual items are usually strung together in this way. In the case of Brecht's play, translators can choose a genderless title and thereby remove a lot of further problems. More important, if we take Quine's uncertainty seriously, translators will never have anything like complete information about these games. They could be playing the stock market rather than chess. After all, the translator calculates risks and takes chances without really being aware of how the elements will fit together in the mind of the end receiver. Indeterminacy means the translator has no certainty that all possible options have been seen, or that future decisions will be entirely determined by the previous ones.

Taken in that sense, as an approach to decisions made on the basis of *incomplete* information, game theory might also teach us to live with indeterminacy. That link opens onto the huge field that has not been fully explored by translation theorists.

6.4.6 Non-linear logic

Levý's example starts from a kind of linear logic, of the kind "If A, then B" (if the title is rendered one way, there are direct consequences down the line). The entire equivalence paradigm might have a similar basis: "If A in the input, then B in the output." This mode of thought combines the Aristotelian principles of identity ("A cannot be B"), non-contradiction ("A cannot be true and false at the same time"), and the excluded middle ("If A is true, then the opposite of A is false"). Indeterminism questions all of those principles, since it allows doubt about the identity of different occurrences of A (a word has different meanings in different texts); it allows that a proposition can be partly true and partly false; and it recognizes shades of meaning between A and non-A. Since indeterminism has informed virtually all sciences, there is now a rich array of alternatives to linear thought, and non-linear principles can be seen as underlying many of our loose "ways of living with indeterminism." Some attempts have been made to apply them to translation theory, with significant overlaps:

- *Heuristics*: Folkart (1989) distinguishes between two ways of translating: "teleological" (the linearity suited to equivalence) and "heuristic," where the interpretative processes give translations that could not have been predicted on the basis of the start text alone (there is a lack of "reversibility"). This lack is conceptualized in terms of entropy, which is a measure of the chaos in a system. Folkart's distinction between two ways of translating partly maps onto my notions of natural and directional equivalence, although it more radically questions causation in cases of directionality.

■ **Visualization**: A particular kind of heuristics is based on seeing a text as a scene, and resolving difficult translation problems by viewing the scene in different ways. Kussmaul (2000) recommends that translators use techniques like zooming, focusing, or perspective change in order to find creative solutions: when you "just can't think straight," you are probably translating creatively. This non-linear approach draws on scenes-and-frames semantics, which was of interest to others in the *Skopos* paradigm.

■ **Cybernetics**: Holz-Mänttäri (1990: 71–2) similarly criticizes the linearity of "If A in the start text, then B in the translation" and proposes that the translator is dealing with information flows in a cybernetic system: "Guidance is not in terms of an endpoint to be reached, but from the relations between the flows, marked by [the fiction of] 'functional constancy' as the system's Not-Yet-Being and Not-Yet-Conscious" (my translation— the latter terms come from the work of Ernst Bloch). This cybernetic model of forces and flows connects with theories of emergence, complexity, and chaos, albeit retaining the idea of teleological action.

■ **Complexity theory**: Longa (2004) also draws on complexity science to radically question assumptions of causal links between input and output. Just as in non-linear dynamics "a small difference in the initial conditions triggers very divergent effects, because the initial difference increases exponentially" (2004: 204), so a translation cannot be predicted on the basis of linguistic features alone. This non-predictability can be measured in terms of chaos, understood here as an absence of organization. Outcomes are thus not caused directly, but "emerge" from the complex interactions of many different factors (text, client, readership, rate of pay, ideologies, limited knowledge, etc.), making each translation a unique occurrence.

■ **Risk analysis**: Pym (2005) presents a model where translators do not seek equivalence but instead manage the risk of their solutions failing to achieve basic aims (like getting paid). This is based on calculations of the *probability* of failure, rather than any certitude of match. Probabilistic calculations of this kind transgress the excluded middle but still assume an identity of aims and assessments of causation, and thus some degree of linearity. A variant on this is analysis of how translators manage guesses about equivalence (Künzli 2004; Angelone 2010).

■ **Fuzzy logic as partial set membership**: The term "fuzzy logic" can be understood in two ways. The most common is where an element can be a member of two different sets but to different degrees: a solution might be 80 percent foreignizing and 20 percent domesticating, for example: when "McDonald's" signs appear all over the non-American world, they are foreignizing because from a foreign culture yet domesticating because, for the mostly young clientele, they have always been there. The notion of "multiple membership" is not entirely new: Vinay and Darbelnet recognized that a translation solution can be in several categories at once (2.3 above), and Pym (1992b) talked about non-binarism when solutions are judged "Right, but..." and "Wrong, but..." (i.e. solutions are only right or wrong to a degree, on some levels but not on others). Mathematical calculations of "fuzzy matches" in translation memories (see 7.5.4 below), although not based on non-linear logic, nevertheless mean that users of translation memories are negotiating *degrees of correctness* all the time.

■ *Fuzzy logic as simultaneous set membership*: Another kind of fuzzy logic is when an element is a full member of two sets at the same time, depending on the perspective of the observer. A European Union law, for example, usually results from a complex translation and rewriting process, but since all language versions are equally valid, the laws are technically *not* translations of each other. That is, they are translations in terms of production processes, but they are not in terms of law. Monacelli and Punzo (2001) describe how military translations are not judged "equivalent" until authorized up in the chain of command, so the further the translation moves from its place of production, the more "equivalent" it becomes.

■ *Wisdom*: Marais (2009, 2013) posits that translator education in development contexts must be based on an awareness of complexity and that the search for solutions should be guided by "wisdom," understood as a capacity to see several sides of a whole question simultaneously, and then to make decisions oriented by ethics. This might connect with theories of cooperation, where translators are called upon to assess the efforts and interests of multiple actors and to decide in such a way as to seek "mutual benefits" (Pym 2012: 133–60).

■ *Ecology*: A series of conferences have approached translation in the following terms: "Regarding the scene of translation as a holistic eco-system, ['eco-translatology'] describes and interprets translation activities in terms of ecological principles of Eco-holism, the Oriental traditional eco-wisdom, and Translation as Adaptation and Selection" (announcement of 2013 eco-translatology conference). This would seem to bring together some of the above strands, albeit in the vaguest of terms.

These theories are all saying similar things, but in different ways and to different degrees. Some can be formalized in fairly precise terms, others less so. Some radically question translation as a goal-driven activity (and thus all linearity), others do not. All of them, though, would be questioning the Western tradition of linear logic, with its dominant binarisms. In listing the theories in this way, I hope to illustrate, first, that non-linearity is not non-Western and not particularly new, and second, that the principles can connect with ideas for translator education.

6.4.7 Theories of semiosis

What happens if we accept that we do not have access to any intention behind an utterance? Let us say, we have the word *gavagai* and we want to know what it means. We are really asking what the word "stands for"; we are treating it as a "sign." However, we can only produce *interpretations* of whatever it stands for, and those interpretations will be further signs, which will then be subject to further interpretations. At no point can we be sure our intention corresponds to anything that was there before the sign was produced (the speaker's idea, for example). Our renditions thus constantly move meaning forward, rather than back to anything in the past. This would be despite the backward-looking positions adopted by thinkers like Heidegger. In terms of the nineteenth-century philosopher **Charles Sanders Peirce**, we are involved in "**semiosis**":

> By semiosis I mean an action, an influence, which is, or involves, a cooperation of three subjects, such as a sign, its object and its interpretant, this tri-relative influence not being in any way resolvable into pairs.
>
> (Peirce 1931/1958: 5.484)

This has been of importance for translation within **semiotics** (the study of signs) (Gorlée 1994; Stecconi 2004). If we follow **Umberto Eco**'s reading of this theory (Eco 1977), the "**interpretant**" is a sign that acts as the interpretation of a previous sign. Semiosis is the process by which signs "grow," as Peirce puts it, potentially in an unlimited way. For example, if you look up a word in the dictionary, you find that the "meaning" is a set of different words. We could then look up the meanings of those words, and so on *ad infinitum*, until the dictionary is exhausted, the language itself will have changed, and we will have to start again.

Eco (1977: 70) describes the interpretant as assuming many different forms, of which "translation into another language" is just one. Other theories, however, have been inclined to see translation as operating in all types of interpretation (see 8.3.1 below). The important point is that the very nature of semiosis makes the processes keep going. That is what translation, in the widest sense, could be doing in the world.

The Russian linguist **Roman Jakobson** was paraphrasing Peirce when he wrote that "the meaning of any linguistic sign is its translation into some further, alternative sign" (1959/2012: 127). This effectively reverses traditional translation problems: rather than represent a previous meaning, translation would be the active *creation* of meaning. Jakobson, rather like Eco, recognizes translation as operating in a very wide sense. He finds translation both within languages and between them, as well as between different kinds of signs (as when a painting represents a poem).

Theories of semiosis are not always revolutionary, however. For instance, when Jakobson announces a theory of general translation (the creation of meaning itself), he immediately refers to just one kind of "**translation proper**," understood as translation across languages. The same reduction to "translation proper" is found in Eco (2001), when he opposes translation to other kinds of "rewriting." Neither Jakobson nor Eco want to lose the Western translation form. For Jakobson, "equivalence in difference is the cardinal problem of language and the pivotal concern of linguistics" (1959/2012: 127); for Eco, each text has its own "intention," which is what should be translated (cf. Eco 2001). The idea of semiosis is strangely present within the discourse of thinkers whose prime search was for certainty. For this group of theories, semiosis has tended to be regarded as dissipation rather than liberation.

6.5 DECONSTRUCTION

Many of the theories dealt with in this chapter could be associated with "deconstruction," a set of critical ideas based on the work of the French philosopher **Jacques Derrida** (see Davis 2001). Deconstruction is a highly indeterminist approach that sets out to **undo illusions of stable meaning** of any kind. Whereas other approaches within the uncertainty paradigm have developed from an earnest search for truth, for a moment of full determinacy, or have measured distances from ideals like equivalence, deconstruction proposes that we should accept that language is not transparent to intentions, referents, or values.

Deconstruction thus does not present itself as a theory (since a theory is supposed to have stable concepts). It is instead a practice, an ongoing use of language on language, revealing the gaps and displacements ("differences") by which semiosis keeps going. The uncertainty that was a problem for other approaches here becomes something to be embraced, as an invitation to discovery and creation.

For example, Derrida (1985) criticized **Jakobson**'s use of "translation proper" for positing that the term was stable in one place (what is "proper," usually defined by something like equivalence) and not in the other places (the rest). The use of terms like "translation proper" is seen as "essentialism," as the false assumption that words have their true meanings (their "essences") somehow embedded in them. We might now say that deconstruction is a critique of all forms of determinism, remembering that Cratylus believed things could determine their "correct" names. In enacting this critique, deconstruction necessarily sees **translation as a form of transformation** rather than as any kind of meaning transfer. Like Heidegger in this regard, Derrida seeks out the "**remainder**," the potential significations that are omitted in the process of translation.

This critique is in the early Derrida (1968) when he analyzes translations of Plato. Derrida observes that the Greek term **_pharmakon_** could be rendered in French as either _remède_ (cure) or _poison_ (poison), but not both terms at the same time (perhaps like the American-English word _drugs_, which can be good or bad for the body). This is seen as a problem not just for translations into French, but for the movement from everyday Greek to philosophical Greek.

Derrida often uses translation to draw out the plurality of texts, revealing their semantic richness and instability. His oft-cited phrase "**_plus d'une langue_**" expresses this plurality. It could be translated as "more than one language" or as "let us have no more of one language," and both readings are in the text. However, Derrida does not seek to remove the special status of the start text. In his treatise on "a relevant translation" (2005) we find him asking how it is possible that Shakespeare could make sense—any kind of sense—well beyond its original historical and cultural location. This mode of translatability is called "**iterability**," attributed not to anything semantic but to the literary institutionalization of certain meaning effects (Davis 2001: 30–5). The text can thus be seen not as a set of obligatory orders (as it would in a deterministic world) but as a **phantom**, an image that organizes the range of translational variants without fixing them in a deterministic way. The foreign text returns, like the ghost of King Hamlet, but only as a spirit that can hope to guide without acting directly (Derrida 1993: 42–3). This kind of relationship has been explored by the American theorist **Douglas Robinson** (2001), who relates it to mystical theories of "**spirit channeling**," without any essentialist claim to sameness.

Derrida's most perceptive comments on translation are in texts where he investigates entities that are at once present and absent. This is the context in which we find the discussions of ghosts, after-life, survival ("living-on"), and the apparently permeable border between life and death (Derrida 1979, 1982/1985, 1985, 1993). The concept of translation, as a process more than as a product, enters as a model of how a voice can cross a border and continue, transformed. For this, Derrida picks up the notion of "**after-life**" (_Fortleben_, "prolonged life") that **Benjamin** (1923/2012: 76) used to describe the way a translation can continue the life of the text (see 8.3 below).

On the other hand, when Derrida comes to actual translations, he is remarkably conservative. In some early texts he sees translation as an inferior activity, "a technique in the service of language, a _porte-parole_" (1967: 17–18; cf. 1972: 226). When analyzing the *pharmakon* example he takes delight in challenging the "official translations" and pointing out how they should be improved (1972: 80). Even when looking at the French translations of Hamlet (1993: 42–7), Derrida is remarkably prescriptive, finding no translation on the level of the original, and predictably preferring the most literal version. For as much as his theorization went one way, his authoritarian stance tended to prevail in contact with actual translations.

The Brazilian theorist **Rosemary Arrojo** has perhaps been the most consistent in her application of deconstruction to translation. We find her enlisting deconstruction (along with psychoanalysis) not just in her attacks on assumed meaning transfer (Arrojo 1993) but also against essentialist feminist approaches to translation (1994), against ideal symmetrical relations (1997), and generally against all illusions of stable meaning (1998). As in Derrida, Arrojo sees deconstruction as a practice, a way of using language to analyze language, and thus as a way of using language to translate. For example, Arrojo (1992) proposes the Brazilian term **oficina de tradução** to translate the American term *translation workshop* (the practice class where students work together on literary translations). The translation is then shown to come under the category of "right, but …" The Brazilian *oficina* is the standard equivalent of *workshop*, but the word also has the values of "place of work" or "place for the exercise of a profession (*ofício*)." Arrojo (1992: 7–8) says *oficina* can also mean "laboratory," "place for the machinery or instruments of a factory," and "place where cars are repaired" (*workshop*, indeed). If we translate *workshop* as *oficina*, we are thus bringing slightly different meanings, different images, new questions. Is this a question of adapting to the new target culture? Interestingly enough, the Brazilian poet and theorist Haroldo de Campos (1962/1976) had previously called for a "text laboratory" where linguists and artists would work together on translations. But an *oficina* is not quite the same thing as a *laboratory* (not even in Brazilian Portuguese). As Quine might have predicted, both can mean *workshop*, but they maintain a dynamic difference. Arrojo's translation can thus continue to produce meaning, moving the semiosis on.

The simple lesson of deconstruction is that **translation always involves transformation**. That would seem a logical consequence of indeterminacy. The task of the deconstructionist would be to make readers aware of this. Rather than provide ready-made solutions, the deconstructionist would use indeterminism in order to make readers think. We are made to engage in an experience (perhaps as in Augustine), in a dialogue (perhaps as in Locke, although without final consensus), or in a situation where readers themselves have to create knowledge (as in constructivism).

6.6 SO HOW SHOULD WE TRANSLATE?

If we accept all or any of these theories, how should we translate? Unfortunately, very few theories are particularly helpful in this regard. Model examples do not abound, and there is a reason for this. In the end, from the perspective of indeterminism, **each individual translator decides**. After all, if there is no certainty, how can any theory presume to tell us what to do?

Despite this reluctance to prescribe, some theorists have tried to find some practical benefits in heightened awareness of uncertainty. In his survey of hermeneutic theory, **Simon S. C. Chau** (1984: 76–7) claims that translators might be affected in the following ways (here I paraphrase):

- They become more **humble**, as they are aware of their existential limitation in relation to the translation.
- They become more **honest**, as they admit that neither their reading nor their rendering is canonical.
- They become more **efficient** interpreters, as they realize that apart from employing various scientific means to understand the source, they must "lose themselves" in the communion before any valid interpretation comes about.
- They become more **confident**, as their personal creativity is affirmed—they are not haunted by the myth of *the* reading and *the* translation.
- They become more **responsible**, as they realize the active creative role of the translator.

This is an optimistic list: it does not envisage the translator's "confidence" (perhaps Gadamer's "prejudice") becoming excessive and overriding; it does not worry that "humility" might lead to self-doubt. The list is not as subtle as the virtues in **Antoine Berman**, who optimistically proposes that the hermeneutically trained translator will respect the foreign author as an "other," resisting the temptation to domesticate the marks of foreignness (domestication would be unethical "ethnocentric" translation): "The essence of translation is to be an opening, a dialogue, a cross-breeding, a decentering" (Berman 1984/1992: 4). This in turn differs from the calculated pessimism of **Paul Ricœur**, who talks about transla-tion in terms of a secret "fear" and even "hatred" of the foreigner (2004: 41) and sees the translator as maintaining "distance within proximity" (2004: 52). All these qualities, good or bad, tend to concern the translator's relation with the *start* text or author, far more than they concern forward-looking relations with clients or readers.

　　Those aspects concern the translator more than the actual process of translating. If you look for proposals about the way you should translate, you find that the uncertainty paradigm is broadly compatible with a few prominent ideas that come from elsewhere. One prime lesson was taught by the French theorist **Georges Mounin** in 1963: translators tend to **"over-translate,"** to explain everything in order to make texts easy for their readers. This would be on the "domestication" side of **Schleiermacher**'s classical dichotomy. Many inde-terminist theories see this as a shortcoming; they tend to favor **"foreignizing"** strategies, the ones that make the reader aware that the text is a translation. The most developed notion of this preference is perhaps **Philip E. Lewis**'s concept of **"abusive fidelity"** (1985/2012), derived from Derrida's work on translation. Lewis values translations that do *not* adopt the norms of the target culture, and which instead try to follow the start text so closely (hence "fidelity") that the result will sound strange to most readers. This, says Lewis, should be done only at points in a text where there are meanings to be explored ("a deci-sive textual knot," 1985/2012: 227). "Abusive fidelity" could be a recommendation for anyone who wants to develop a philosophical reading of a text. But can it seriously be proposed as a general translation method? Perhaps not, given its restriction to selected points in great texts (see Davis 2001: 87ff.) and its apparent indifference to the economies of translating. However, the practice of "abusive fidelity" can bring the receiver into a space between two languages; receivers are made aware that there is no meaning transfer as such. The result would ideally be what **Marylin Gaddis Rose** (1997) calls **"stereoscopic reading,"** taking place in an "interliminal space," where both languages are present.

　　Beyond these few concepts, most approaches that oppose "domestication" or "fluency" also claim to raise awareness of indeterminacy. I mentioned some of these modes in the chapter on directional equivalence, picking up a line of thinkers that runs from Schleiermacher through to Gutt and Venuti. It would be wrong to place those thinkers entirely within deconstruction, since none of them consistently doubts the translator's capacity to understand the start text. However, the same theorists would certainly want to make the reader work; they do not want translators to provide ready-made solutions, at least not for all translations. In this they meet up with indeterminism in seeking a complex reception experience. In **Schleiermacher** and the German Romantic school we find calls to translate in ways that allow features of the foreign text to influence domestic syntactic patterns. **Gutt**, for his part, would oppose moves to translate the Bible as a modernized story (updating things like cultural practices or units of measurement); he prefers translators to provide readers with enough information ("communicative clues") for them to approximate the source location. As for **Venuti**, his call for translations that "resist fluency" privileges the use of non-standard variants in the target language. One of the theoretical bases for this is a deconstructionist critique of linguistics, since Venuti sees mainstream linguists as excluding the parts of language that are unsystematized and thus count as a "**remainder**" (see Venuti 1998). This critique unfairly overlooks much of contemporary linguistics (especially the sociolinguistics of variation), but it does help raise awareness of uncertainty.

Uncertainty is something that translators are often conscious of, along with revisers, editors, translation critics, and indeed anyone else who is able to read both start text and translation. They might not have a word for it, but they know it is there. They constantly find themselves in situations where they have to decide, without certainty, between different interpretations or renditions. Awareness of indeterminism might be considered in some way **internal** to the profession. **External knowledge**, on the other hand, would characterize a reception process in which no doubts are raised about the way the translation represents an absent text. Seen in these crude binary terms, awareness of indeterminacy would be well served by any mode of translation able to extend internal knowledge as far as possible into the external sphere. If you can translate in such a way that points of indeterminacy are revealed rather than hidden, we might approach a situation where the end-users of translations are also translating.

6.7 FREQUENTLY HAD ARGUMENTS

Given the importance of the uncertainty principle in twentieth-century thought, these theories have sparked relatively little debate within Translation Studies. Part of the reason could be geographical. **Deconstruction** has been particularly important in literary studies in the **United States**, a country where Translation Studies was slow to develop. Across the world, university departments of literature or cultural studies have taken their lead from the United States, and have thus paid due attention to deconstruction, and rather less to translation. Parallel to this, the many institutions where translators are trained have tended to take their lead from **Europe and Canada**, where translation is necessary for the workings of multilingual societies and indeterminacy is not especially what those societies want to know about. Few translator trainers have read these theories, and even fewer have seen value in the complexities. With isolated exceptions, the problematics of uncertainty have mostly been allowed to go their own separate way.

One exception is an exchange between **Rosemary Arrojo and Andrew Chesterman** (Chesterman and Arrojo 2000). Arrojo represents deconstruction; Chesterman offers something like philosophically aware descriptive studies. In their joint article, the two agree on a remarkably long list of things that can be done in Translation Studies. They show that an academic discipline can allow for exchange between paradigms. At one point, however, Chesterman argues that the relation between a translation and its start text cannot be characterized by difference alone, since **meanings have *degrees* of stability** (as well as degrees of difference, as in the "family likeness" metaphor). Arrojo does not accept this: "Meanings are always context-bound," she argues. "Depending on our viewpoint and our circumstances, we may perceive them to be either 'more' or 'less' stable but all of them are always equally dependent on a certain context" (Chesterman and Arrojo 2000: Ad.10). Arrojo wants no part of the "more or less." For Arrojo, for consistent deconstruction, to analyze degrees of similarity would mean accepting the ideal of possible sameness ("more or less" with regard to what?), and thus falling into essentialism. At this point, the two paradigms touch but separate.

Beyond that particular exchange, there have long been behind-the-back mumblings. I summarize a few general complaints:

6.7.1 "The theories are not useful to translators"

Theories of indeterminacy offer few guidelines that might be of practical use to translators. They would seem to be **theories for theorists**. Translators, on the other hand, are rarely paid for showing indeterminacy to the world. That said, indeterminism could be of some practical consequence for the way translators are trained, and opposition to commercial criteria might prove one of the paradigm's more profound contributions.

6.7.2 "The theorists are not translators and do not care about translation"

This is a belligerent version of the above. Many of the thinkers cited in this chapter are philosophers or literary theorists, more than they are translators. However, when Heidegger traces differences between German, Latin, and Greek, or when Derrida teases out the various gaps found in translations, they are using translation to do philosophy. Who would say they are not translating?

6.7.3 "The theories lead to a lack of rigor"

A fairly common complaint about **deconstruction** is that it leads to situations where "anything goes" (see Eco *et al.* 1992). Clever critics can locate any meaning in any text, proving nothing but their own cleverness. Part of the problem is that deconstructionist writing is relatively easy to imitate, and pretentious third-raters can display a thousand trivial interpretations, filling their texts with unbearable puns. Derrida, however, was anything but gratuitous. His close, careful readings are marked by punctilious attention to detail. If anything, Derrida's practice displays an excess of cold rigor. Like translation itself, deconstruction has practitioners at all levels, and there is no need to discredit the entire paradigm because of the abundance of facile extensions.

6.7.4 "Indeterminism is of no consequence"

A further debate concerns the **"So what?" response**. The criticism is that, if two or more translation solutions are valid, the theories producing them have no effect on the actual practice of translation. Granted, indeterminism quite possibly does not interfere with the everyday practice of translation. It should nevertheless concern any search for certainty, and thus most kinds of theorization. When you make selections between various possible solutions, you should realize you are usually dealing with problems that are more complex than "right" versus "wrong."

6.7.5 "These theories are merely oppositional"

This criticism takes some indeterminist theories to task for being too ready to expose the inadequacies of all other theories. As I have indicated, you cannot simply assume all theories of equivalence to be "transmissionist" or "essentialist." You cannot categorize all theories prior to Derrida as somehow "determinist," "prescriptive," or "authoritarian." Indeterminist theories have been around for a long time, and they interact in quite subtle and contradictory ways with the other paradigms. Determinist theories of expression can give indeterminist theories of translation, whereas indeterminist theories of expression (the arbitrariness of the sign) potentially allow translation to be encoding and decoding. In this situation, simple opposition is extremely reductive.

6.7.6 "Deconstruction prescribes what translations should be"

This is one of the criticisms made by **Raymond van den Broeck** (1990), who views Derrida (1985) and Lewis (1985/2012) as calling for little more than a particular kind of "deconstructive translation" (1990: 54). Van den Broeck thus sees deconstruction as being opposed to Descriptive Translation Studies. The critique seems based on a misunderstanding, since the uncertainty paradigm obviously does far more than prescribe one ideal way of translating. If "abusive fidelity" is the mode of translating best suited to deconstruction, this does not mean that indeterminism cannot be found in all modes of translating across the board. Cannot a deconstructionist approach, which is basically a way of interpreting texts, be applied to any translation at all?

6.7.7 "Linearity is part of the translation form"

Indeterminism would suggest that non-linear logic is particularly well suited to the analysis of translations, since there are weak causal links between input and output, and a complex range of factors involved. One might nevertheless object that non-linearity fails to describe the social function of equivalence beliefs, which operate precisely to construct assumptions of linear causation. Further, those beliefs are based on assumed lines between languages, and often on the illusion that national borders separate languages and cultures (Pym 2003). Just as second-language acquisition studies have had to analyze not just what people learn, but also their beliefs about learning, so translation theory should consider not just the non-linear relations but also the very *linear beliefs* associated with translation.

6.7.8 "Indeterminism is debilitating"

A good number of "committed" approaches to translation see themselves as acting on behalf of causes that are more important than translation: sexual equality, anti-capitalism, anti-globalization ("minoritization"), anti-imperialism, and so on. For these approaches, theory should change the way people think and act, and the more uncertainty one reveals, the less people are going to be moved to action. You do not take to the streets to defend fuzzy logic. In criticizing the essentialist certainties of feminism, Arrojo thus weakens the connection between theory and motivation. On the other side of the coin, we might see the national harmonies of eco-translatology as precluding oppositional action, and accepting the political status quo.

6.7.9 "These theories do not help us live with uncertainty"

Many of the theories are not only bluntly oppositional with respect to other paradigms but also fail to seek ways in which professional practice effectively works with indeterminism. I have nevertheless listed a fair bunch of ideas that could help us come to terms with indeterminism in fairly practical ways. Much more could be done in this regard. We could look closely at the way disciplines like physics and economics deal with uncertainty. Most empirical sciences are living with uncertainty, and translation theory is only exceptional in that it took us so long to realize it.

None of these arguments seems strong enough to undermine the indeterminist paradigm. Whatever kind of translation theory you choose to develop, you must learn to live with uncertainty.

Just as it has been attacked, so the indeterminist paradigm has been able to attack rival approaches to translation. Deconstructionists like Rosemary Arrojo (particularly 1998) tend to see all traditional translation theory as being based on equivalence, which they criticize for being essentialist. That critique is easy enough to make. But it could be extended into the other paradigms as well. When *Skopos* theory names its dominant factor as this *Skopos* we have called "purpose," is that not also an essentialism, an assumption of stable meaning? And when Descriptive Translation Studies presumes to be doing science by separating the object of study from the subjectivity of the researcher, is that not similarly an untenable and essentialist divide? Thus extended, the indeterminist paradigm could claim to be the only satisfactory way to come to terms with uncertainty. There would then be no way to turn but "to the text itself and hence to a concern with language" (Benjamin 1989: 86). Translation theory would be endlessly tracing transformations between languages, in the spirit of Cratylus, Heidegger, and Derrida.

And yet that is not the turn that history is taking.

SUMMARY

This chapter started from the simple idea that translators cannot be absolutely certain about the meanings they translate. This is seen as a problem of determinism, in the sense that a text does not fully cause (or "determine") its translations. I have identified two kinds of theories that accept this uncertainty. Some theories assume that the (great) text is full of meaning in a way to which translations will be adequate. Those theories are thus determinist with respect to expression and indeterminist with respect to translation. Other theories, however, assume uncertainty to be a feature of all communication. They are indeterminist with respect to both start texts and translations. Seen in this way, uncertainty becomes a problem that the translator has to resolve. I have identified several ways in which translators might come to live with uncertainty. You can, for example, trust that religious faith or mystical illumination will guide you; you could enter into extended dialogues in order to reach social consensus about meaning; you can accept that your position influences what you find in a text, so it is worth analyzing your own motivations; you can see translation as the way in which all meaning is constructed; you can see translating as a game in which we make moves and place bets, in a complex world theorized through non-linear logic. Finally, the practice of deconstruction is one further way of dealing with uncertainty, based on translating or analyzing translations in such a way that the points of indeterminacy are revealed rather than hidden.

SOURCES AND FURTHER READING

The third edition of *The Translation Studies Reader* (Venuti 2012) has texts by Benjamin, Jakobson, Berman, Lewis, and Derrida, with Quine and Levý in the first edition only. Munday (2012) has summary accounts of Benjamin and Derrida. The best introduction is still Davis (2001). George Steiner's *After Babel* (1975) gives much room to hermeneutic tradition and a questionable reading of Walter Benjamin's essay as Kabalistic. Steiner's general view is ultimately a determinist theory of expression underlying an indeterminist view of reception. There are better commentaries on Benjamin's essay, which has been fetishized by English-language literary criticism. Students are advised to tackle Benjamin's text before and after reading the commentaries. Marylin Gaddis Rose's *Translation and Literary Criticism* (1997) includes an application of Benjamin to the teaching of literary translation, displaying keen awareness of the way indeterminism underlies the "stereoscopic" reading of literary texts. Rosemary Arrojo's books in Portuguese (1992, 1993), along with her articles in English, are a constant demonstration of the way deconstruction can reveal contradictions and inconsistencies in other theories of translation. Numerous other authors in the deconstruction camp are more interested in translation as a metaphor, construing translating itself as deconstructive practice. At that point, they blend into the "cultural translation" paradigm (Chapter 8 below).

Suggested projects and activities

The activities listed here are designed to make students think beyond the binarisms of right vs. wrong. However, students should also be invited to challenge the certitudes upon which other translation paradigms are based.

1   Return to a translation you have done, in prose and preferably not highly technical. Select a start-text sentence and rephrase it, in the start language, in as many different ways as you can. Now look at your previous translation of that

sentence. Did your translation follow the *form* of the sentence you found, or the form of one of the variations you have now produced? Why?

2   Try the same exercise for a line of verse, and again for a sentence from a highly technical text. What is different in each case? Could we say that the language is more determinate (more fixed, or less open to interpretation) in some cases than in others?

3   Working in small groups, students write two sentences, one that they think cannot be misinterpreted (i.e. is relatively determinate) and one that they think could be interpreted in different ways (i.e. has ambiguities or is otherwise rela-tively indeterminate). They then have these sentences translated into another language, then back into the start language (by a student who has not seen the original). The operation can be repeated for as many languages as are available, with the starting point always being the previous translation into the start language. You can do this with a sheet of paper that is folded over so that the translator cannot see the previous translations. The groups then see what has happened to their sentences. They can use this information to answer questions like the following: a) Did the most indeterminate text undergo the most changes? b) So does equivalence apply to some texts more than others?

4   Repeat Activity 3 but use the automatic translation programs Babelfish and Google Translate for the translations and back-translations. What do you find? At what points do human and machine translation reach a level where the successive translations introduce no new modifications? Why?

5   Activities 3 and 4 are versions of a game called "telephone" in the United States. Look up the other names this game is known by around the world. Why should the same game have so many different names? Are there correct and incorrect names for the game?

6   Is the linguistic sign arbitrary? Consider the names of the heroes and the villains in films or comics. Could the names be changed, or are some sounds well suited to villains, and others appropriate for heroes? Why is "Darth Vader" such a good name for an evil character (see Crystal 2006)? Do these strangely appropriate sounds work the same way in other languages? If not, how should they be translated?

7   Walter Benjamin intimates that the French and German words for "bread" cannot translate each other because they evoke different kinds of bread. Is this really true? Find a sizeable literary text online and do a search for the terms for "bread." How often do those terms really refer to a general kind of bread that is found in one culture only? What does this tell us about the linguistic or cultural units that translators actually work on?

8   Do a web search for texts presented as translations of Rimbaud's poem "Voyelles" (in 2013 seven could be found here: http://www.brindin.com/pfrimvoy.htm). Can you find any that you would not call translations? At what point does a version cease to be a translation? What does this say about translation as a constant creation of new meanings?

9   For any text, compare the translations done in class, noting the points where the solutions are all the same and where they are different (cf.

Campbell 2001). What is the relation between indeterminacy and the points with many different translations? Are the points "decisive textual knots" (Lewis)? Are they the most difficult translation problems?

10 Act out an encounter where information is exchanged (e.g. asking for street directions, or giving advice on how to cook a dish). At a key point, one of the actors has to request information in as many different ways as possible, and the other actor responds accordingly. Can the same request be made in numerous different ways? Or does each different formulation receive a different response? Compare this with the "so what?" argument formulated by Chomsky and Katz.

11 Some theories of languages as world-views say that translation is impossible. But how can anyone know there is a world-view that is not like their own? Use the Internet to find out about the research done by Humboldt, Sapir, and Whorf. In the course of their research, do you think they used translation in order to learn about a language that was not their own?

12 Freeman (1999) claims that the American anthropologist Margaret Mead was lied to by the young Samoan girls who were her "native informants." Is this case like Quine's *gavagai* example? Was the hoax due to indeterminacy? What does it say about ethnography as a kind of translation?

13 Consider the following passage from the American philosopher Richard Rorty:

> The thought that a commentator has discovered what a text is really doing—for example, that it is *really* demystifying an ideological construct, or *really* deconstructing the hierarchical oppositions of western metaphysics, rather than merely being capable of being used for these purposes—is, for us pragmatists, just more occultism.
>
> (in Eco *et al.* 1992: 102–3)

Is this a fair criticism of the way deconstruction has been applied in translation analysis? On the basis of the description in this chapter, would there be any profound differences between "constructivism" and "deconstruction"? Do an Internet search for these terms and try to characterize the different academic fields they are used in.

14 Rosemary Arrojo refuses to discuss whether meanings are "more or less" stable. Is she right to do so? Here is her argument on this point:

> Meanings are always context-bound. Depending on our viewpoint and our circumstances, we may perceive them to be either "more" or "less" stable but all of them are always equally dependent on a certain context. A proper name such as the University of Vic, for example, only makes sense to those who are familiar with the explicit and implicit context to which it belongs and which makes it meaningful. The same certainly applies to notions such as democracy, which may be perceived by some to be less stable. If we ask Fidel Castro, or Augusto Pinochet, for instance, what "democracy" is, their answers will certainly indicate that there is nothing "unstable" about their

definitions of the concept, no matter how different they may end up to be. Both Castro and Pinochet will be sure that each of them has the right, true "definition" and that the other one is wrong. The implications of such statements for translation are certainly essential and far-reaching and they may be summarized as follows: no translation will ever be definite or universally acceptable, no translation will ever escape ideology or perspectivism.

(in Chesterman and Arrojo 2000: Ad.10)

How might this position relate to what can be discovered in Activities 1, 2 and 3 above? Do you agree with Arrojo?

15 Jakobson and others see all meaning-production as translation. So what do you make of the following passage from George Lakoff (1987: 312)?

The difference between translation and understanding is this: translation requires a mapping from one language to another language. Understanding is something that is internal to a person. It has to do with his ability to conceptualize and to match those concepts to his experiences on the one hand and to the expressions of the new language on the other. Translation can occur without understanding and understanding can occur without the possibility of translation.

16 Venuti (2013: 235, 243) argues that American literary translators should produce more theory, since non-theoretical accounts lack "precision." Is there any precision in theories of indeterminacy?

CHAPTER 7

Localization

Localization usually refers to the translation and adaptation of software, instruction manuals, and websites. This chapter explores the field as a paradigm of translation theory. Although some see localization as an unconstrained form of adaptation, the way it operates in the localization industry usually involves the use of quite extreme constraints. This is partly due to the use of new translation technologies, to various types of "internationalization" as generalized one-to-many translation, and to non-linear modes of text production and reception (which have nothing to do with non-linear logic). Here I run through the main concepts of localization theory and a few of the technologies. The end of the chapter asks whether translation is part of localization, or vice versa, and what the cultural effects of localization might be, particularly with respect to the increasing numbers of volunteer translators. I will generally argue that the basic concepts of localization have a great deal to say about the way translation is working in a globalizing world.

The main points in this chapter are:

■ The localization industry responds to the problem of uncertainty by creating artificial languages and cultures.

■ Localization is the preparation of a product for a new locale.

■ A locale is a set of linguistic, economic, and cultural parameters for the end-use of the product.

■ What makes localization a new paradigm is the key role played by *internationalization*, which is the preparation of material so that it can be translated quickly and simultaneously into many languages.

■ Although electronic translation technologies are not to be equated with localization, they enhance the role of internationalization.

■ One effect of the technologies is to promote *non-linear* modes of text production, use, and translation.

■ Localization may be seen as a partial return to equivalence in that it uses fixed glossaries and promotes decontextualized translation. The opposition between "standardization" and "diversification" as localization strategies is also reminiscent of natural and directional equivalence.

7.1 LOCALIZATION AS A PARADIGM

At the beginning of this book I described a strong paradigm based on equivalence. Since equivalence was supposed to be a scientific, objective paradigm, it was seriously challenged by the principle of uncertainty. From that conflict, translation theorists have developed at least three ways of responding. The purpose-based paradigm responded by moving theory closer to practice, reducing equivalence to a special case and insisting that translators and their clients negotiate in order to translate. In parallel, Descriptive Translation Studies made equivalence a quality of *all* translations, no matter how good or bad, and set about describing the shifts and transformations that translators produce. A third response is the indeterminist paradigm itself, particularly deconstruction, which sets about undoing illusions of equivalence as a stable semantic relation.

These three responses all deserve to be called paradigms. Each is coherent within itself, and they are different from each other to the extent that people working in any one paradigm genuinely have trouble appreciating theories from others. If that much can be allowed, we must also recognize at least one further paradigm. The ideas and practices increasingly brought together under the label of "localization" do not constitute a translation theory in any strong academic sense; they are perhaps just a set of names-for-things developed within certain sectors of the language industry. On the other hand, those concepts provide a coherent response to the problem of uncertainty. If languages and cultures are so indeterminate that no one can be sure about equivalence, then one solution is to create *artificial* **languages and cultures** in which relative certitude becomes possible. That is a viable solution. But why should it be called "localization"?

7.2 WHAT IS LOCALIZATION?

I start with a tale that simplifies history. Back in the 1980s, the American company Microsoft was developing software for the North American market and was translating the software into the main languages of other markets (English to German, English to French, English to Spanish, and so on). That was fine for as long as there were just a few foreign markets. However, as the number of markets grew, the **one-language-to-one-language transla-tion** model was seen to be inadequate and expensive. The software required not just replacement of the pieces of language in the menus, dialogue boxes, and Help files, but also attention to a long list of apparently minor details like date formats, hotkeys, punctua-tion conventions, and user contracts. Some of those things concern translation; others require the technical expertise of a product engineer; and still others require telecommuni-cations technicians, terminologists, marketing experts, and lawyers. Together, such tasks are carried out by teams, of which translators are a part. The entire process is then called "localization," of which translation is a part.

Language and culture tasks in the localization of software

Software localization manuals give lists of problems and tasks like the following, only some of which concern traditional translation:

- Time conventions: Different cultures have different ways of presenting clocks and calendars (11.04.14 means November 4th 2014 in the United States and the 11th of April 2014 in virtually everywhere else in the English-speaking world; and Chinese English puts the year first).
- Numbers: Different cultures (and different companies!) use different punctuation in the presentation of numbers. For example, the English number 1,200.01 becomes 1.200,01 in traditional Spanish, 1 200,01 in reformed Spanish (and the International System of Units), and 1 200.01 in Iberian Spanish that now officially tolerates partial interference from English (and/or from the International System of Units).
- Currencies are different, as are the ways in which they are presented.
- Some scripts move left to write, others go right to left.
- Hotkeys may be reallocated (for example, in English Control+O opens a document, in Spanish it is Control+A for "abrir"). But then you have to make sure that the command Control+A is not being used for something else. In fact, the complications are so great that the more professional Spanish programs just stay with Control+O.
- Examples and colors need to be adapted to local tastes.
- Products must conform to local legal, fiscal, safety, and environmental requirements.
- Products also have to be adapted to local standards with regard to telecommunications, measurement units, paper sizes, and keyboard layouts.

"Localization" can involve a wide range of tasks; it usually concerns information technology and marketing, as well as language skills. The definitions of "localization" reflect this by talking about **products rather than texts**, and describing the process in terms of the "preparation," "tailoring," or "adaptation" of the product for a new situation. That shift is important. Some even more significant shifts, however, come from the other terms with which "localization" is associated. The first of these is the small word "**locale**," which denotes a set of linguistic and cultural parameters defining the context of end use. It is a nice short term to replace wieldy expressions like "target language and/or culture." It also implicitly recognizes that translators have rarely worked for entire languages or cultures; our audiences are usually local markets, locales, for which the term was missing.

The important point is that the localization paradigm involves more than the mere term "localization."

The key concepts of localization

The basic terms of localization can be defined in several ways. The first three definitions below were proposed by the now-defunct Localization Industry Standards Association (LISA) in 1998:

- *Localization* involves taking a product and making it linguistically and culturally appropriate to the target locale (country/region and language) where it will be used and sold.
- *Internationalization* is the process of generalizing a product so that it can handle multiple languages and cultural conventions without the need for re-design.

Internationalization takes place at the level of program design and document development.

■ **Globalization** addresses the business issues associated with taking a product global. In the globalization of high-tech products this involves integrating localization throughout a company, after proper internationalization and product design, as well as marketing, sales, and support in the world market. This meaning is more specific than the general process of economic globalization.

■ **One-to-many**: This is a term for translation processes that go from an internationalized version to many target-language versions simultaneously. It is not to be confused with the term "one-to-several" coined by Kade to describe the way one start-language item can correlate with many target-language items (see 3.2 above).

■ **Partial localization**: A localization process in which not all the user-visible language is translated, usually to save costs when working into a small locale.

■ **Reverse localization**: A localization process that goes from a minor language into a major language (Schäler 2006).

■ **CAT**: The traditional acronym for Computer-Aided Translation, used to describe translation-memory and terminology-management suites as "CAT tools." The term is misleading, since almost all translating is done with computers these days, so all processes are "computer-aided" to some extent.

7.3 WHAT IS INTERNATIONALIZATION?

There might appear to be nothing new in localization: the term could simply refer to traditional translation plus a certain amount of "adaptation." That would be nothing new: *Skopos* theory had already seen that many translators carry out numerous tasks beyond the production of translations (hence the concept of "translatorial action"). There are nevertheless several things that are genuinely new in localization theory.

   Let us go back to the American software program that has to be localized for a series of European markets (French, German, Spanish, and so on). In many instances, those individual localization projects are going to face the same difficulties, in the same places in the programs, even though their solutions will often be different. These particular places are of the kind we have listed above: date formats, currency references, number presentations, and so on. Those are also the places where the American software turns out to be specific to American cultural preferences (for example, in using MONTH, DAY, YEAR as a date format). At those points, there is no real need to translate each time from the American version into all the different target versions. That would involve negotiating a huge number of cultural differences and running enormous risks of error. Greater efficiency comes from taking the American-specific elements *out* of the program and replacing them with generic elements, as far as possible.

   What has happened here? In traditional translation, you move from a start text to a target text:

Figure 7.1a   A very simple model of traditional translation

In localization, on the other hand, you move from a start to an intermediary version. The production of that intermediary version is called "**internationalization**," and the thing produced is the "internationalized" version. This is a bad name, since nations have nothing to do with it (which is why we have the term "locale," after all). But I am not here to correct the industry. The general model now looks like this:

Figure 7.1b   A simple model of translation plus internationalization

Internationalization has prepared the product prior to the moment of translation. This makes the translation processes easier and faster. Localization can then work directly from the internationalized version, without necessary reference to the initial text, and can do so into many languages simultaneously, in a **one-to-many** workflow. This brings greater efficiency, with many localizations happening at the same time, producing many different target versions:

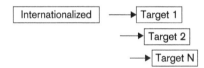

Figure 7.1c   A model of localization

The simultaneous production of target versions has its logic. Economic globalization means that major products (like a new version of Microsoft's operating system) are released at the same time in many locales across the globe, with similar marketing formats and publicity campaigns. The age of "**simultaneous shipment**" requires rapid localization, not just of the products but also of the marketing material.

As a general concept, internationalization can take several forms, some of which go beyond what the industry might want to recognize as internationalization. At one extreme, it can involve putting **more information and more potential formats** into the product to be localized. The localizer then only needs to consult the glosses or select the appropriate option. Perhaps the most successful model of internationalization of this kind is the development of **character encoding**. Back in the days when software existed in English and little more, the 7-bit ASCII encoding was enough: it allowed for 128 different characters. Then, when IBM started to distribute internationally, it found that an 8-bit set was needed to cover all the accents and symbols of Romance languages: this allowed for 256 different characters. Nowadays, with extensive globalization, we have moved to the 32-bit USO or Unicode encoding systems, allowing for over four million characters (for USO). All characters are now encoded in the larger systems, including those that had simple encoding in the previous systems. The code carrying the information thus expands enormously, but the characters of potentially all locales can thus be represented. This would be the technological logic of internationalization: **expand the start text**, so that all localization possibilities are allowed for.

At the other extreme, internationalization can make a text **simpler**, reducing surface-level variation through the use of **controlled language**. When a document has a limited number of syntactic structures and a completely controlled multilingual terminology, as in the case of "Caterpillar English" for heavy machinery, the localization process can happen almost automatically, through the use of machine translation plus reviewing. Later I will return to various modes of internationalization between these two extremes.

Thanks to internationalization, the fundamental message of localization is not just that products need to be adapted to new users in different cultures. The inclusion of internationalization means that those adaptations have to be **thought about from the very beginning**, and planned for at every stage of product development. Translation is usually considered to be something that comes later, after the start text has been produced. Localization, on the other hand, should involve a complete re-think of the way products and texts are produced.

This restructuring of processes is sometimes called "**globalization**," since it is designed to address a global market. A company might decide to "go global" by introducing processes of internationalization and localization. Some care should be taken with this term, however. "Globalization" more generally refers to the development of transnational markets, with major economic and financial consequences. Just to confuse the issue, Microsoft uses the term "globalization" to refer to what we have called "internationalization." Here I will stay with the few terms so far described: within a company that has been **globalized**, products are **internationalized** so they can then be **localized** quickly and simultaneously, and part of that localization process is **translation**.

7.4 IS LOCALIZATION NEW?

If seen as cultural adaptation, localization probably adds nothing new to existing translation theory. After all, the priorities that *Skopos* theory gives to end-purpose could also justify a wide range of adaptations. On the other hand, if you see **internationalization** as a key part of localization, then there is something new. Is this concept, or anything like it, to be found in any other paradigm of translation theory? One could perhaps argue that taking out or reducing culture-specific elements can be justified by theories of natural equivalence, where a neutral *tertium comparationis* or underlying kernel was once sought as a guarantee that the same thing was being said (see 3.4 above). However, you would have to scour many hundreds of pages to find ideas of working from an intermediary version. Internationalization, I suggest, is a new element of theory.

This is not to say that one-to-many work cannot be found in some translation projects, in relay interpreting, and in screen translation. A Hollywood film will usually *not* be translated (for dubbing or subtitling) from the original screen version or from the original script. The translations are increasingly done from a script especially prepared for translators across the globe, which incorporates glosses on culturally specific items, on necessary cross-references within the film text, and indeed any other kind of note that can avoid translation mistakes before they happen. Those prepared scripts might count as internationalized versions. In similar fashion, many Bible translation projects are nowadays carried out by referring not only to the Hebrew and Greek texts, but to the software known as Paratext, which brings together those texts, other translations into many languages, explanatory glosses, and sophisticated concordancing tools. That might be an instance of internationalization (expanding the source) plus localization. Perhaps more significantly, the actual translations are carried out by teams of native speakers of the many hundreds of minor target languages, with the help of expert "translation consultants" who know Biblical scholarship and who can work with several teams at the same time. The presence and function of the "consultant" might also be seen as a humanized instance of internationalization. These practices provide interesting comparisons with software localization.

The models can be taken further still. For instance, consider the way **international news** is put together and translated. An event occurs, producing initial reports; the texts are then put into the format of an international news service like Reuters; those "internationalized" versions are then localized by newspapers, radios, television networks, and websites, some with interlingual translation, others without, but all with adaptation. The terminology of localization can describe the overall process. Similarly, **multilingual websites** have to be developed in such a way that the localizations are thought of from the outset, in the initial design and engineering. The localizations then necessarily work from an internationalized version.

There is thus a range of translation practices that operate in ways similar to the model of internationalization plus localization. Not all those practices are new. The use of localization theory to describe those processes is nevertheless not only new, but also useful. Once you extend the terms and concepts outward from the software industry, you start to see a few general trends in the way economic globalization is affecting translation.

As a rule of thumb, the more global and instantaneous the medium, the more the medium welcomes internationalization plus localization. The more traditional, monocultural and diachronic the medium (sending messages across centuries, for example, as in many literary ideologies), the more you find traditional binary models, where translation moves from start to target each time. However, even within literary translation, the terms of localization are not completely lost. The Canadian-based publisher Harlequin, for example, can put out the same novel in some 24 languages and about 100 locales, in each case not just translating but also editing the text to suit local expectations about length, morality, and styles of story-telling (cf. Hemmungs Wirtén 1998, who calls this kind of localization "transediting").

You could still argue that, even within these workflows, translation remains translation at each particular step. So perhaps no new theory is needed? Is there really no new paradigm at work? Yes, translation is probably what it has always been, at some very basic level. Yet the consequences of localization do not stop at the production of internationalized versions. Technology has taken things a few steps further.

7.5 THE ROLE OF TECHNOLOGIES

Recent years have seen a tendency to offer courses on "localization" that basically teach students how to use a series of electronic tools: translation memories, software localization tools, terminology management tools, and increasingly integrated machine translation, with perhaps a content-management system or project-management tool as well. Despite the courses, those tools should not be equated with localization as a paradigm. The tools are there; they are certainly used in the localization industry; but translation memories, machine translation, and terminology management can work without any kind of localization going on, and internationalization and localization can be carried out quite independently of the tools. Localization theory is one thing; electronic tools are something else.

At the same time, careful attention should be paid to the effect that the tools have on the overall work processes. In general, the various technologies allow language to be processed in a paradigmatic way. That is, they show the alternatives available at particular points in a text, interrupting the syntagmatic or linear dimension of language. You might think here of the simplest electronic tools, which are among the most useful. As you write with word-processing software, a spell-checker automatically compares your words with an electronic dictionary. If you are unsure of the spelling or appropriateness of a word, you can quickly consult a list of suggested spellings or synonyms. The tool thus gives a vertical list of alternatives, in addition to the horizontal flow of the text. That list is paradigmatic. It interrupts the syntagmatic flow. The technology **imposes the paradigmatic on the syntagmatic**. All translation technology does this to some extent.

How do technologies relate to internationalization and localization? To answer this, we have to consider a few tools in greater detail.

7.5.1 Management systems

Years ago, a team of translators might have been employed to render a whole software program or company website into a particular language. To understand that process, you might consider the user-visible parts of the program or website as a text, and you then assume that translators would render the whole of that text, with each translator more or less aware of the overall product. In short, everyone would be aware of what was going on. Nowadays, software and websites are rarely developed in this way. What you find tends to be a constant flow of **modifications and updates**, as one version gradually evolves into another. Just as new translations of the Bible incorporate findings and solutions from previous translations, so new localizations of software and websites make use of the material produced in previous localizations. This means the translators no longer work on whole texts, not even on whole internationalized versions, but only on the **new additions and modifications**.

The result is a radical change in the way translators are made to think. What they receive is not a coherent whole. It is more commonly a list of isolated sentences and phrases, or sometimes new paragraphs, one on top of the other, as a set of vertically arranged items. The translator has to render them in accordance with a supplied glossary, which is another paradigmatic document, with items one on top of the other. The work is thus doubly vertical, paradigmatic, rather than horizontal, syntagmatic.

Where is the technology here? Imagine a company that has countless documents on all its products and operations. The company markets its products in seven different languages, contacting its customers through a multilingual website, user manuals, and publicity material. When an updated version of a product is being prepared, the company is not going to rewrite and translate the entirety of all its previous documents. It somehow has to isolate the additions and modifications, and to coordinate them so that the end output is appropriate to all the media in which it is going to communicate. The key challenge is not getting the translations done, but keeping track of all the pieces. To do this with any degree of efficiency, the company has its information ("**content**") broken down into units, usually of one or several paragraphs ("**chunks**"), in such a way that these units can be updated individually and combined in new ways to suit new purposes. **Content-management systems** allow this process to be controlled with some efficiency in one language; **globalization**

management systems allow content to be coordinated in many language versions. A change introduced in an English segment might thus automatically signal that changes are needed in the corresponding segments in other language versions.

What the management system prepares for translators are the lists of "**translatables**," along with the list of glossary entries that are to be respected. The translators no longer have access to any overall view of the text or the project. They have no possibility of carrying out the extra-translational tasks envisaged by *Skopos* theory, since they have very few clues about what the communicative purpose is. In effect, all questions of strategic planning have moved to the project manager or perhaps to a marketing expert, while the global project as a set of texts is now held by the technology, in the management system.

7.5.2 XML

Another level of coordinated control is made possible by XML (eXtensible Markup Language), which is a technical standard used to exchange content. Basically, information is tagged so that it can be retrieved later. The following is an example of a simple XML text:

```
<item>
<title>Pride and Prejudice</title> was written by <author>Jane Austen</author>
in <year>1813</year>.
</item>

<item>
<title>Alice in Wonderland</title> was written by <author>Lewis Carroll</author>
in <year>1866</year> .
</item>
```

By tagging texts in this way, you can later retrieve just the information on authors, for instance, for a textbook on literature. You might also retrieve information on dates, perhaps to create a chronology of publications between 1800 and 1850. XML is a way of writing texts so that their elements become available for easy re-use in future texts. For as much as translation theorists have been repeated that meaning depends on context, here the aim is to prepare texts so they can be used in many different contexts.

When management systems and XML are used in localization projects, something quite profound happens to the nature of the texts involved. On many levels, and in many ways, texts are being broken down into fragments that then become available for re-use. New texts are pieced together from those fragments, in a way that is no longer linear: the text producer does not start from a beginning, move to a middle, and finish at an end, as Aristotle assumed in his *Poetics*. Texts become **reorganizations of re-usable content**. Nor are these texts *used* in a linear way, starting at the beginning and moving toward the end. Think of how you use a software Help file, or an operation manual for an appliance, or a website. The use of these texts (no longer a "reading") is mostly non-linear, based on indices, hyperlinks, or a Find function.

When texts are regularly *produced* in a non-linear way, and *used* in a non-linear way, it comes as no surprise that they are *translated* in a non-linear way.

To take a banal example, the translator may have to render the English term "Start," which could be a noun or a verb, depending on the co-text (other neighboring words in the text) or context (situation of future use). What happens when the translator can see neither co-text nor context? Do you translate the noun or the verb? This is where the relation between localization and translation becomes problematic. Note, though, that the problem is *not* in the theory of internationalization (ideal internationalization would have had the term tagged with a grammatical function). It ensues from the complexity of the work process itself, and from the nature of the technologies able to handle that complexity.

The change is far-reaching: it touches the fundamentals of translation theory. Once upon a time, in the days of comparative linguistics and natural equivalence, translators were seen as working on terms and phrases. With the development of text linguistics and functionalist approaches, translators were increasingly seen as working on *texts*. In the purpose paradigm, where importance is attached to the client's instructions and different communicative aims, the translator was viewed as working on a *project* (text plus instructions, and perhaps plus information on a few cultural and professional contexts). This vision holds true in the field of localization, of course, since the projects have become so complex that they are handled by specialized project managers. From the perspective of the translator, though, the work increasingly involves an ongoing series of updates and modifications: the translator is engaged in a **long-term localization "program,"** rather like the maintenance programs that you use to have your car serviced regularly. The frame has moved from sentence to text to project, then right back to where we started from: translators work on terms and phrases, as in the good old days of comparative linguistics, or of phrase-level equivalence.

7.5.3 Translation memories

Since localization projects are complex, they are frequently allied with technologies that are useful for controlling complexity. Not by chance, the technologies have evolved at the same time as localization practices (commercial translation memories date from the early 1990s). The catch is that the technologies do something quite different from the idea of cultural adaptation that is sometimes invested in the term "localization." This is one of the major contradictions of the paradigm.

All electronic language technologies are based on enhanced **memory capacity**, which is why they enable re-use. **Translation-memory tools**, as the name suggests, bring this capacity closer to the process of translation. Translation memories basically store previously translated sentences or phrases ("segments") in such a way that start segments are matched with target segments (thus storing "bi-texts"). (Note that the resulting databases are superficially like the one used in corpus linguistics, except that corpus linguistics has little to do with the development or professional use of these systems.) As the translator moves through a text, all the segments that have been translated previously can be brought up onto the screen; they do not have to be translated again. The translator effectively only has to translate the new segments. Further, the translation memory can bring up previous translations that are only partly like the one to be worked on, thus presenting a range of "fuzzy matches." For example, if you have translated "the big red car," you will have almost all the elements required to translate "the big blue car." The translator then only has to change the elements that are not a complete match. The idea is simple and effective.

For text genres that are highly repetitive, there are real gains in the translator's **productivity**. More significant, though, is the way translation memories tend to impose uniform terminology and phraseology across projects, ensuring that different translators use the same kind of language. From the client's perspective, and for many of the managers co-ordinating the work of translation teams, this is one of the major benefits of translation memories: **increased consistency** can be just as important as any gain in productivity.

This means of control is further extended when the translation-memory suites are integrated with **terminology tools**. The translator receives not only the translatables and the translation memory, but also the terminology to be followed when carrying out the translation.

7.5.4 Data-based machine translation

The main recent advance has been the integration of machine translation into translation-memory systems. In some cases this is fairly simple. If the translation memory does not give you a full or fuzzy match, it can present a suggested translation drawn from an online machine translation system. The translation may not be perfect, but it is usually good enough to justify a revision process ("post-editing"). Yet there is a lot more happening in machine translation than this simple "Plan B" approach.

Translators have spent decades claiming that machines will never be able to translate. Now we have to reconsider what that means. It is easy enough to feed text into an online machine translation system and make fun of the results. But for many language pairs, we are now at the stage where it is quicker to "post-edit" machine-translation output than to start translating from scratch (Pym 2009; García 2010), and the differences in quality may not be all that significant.

The more successful machine translation systems are "**data-based**" or "**statistical**." This means that, in addition to linguistic mapping rules, they are able to search through large databases of bi-texts, propose the most statistically likely pairs, and determine which of them are well-formed in the target language. This is what Google Translate and Bing Translator are doing, online and for free, and the most accessible integration of machine translation into a translation memory is Google Translator Toolkit, also online for free. Since a lot of people are using these services, they have a revolutionary potential, well beyond localization. On the one hand, these systems allow a **virtuous circle**: the more the machine-translation outputs are used intelligently and post-edited, the more good bi-texts are fed back into the system, the bigger the paired databases become, so the matches become better, the tool will be used more, and so on. Eventually everyone should have serviceable translations for free. On the other hand, though, there is a **vicious circle**: when people think that raw machine translations are usable without post-editing, they feed bad translations back into the system, the matches become worse, and the system fails.

Which of these processes will win out? The simple way to avoid the vicious circle is for each company to have its own in-house statistical machine translation system, which will thus become little different from a large translation memory. Translators working for the company will all be either pre-editing texts to prepare them for the system, or post-editing machine-translation output. We might not want to call them "translators" anymore, but that problem was solved by the concept of "translatorial action," way back in *Skopos* theory (4.3 above).

In the public domain, however, these technologies still have the potential to alter the way our societies view and use translations. And public education should be the main factor in tipping the balance between the virtuous and vicious circles.

7.5.5 Volunteer translation

If you have a system that improves the more it is used, you logically need a lot of people to use it. A system like Google Translator Toolkit, released in 2009, uses this logic by providing a free online translation memory system that by default incorporates machine translation suggestions. That is, as you translate, you can build your translation memories at the same time as you post-edit machine translation output (do not confuse this with the machine translation system Google Translate). In exchange for this free tool, the translations you produce are by default fed into Google's databases, thus improving their system. The more people get involved in the system, the better it works, so the more people will be involved, and so on. This is how a private company can solve a lot of translation problems by giving us something for free—you use the system, but Google gets your translations.

This appeal to public involvement can be seen in the settings of Google Translator Toolkit, which explicitly caters for the group translation of websites and Wikipedia articles. The system is designed for projects where translation is not only going to be done on a voluntary basis, but it is likely to be done by a group of translators who communicate with each other online. The technology moves us toward new kinds of work arrangements, presenting a major challenge to individual professional paid translators.

There are many names for the incorporation of volunteer translators in this way. Popular references are to "**user-generated translation**," "**crowdsourcing**" (as a poor rhyme on "outsourcing"), "**community translation**," and "**collaborative translation**." None of these terms focuses on what might be the most innovative element: under all these rubrics, the work is going to be voluntary, and for that simple reason I believe that "voluntary translation" is the most suitably provocative name for the thing.

Volunteer translation is sometimes carried out by a community of users, as in the case of Facebook or Twitter. This makes social sense. After all, the people who use these social media are probably the ones best suited to decide on the most appropriate translations, and who will most directly benefit from the results. In the case of the Facebook crowdsourcing system, users propose possible translations (mostly for less-than-transcendental segments like "Who are you looking for?"), then the users themselves vote on the most appropriate suggestion. The translation process is thus significantly socialized. In more committed cases such as Greenpeace or Amnesty International, we might more readily say that the work of volunteer translators constitutes active intervention, an empowering democratization of translation technology. Activists point out, correctly, that remunerated translation services tend to be for the texts of *official* culture, so volunteers are required to translate alternative, resistant cultural forms (cf. Boéri and Maier 2010).

In all such cases, various technologies are being combined to make translation far more than the individual professional activity that it is traditionally conceived as. Some professional translator associations have already begun to point out the dangers of placing undue trust in public technologies and volunteer translators. At the same time, though, there is little reason why interested users should not be well positioned to decide on the most suitable translations: Facebook fans know what works for their particular class and generation, and Greenpeace activists are likely to be quite good at finding the right ecological terms for their particular locales. Translation quality may ultimately not be the major problem. On the other hand, there might problems with respect to cross-product consistency, style sheets, workflow deadlines, and corruption by intruders. Because of these aspects, the way ahead may be to seek cooperation between volunteers and professionals, with the two groups intervening at different stages of the workflow.

7.5.6 Technology and the return of equivalence

I return to the fundamental question: Are these memory technologies necessarily part of the localization paradigm? There seems little justification for a straight correlation. After all, some translators can use translation memories to translate novels, in a quite traditional way. There seems to be no reason, on the level of translation theory, why such uses should be called "localization."

Clearly, we have to ask what specific *uses* localization processes make of technology. The following points can now be made:

- When translators receive a text along with translation memories and term databases, the effect on translation is functionally similar to internationalization. That is, the text-reuse technologies are operating as forms of pre-translation. Just as Unicode and controlled writing attempt to resolve localization problems before they surface, so translation memories and term bases do translation work before the translator enters the scene. The generality of repetition (text re-use) precludes the specificity of situation (this translator, with this text, for this purpose). In effect, **the technologies are being used for a wider kind of internationalization**, and to that extent have become fundamental to what is new in localization.
- When translators are simply calling up memories of their own previous translations, they are usually free to *alter* the matches and keep the improved memory as part of their work capital. However, when companies use online translation memories for projects involving teams of translators, those translators have no effective **ownership of the memories** and thus little self-interest in correcting false matches. Indeed, translators are often instructed *not* to alter the full matches, no matter how wrong the matches appear, and the translators are consequently not paid for those matches (although they are paid at varying rates for fuzzy matches). When this happens, the actual work process of the translator is altered substantially: since the previous matches are not looked at, textual linearity all but disappears, and equivalents are cognitively restricted to segment level.
- Translation decisions within localization projects also involve **conflicts of authority**. Where text re-use technologies present an "authorized" solution, the translator is likely to opt for it, even when alternative solutions are readily available or even clearly necessary. It may be that translators only correct the memories when they have the self-assuredness of experience in the particular field, perhaps a rather healthy pay-check, no deadlines, and ideally a strong ethical dedication to quality communication, all of

which would seem to be a combination of factors rare within the frame of localization. Note that such corrections, which go from the specific situation to the general database, run counter to the underlying logic of internationalization, which would ideally have all movements flow from the database to the situation.

■ In projects where several translators are involved simultaneously, the re-use technologies result in texts where sentences or segments will be culled from different co-texts and contexts, probably rendered by different translators. Bédard (2000) notes the consequent degradation of text quality, resulting in a "**sentence salad**"—the target text will have stylistic features from several different translators and probably many different discursive situations.

■ Because of these problems, localization projects tend to include extensive **product testing** and **document reviewing or revision**, depending on the level of quality required. In this way, the negative effects of the internationalization processes (all concerning pre-translation) are to some extent countered by a series of checking processes (post-translation). Reviewing becomes an extremely important part of the translation process, meriting its own theorization.

So what kind of **equivalence** is involved in localization? The answer must depend on what part of the localization process we are talking about. With respect to internationalization, and indeed from the perspective of the language worker employed as a translator and nothing but a translator, the reigning ideal is undoubtedly equivalence at sentence or phrase level, reinforced by equivalence at product-function level (the user either pushes the right button or they don't—and that is often what really counts). If we compare this with the theories of the 1960s and 1970s, we find that this "internationalized" equivalence is no longer "natural" (contextualized by the dynamics of social language and culture) or "directional" (with one-off creativity). It has become fundamentally **standardized, artificial**, the creation of a **purely technical language and culture**, in many cases the language of a particular company.

At the same time, beyond the technologies, there are typically two ways in which localization projects can be oriented. On the one hand, the multilingual contents may be strongly centralized and reproduced in all target languages, resulting in an extreme **standardization** of localization projects. On the other, contents may be highly adapted to the specific norms and tastes of the target locales, in accordance with a decentralized **diversification** approach. In terms of the models touched on in this chapter, "standardization" would mean that internationalization plays a key role, whereas "diversification" should give greater scope to adaptation. The underlying binarism is also fundamental in the organization of international advertising campaigns. What is intriguing here is that the opposition between standardization and diversification recalls the classical oppositions we saw in theories of **directional equivalence** ("formal" vs. "dynamic," etc., see 3.4 above). There is thus a certain return to the modes of thought used with respect to both natural equivalence (in the consequences of technology) and directional equivalence (in the alternatives facing communication policies).

I hasten to add that localization does include moments (in text composition based on content management and in post-translation editing) in which equivalence is certainly *not* the order of the day. In those moments, **addition and omission are legitimate strategies**, to an extent not envisaged in classical theories of equivalence. Further, cultural adaptation may require degrees of transformation that go well beyond the classical limits of translation but can be justified within the purpose paradigm. Far more can happen within localization than was contemplated by the standard theories of equivalence. The catch, of course, is that the new things, the adapting and the editing, tend not to be done by people employed as translators.

7.6 TRANSLATION WITHIN LOCALIZATION?

We are now in a position to deal with an apparent **contradiction between the discourse and the work processes of localization**. The ideology of localization is based on cultural diversification, yet the principle of text-reuse is that language is *not* dependent on specific situations, and thus, in theory, does not have to be adapted. The contradiction is more apparent than real because different things are happening at different levels, or at different stages: text re-use is an affair of technology and internationalization, whereas adaptation is something that tends to be done by policy-makers or marketing experts. The more problematic aspect is where translation fits into those stages.

Tasks in the localization of software
The following steps might be taken when localizing software (adapted from Esselink 2000: 17–18):

Analysis of Received Material
Scheduling and Budgeting
Glossary Translation or Terminology Setup
Preparation of Localization Kit (materials for the translators)
Translation of Software
Translation of Help and Documentation
Processing Updates
Testing of Software
Testing of Help and Publishing of Documentation
Product QA and Delivery
Post-mortem with Client

A localization project can involve numerous tasks, from the moment the material is received through to "post-mortem" discussion with the client. Those are the things that project managers have to consider. Translation is usually presented as just one or two of those steps, so the managers logically conclude that **translation is a small part of localization** (as indeed is the case in Gouadec's workflow model, 4.8 above). Seen in terms of the tasks, that is entirely correct. Translation has become the replacement of user-visible natural-language strings (i.e. the pieces of non-code that users of the product will have to interact with). That is quite probably the least interesting part of localization, both for practitioners and for theorists. The higher costs (and the substantial profits) are in tasks that are wider than simple translation: product internationalization, the identification and extraction of translatables, structuring hierarchies of target languages in terms of market priorities, organizing complex language-service teams, drawing up schedules, testing localized products, post-editing translations, creating cooperative working relations between specialized service companies, using or developing appropriate software for localization, and working with controlled writing. In short, no matter which model of localization you choose, the replacement of natural-language strings ("translation") is going to look like a minor part. The breakdowns of budgets often rate "translation" at less than a third of the total costs.

This operative reduction of translation lies behind the reliance on "artificial" equivalence. It also effectively separates translation from the wider fields of action sought by the purpose paradigm, even when the fundamental concept of localization would be in agreement with those approaches. Needless to say, it has no place for uncertainty. The localization frame brings translation back to square one.

7.7 FREQUENTLY HAD ARGUMENTS

Although these dilemmas concern nothing less than the form of translation, there has been little debate about localization among translation theorists. This is partly because of the nature of localization discourse, which is the stuff of guru experts, new terms for new trends, hype about technological advances, quick industry surveys, and ideologies straight from globalizing capitalism. The industry experts have no need for careful theoretical concepts.

Perhaps for the same reasons, academics have shown little inclination to take the localization industry seriously, at least not in any sense that could threaten fundamental beliefs about translation.

A relatively informal and under-informed milieu thus provides the background for the current arguments, of which I offer a few.

7.7.1 "Localization is a part of translation"

The localization industry generally sees translation as part of localization; theorists from other paradigms sometimes see the relation the other way round—for them, localization is just a special kind of translation. The solution could be for speakers to explain exactly what they mean by "translation," as Locke would have recommended.

7.7.2 "There is nothing new in localization"

This is the main weapon used by those who see localization as a part of translation (i.e. standard translation theorists, particularly from *Skopos* theory). I have argued that the effectively new elements in localization are internationalization and the consequent process of one-to-many translation. Others tend to argue that the various text re-use technologies are what is really new, and that the technologies are not specific to the localization industry. Either way, there is something new.

7.7.3 "Localization belittles translators"

This statement brings together various aspects: the restricted sense of translation as segment-replacement, the tendency to ensure that translation memories cannot be owned by the translators who produce them, the distribution of costs and financial rewards away from translation, and the extreme time constraints typically placed on translation work. Some within the industry claim that these are advantages: translators are now able to focus on what they apparently do well (translation), without having to worry about all the techno-logical aspects of product engineering and formatting, and without having to concern themselves with aspects better handled by marketing and engineering experts. On the other hand, voices within the industry also claim that translators have the intimate cultural knowledge that might ensure the success of products in new markets, and that they should thus be listened to at more than phrase level.

7.7.4 "Localization leads to low-quality communication"

There are several things here. Many within the industry express concerns about the linguistic qualities of translations due to the use of team translating with translation memo-ries and machine translation. Others are more worried about the accumulation of errors in the translation memories. Still others focus on the relative invisibility of images and of the communication situation, assuming that this will lead to decontextualized communication. At present, none of these doubts is based on irrefutable empirical evidence, and all appear to concern the use of translation memories and machine translation rather than the key concepts of localization itself.

7.7.5 "Standardization reduces cultural diversity"

This criticism is sometimes made of the localization industry in general. However, standardi-zation most properly belongs to the "internationalization" side of localization, and consider-able cultural adaptation is still conceivable in terms of the localization paradigm. The argument should focus not so much on the communication strategies as on the **range of cultures and languages** that are affected by the localization industry. For the more global products, the lists are impressive (for instance check the "language and region" settings in Microsoft Office). Beyond commercial self-interest, that is not a minor virtue. The entry of a language into electronic communication, with standardized scripts and Unicode identity, may well do more to enhance its longevity than will several hundred studies by well-intentioned cultural theorists. The very existence and relative prosperity of the localization industry could thus *enhance* linguistic and cultural diversity, quite independently of the standardized or diversi-fied communication strategies that are adopted within individual localization projects. At the same time, however, the major act of cultural change is probably the introduction of elec-tronic communication itself, the consequences of which can be far-reaching and are quite possibly common to all cultures that adopt the medium. The tendency toward non-linearity, for example, would seem to be written into the technologies. One might expect it to become a feature of certain genres in all communities that adopt electronic communication.

On most of these issues, the jury is still out.

7.8 THE FUTURE OF LOCALIZATION

Since localization is of importance because of its association with **economic globalization**, let me sketch a simple theory of how that relation works (for the complexities, see Cronin 2013).

As technologies reduce the costs of transport and communication, there is increased mobility of capital, merchandise, and labor, and this requires massive crossings of cultural and linguistic boundaries. Those crossings tend to require language learning (when the relation is long-term, as in the movement of labor) and translation (when they are short-term, as is increasingly the case in the movement of capital and merchandise). The **long-term relations** tend toward the use of lingua francas, especially in the relations of production. Experts from different professions and different primary cultures will come together to work in a multinational space, where they will speak English, or Chinese, or whatever is the dominant language to be learned.

Short-term relations, however, are better served by translation. No one is going to learn a language just to sell one product over six months. The whole commercial logic of translation could be based on the calculation that, in the short term, it is marginally cheaper to use translation than to learn whole languages.

We thus have some languages being learnt as second or third languages over the long term and by people from many different provenances. Those become the languages of globalized production. Then there are other languages that are used in strong and advanced relations of production on the national level, or that form large and/or wealthy locales. Those become languages of both production and consumption: end-users will demand products in their languages. Finally, at the extreme, some languages are virtually only learnt by mother-tongue speakers and the occasional translator. Where they are not associated with enough wealth to form a viable market, those languages may effectively be excluded from consumption. If you speak Ao-Naga and you want to use a computer, you learn enough English or Bangla to do so.

Such is the translational logic of what has been called the "**world language system**" (de Swaan 2002). The general picture is of a hierarchy where some languages are central and used for production, others are semi-central and impose strong constraints on consumption, and still others are virtually excluded from the relations of production, consumption, and translation. The result is strangely like the dynamics and ideologies of the medieval hierarchy of languages.

Within this hierarchy, translation tends to move from centralized production to semi-central consumption. This often means going from English to all the major languages of the world. There have been some similar movements from other languages, for instance from Japanese for the initial market for video games, or from Korean for computers, cars, and ships produced by *jaebeol*. English is certainly not the only language of international production, yet the logic of the one-to-many movement remains the same.

Economic globalization can thus explain why the one-to-many configuration is so important. That is why the logic and ideologies of localization are pinned to the development of economic globalization.

Localization is marked by a **strong directionality**, moving from the central languages toward the more peripheral languages. This directionality is so pronounced that movements in the other direction have been called "**reverse localization**" (Schäler 2006). For example, we might find translations *into* English for 1) specialist sectors that require information on other cultures, including feedback on consumption patterns, and 2) easy exchange into third cultures, in a situation where the central language becomes a kind of "**clearing house**" (a Romanian bank will announce investment opportunities in English; French philosophy is sold in English in eastern Europe; for that matter, Newton wrote in Latin, still the clearing-house language for scientific production in his day). Only the second of these reasons bears relation to localization, where it acts as yet another kind of internationalization. Note, however, that these examples of "reverse localization" do not have the initial one-to-many configuration. On the contrary, these examples suggest a preliminary pattern of "many to one," before the stronger sense of localization can begin. As economic globalization increases, reverse localization should become more frequent.

More problematic is what happens at the other end of the scale, with languages that are marginal with respect to both production and consumption. In software localization, for example, the larger locales receive **full localization** (meaning that all user-visible language is translated and items like hotkeys are adapted); secondary locales will have **partial localization** (perhaps the main menus are translated, but not the hotkeys or the Help files), and still smaller locales receive products that are merely "**enabled**" (you can work in the local language with them but the menus and Help files remain untranslated). And then there are the countless languages for which enabling is not yet possible, since the languages do not have standard written forms, or their written forms as yet have no place in our character-encoding systems, and our technologies do not yet work on the basis of voice alone. This rational commercial logic means that the users who most need Help files and pop-up explanations in the menus are precisely the ones who do not have that information in their own language.

The way localization configures relations between cultures is thus very different depending on which part of the hierarchy you are looking at. Between the central languages, a regime of successful yet artificial equivalence may reign, largely thanks to internationalization. Further down the hierarchy, directionality means that equivalents are imposed through calques or straight loans, as was the case with the downward directionality in the medieval hierarchy of languages. Further down still, decisions not to localize affect language survival, which is one of the major tragedies of our age.

If localization simply followed economic globalization, all cultures might conceivably be caught up in the maelstrom of product internationalization. At the same time, the localization industry has an active self-interest in the defense of linguistic and cultural diversity, in the strength of locales, since that is where markets can be expanded. Beyond the commercial logic, many of our government documents and services are now provided online, using communication systems that follow the concepts and the tools of localization projects. **Accessibility** thus becomes an issue of **democracy** and **social ethics**, and a large part of accessibility is the availability of information in one's own language. Whether in the commercial or the governmental sectors, the processes of localization incorporate powerful technologies that can do much to influence the future of diversity. Rather than spread a regime of sameness, the localization paradigm might actively participate in the saving of difference.

SUMMARY

This chapter has presented localization as something more than a synonym for "adaptation" or a use of new translation technologies. Instead, localization introduces a new paradigm because of the key role played by "internationalization" in allowing one-to-many patterns of translation. This key one-to-many workflow allows the localization industry to meet the needs of globalizing economic relations. Further, the one-to-many processing is enhanced by a series of technologies that have far-reaching effects on the way we produce, use, and translate texts, imposing the paradigmatic on the syntagmatic. The way translators work is thus altered considerably. The global consequence of localization may be an increasing standardization of cultures. However, the paradigm also allows for considerable cultural adaptation, going well beyond the confines of traditional equivalence-based translation. In most respects, the long-term cultural effects of localization remain to be seen.

SOURCES AND FURTHER READING

The third edition of Munday (2012) deals with localization in a chapter on "New Media" (which strangely includes corpus studies). Most of the book-length publications on the paradigm are now quite dated, since the field has changed rapidly, although there is value in *Perspectives on Localization* (2006) edited by Keiran J. Dunne. Pym's *The Moving Text* (2004b) is an attempt to rethink translation from the perspective of localization. The literature in blogs and online magazines is nevertheless plagued by hype, with numerous case studies of the way localization has miraculously transformed companies, and recycled disaster stories about what happens when it is not done by professionals. The Machine Translation Archive (http://www.mt-archive.info) has a wealth of information on many aspects of localization, much of it highly technical. Information on recent developments in technology and markets can be found in the journals *Multilingual* and *Localisation Focus*.

Suggested projects and activities

1 Check your software programs for the presence of "locales." How many locales can you find for your language? In Word, check for the available dictionaries and thesauri. In Office, go to Control Panel/Regional settings and languages. Should we describe these locales as languages or cultures?

2 Offer an explanation for the localization problem in the Catalan dialogue box in Figure 7.2. (You do not need to know Catalan to see it – just consider how would you know when it is Friday the 13th.) Would this error occur in a traditional translation process? How could you solve the problem? For how many languages should you solve it? (Note: Later versions of Microsoft operating systems solve the problem by using internationalization.)

3 Look at the website of a large international organization or company (especially vendor sites like Ikea.com or organizations like the World Bank). Compare the different localized versions. What parts of the localization could be called translation? What parts go beyond translation? Are there any examples of partial or incomplete localization? Is the general strategy one of standardization or diversification (see 7.5.6 above)? Can you tell which version was the source for others?

4 Once you have completed Activity 3, select a *national* company or agency that has a multilingual website (most banks do). It will help if the national company is in the same sector as the multinational one. What are the differences in

Figure 7.2   Catalan calendar from Microsoft Windows XP (2005). Used with permission from Microsoft.

communication strategy between the national company and the multinational one? Is there more or less adaptation in the case of reverse localization?

5   Look up and define the following terms: l10n, i18n, and g11n. What might the full version of t9n be? Can it be found with an Internet search engine? If not, why not?

6   Do an Internet search for companies in your country that advertise "localization" services (the local term is probably from English). Do they also offer "translation"? How do they present the relation between "localization" and "translation"? What particular economic sectors do these companies work for?

7   Look at the official website of your local town or city. If it is multilingual, have the different language versions been localized? If it is not multilingual, what languages do you think it should be localized in? Would you translate *all* the content on the site, or would you select content of interest to non-residents? Would you add new content in some language versions?

8   Should a multilingual website use standardization or diversification as its strategy? What will be the long-term effect on the world's cultures?

9   Check the portals of Google and Yahoo! in as many languages as you can. Do they use standardization or diversification as a general strategy? Does either company try to combine the two strategies?

10   Can team translation produce good results? Check to see the way Facebook has been translated.

CHAPTER 8

Cultural translation

Localization theory came from industry and has incorporated elements of the equivalence paradigm. At roughly the same time, a significant number of theories have been heading in precisely the opposite direction. This chapter looks at approaches that use the word "translation" but do not refer to translations as finite texts. Instead, translation is seen as a general activity of communication between cultural groups. This broad concept of "cultural translation" can be used to address problems in postmodern sociology, postcolonialism, migration, cultural hybridity, and much else.

The main points in this chapter are:

- **"Cultural translation" can be understood as a process in which there is no start text and usually no fixed target text. The focus is on cultural *processes* rather than products.**

- **The prime cause of cultural translation is the movement of people (subjects) rather than the movement of texts (objects).**

- **The concepts associated with cultural translation can complement other paradigms by drawing attention to the intermediary position of the translator, the cultural hybridity that can characterize that position, the cross-cultural movements that form the places where translators work, and the problematic nature of the cultural borders crossed by all translations.**

- **There have been prior calls for wider forms of Translation Studies, and for close attention to the cultural effects of translation.**

- **Cultural translation can draw on several wide notions of translation, particularly as developed in 1) social anthropology, where the task of the ethnographer is to describe the foreign culture, 2) actor-network theory ("translation sociology"), where the interactions that form networks are seen as translations, and 3) sociologies that study communication between groups in complex, fragmented societies, particularly those shaped by migration.**

The paradigm thus helps us think about a globalizing world in which "start" and "target" sides are neither stable nor entirely separate.

8.1 A NEW PARADIGM?

The New Centennial Review, which added the "new" part of its name in 2001, opens its programmatic statement as follows:

> The journal recognizes that the language of the Americas is translation, and that questions of translation, dialogue, and border crossings (linguistic, cultural, national, and the like) are necessary for rethinking the foundations and limits of the Americas.

This use of "translation" is difficult to situate in terms of the paradigms I have looked at so far. How can a whole language be translation? How can two continents have just one language? There seems to be no equivalence involved, no goal-oriented communicative activity, no texts or even translators, and nothing definite enough for anyone to be uncertain about it. What is meant, I suspect, is that **colonial and postcolonial processes** have displaced and mixed languages, and this displacement and mixing are somehow related to translation. But to call all of that "translation" sounds willfully metaphorical. It is "as if" every discourse were the result of a translation, "as if" all the moving people were translators, and "as if" there were a mode of communication available to all. The perplexity behind these questions suggests the passage to a new paradigm.

Numerous examples can be found of "translation" being used in this way. The purpose of this chapter is to survey them to see if they might indeed be parts of a paradigm. I will start from the basics of postcolonial theory, from a reading of the influential theorist Homi Bhabha. This will map out a sense of "cultural translation." I will then step back and consider previous calls for wider forms of Translation Studies, most of them direct extensions of the paradigms we have seen in this book. The survey then considers ethnography (where the term "cultural translation" was first used), postmodern sociology, and a little psychoanalysis. Can all these things constitute just one paradigm? Should the Western translation form be extended in all these directions? The chapter will close with brief consideration of the political questions at stake.

8.2 HOMI BHABHA AND "NON-SUBSTANTIVE" TRANSLATION

The idea of "cultural translation" is most significantly presented by the Indian cultural theorist **Homi K. Bhabha** in a chapter called "How Newness Enters the World: Postmodern Space, Postcolonial Time and the Trials of Cultural Translation" (in *The Location of Culture*, 1994/2004). Part of the chapter discusses the novel *The Satanic Verses* by the Indian-born British novelist **Salman Rushdie**. Bhabha is concerned with what this kind of mixed discourse, representative of those who have migrated from the Indian sub-continent to "the West," might mean for Western culture. He sets the stage with two possible options: either the migrant remains the same throughout the process, or they integrate into the new culture. One or the other. That kind of question is strangely reminiscent of some of the major oppositions in translation theory: should the translation keep the form of the start text, or should it function entirely as part of the new cultural setting (3.4 above)? Should localization seek "diversification" or "standardization" (7.5.6 above)? Bhabha's use of the term "translation" might be justified because of those traditional oppositions. Nonetheless, his basic question more directly concerns fundamental dilemmas faced by migrant families, especially in the second and third generations: for example, which languages do we use in the home? Rather than take sides on these questions, Bhabha looks at how they are dealt with (or better, performed) in Rushdie's novel. You can imagine Bhabha reading Rushdie, then commenting on other postcolonial experiences, and doing all that with reference to translation, looking for some kind of solution to the basic cultural problems of postcolonial migration. He does not, however, cite the classical oppositions I have just referred to; he turns only to Walter Benjamin's essay on translation (6.3.2 above) and Derrida's commentary on it (plus a reference to de Man). One of the difficulties of reading Bhabha is that he presupposes a working knowledge of all these texts, as professors of literature tend to assume. Another difficulty is that he invites us to think these are the only translation theorists around, as readers of this book will hopefully now not assume.

So what does "**cultural translation**" mean? By the time Bhabha gets to this chapter of *The Location of Culture* (1994/2004), he has accumulated quite a few uses of the term in a vague metaphorical way. He has talked about "a sense of the new as an insurgent act of cultural translation" (10), "the borderline condition of cultural translation" (11), the "process of cultural translation, showing up the hybridity of any genealogical or systematic filiation" (83), "cultural translation, hybrid sites of meaning" (234), and so on. In this chapter, a more serious attempt is made to connect with translation theory. Bhabha is remarkably uninterested in the translators of *The Satanic Verses*, even though they were the ones who bore the brunt of the *fatwā* or Islamic condemnation of the novel: Hitoshi Igarashi, the Japanese translator, was stabbed to death on July 11, 1991; two other translators of the novel, Ettore Capriolo (into Italian) and Aziz Nesin (into Turkish), survived attempted assassinations in the same years. No matter: Bhabha is more concerned with the novel itself as a kind of translation. What set off the *fatwā* he claims, is the way the novel implicitly translates the sacred into the profane: the name "Mahomed" becomes "Mahound," and the prostitutes are named after wives of the prophet. Those examples do indeed look like translations; the blasphemy can fairly be described as "a transgressive act of cultural translation"; there is thus some substance to the claim that a certain kind of cross-cultural writing can be translational. Then again, what kind of theorization can allow those few words to become representative of whole genres of discourse?

What Bhabha takes from translation theory is not any great binary opposition (the dilemmas of migration present plenty of those already) but the notion of **untranslatability**, found in Walter Benjamin's passing claim that "translations themselves are untranslatable" (Benjamin 1923/1977: 61; 6.3.2 above). Benjamin actually talks about this untranslatability as being due to the "all too great fleetingness [*Flüchtigkeit*] with which meaning attaches to translations" (1923/1977: 61), and I prefer to see this as referring to the momentary subjective position of the translator (6.3.2 above). Bhabha nevertheless wants nothing of this "fleetingness" (and thereby forgoes numerous possible puns on *Flüchtling* as a "displaced person," a "refugee," an "escapee"). For him, that untranslatable quality of translations is instead a point of **resistance**, a negation of complete integration, and a **will to survival** found in the subjectivity of the migrant. As such, it presents a way out of the binary dilemmas. And this, I suspect, is the great attraction of translation as a metaphor or way of thinking, here and throughout the whole of Cultural Studies: it can cut across binarisms.

To associate resistance with survival, however, Bhabha has to mix this "untranslatability" with the part of Benjamin's essay that talks about translations as extending the life of the original. Benjamin does indeed say that translations give the original an "**after-life**"

(*Fortleben*, "prolonged life"), which, says Benjamin, "could not be so called if it were not the transformation and renewal of a living thing, the original is changed" (Benjamin 1923/2012: 77). Now, to get from "after-life" to "survival," you have to have read Derrida's commentary in *The Ear of the Other* (1982/1985: 122–3), where the claim is made that 1) Benjamin uses the terms *Überleben* and *Fortleben* (does Derrida miss *Nachleben*?) interchangeably to mean "living on," and 2) the one French term *survivre* ("survive," but literally "on-live," "to live on") translates both Benjamin's terms (the topic is also developed in Derrida 1979, 1985). Benjamin's "prolonged life" (*Fortleben/Nachleben*) can thus become "survival" (*Überleben, survie*) in the eyes of Bhabha, and both are related to being on, or in, the problematic border between life and death. In this chicane of interlingual interpretations, a few nuances have been shaved off, with alarming certitude: what for Benjamin was "fleeting" has become "resistance;" what was a discussion of *texts* in Benjamin and Derrida has become an explanation of *people*; what was an issue of *languages* has become a concern within *just one language* (Bhabha writes as a professor of English discussing a novel written in English); what was the border between life and death for Derrida has become the cultural borders of migration; and what was generally a theory of translation as linguistic transformation has now become a struggle for new cultural identities. In short, the previous theorization of translation has been invested in one word ("survival") and applied to an entirely new context. Bhabha knits this together as follows:

> If hybridity is heresy, then to blaspheme is to dream. To dream not of the past or present, nor the continuous present; it is not the nostalgic dream of tradition, nor the Utopian dream of modern progress; it is the dream of translation as "survival," as Derrida translates the "time" of Benjamin's concept of the after-life of translation, as *sur-vivre*, the act of living on borderlines. Rushdie translates this into the migrant's dream of survival; an *initiatory* interstices [*sic*]; an empowering condition of hybridity; an emergence that turns "return" into reinscription or re-description; an iteration that is not belated, but ironic and insurgent.
>
> (Bhabha 1994/2004: 324)

There is no attempt here to relate the notion of survival to anything in the equivalence or purpose paradigms of translation, so perhaps I should not insist too much on Rushdie's use of blasphemous names as actual translations. In Bhabha's reading, there is no particular start text, no particular target, no mission to accomplish anything beyond "resistance." All those things (start, target, purpose, life-and-death) surely belong more to the *fatwā* as a flying arrow destined to punish mistranslations. However, if Rushdie's resistance is indeed a kind of translation, it must also recognize the reading embedded in the *fatwā* even if only to contest it. Indeed, it is only through negation of that reading that the object of cultural translation can properly be described as "**non-substantive translation**," as Bhabha himself is reported as calling it (in Trivedi 2007: 286). What we have, though, looks more like a diffuse kind of longing ("to dream") that comes from the position of a translator, situated on or perhaps in the borders between cultures, defined by **cultural hybridity**. From that perspective, something of Benjamin's "fleetingness" can then be recuperated when Bhabha refers to the indeterminacy of the hybrid: "The focus is on making the linkages through the unstable elements of literature and life—the dangerous tryst with the 'untranslatable'—rather than arriving at ready-made names" (Bhabha 1994/2004: 325). This is generalized in the formula: "Translation is the performative nature of cultural communication"

(1994/2004: 326), which can perhaps only be understood in terms of Bhabha's closing winks to all kind of borders between and within cultures, not just those due to migration but also those of all minority cultures: Bhabha mentions feminism, gay and lesbian writings, and the "Irish question." Wherever borders are crossed, cultural translation may result.

As a piece of theorizing, Bhabha's text does not choose between the alternatives it presents. Should the migrants remain unchanged, or should they integrate? What should be their home languages? How should mainstream Western culture react to cultural hybridity? Such questions are not solved; they are dissolved. Bhabha simply points to this space between, elsewhere termed the "third space," where the terms of these questions are enacted. Once you see the workings of that space, the questions no longer need any kind of "yes" or "no" answer.

The sense of "translation" here is far wider than the texts we call translations. This theoretical approach is quite different from the descriptive studies that look at the way translations have been carried out in colonial and postcolonial contexts. Bhabha is not talking about a particular set of translations, but about a different sense of translation.

You can perhaps now understand why the American journal bravely declared that "the language of the Americas is translation." In fact, such claims might now be rather tame. In a world where major demographic movements have undermined categories like "a society," "a language," "a culture," or "a nation," any serious study requires new terms to describe its objects. "Translation" is one of those convenient terms, but so too is "emergence" (things are emerging and submerging in history), "hybridity" (extending Bhabha, every cultural object is a hybrid), "complexity" (there is no one-to-one causation), and "minoritization" (which would recuperate the role of elements excluded by the supposition or imposition of a linguistic or cultural "system"). Translation is only one of a number of terms, but it has become a popular one. And Bhabha is only one of a number of theorists working in this field, but he is perhaps the most influential.

Does this theorizing have anything to offer the other paradigms of translation theory? One might be tempted to dismiss Bhabha as no more than a set of vague opinions, presented in the form of fashionable metaphors. At the same time, if you do accept this as a paradigm of translation theory, it reveals some aspects that have been ignored or side-lined by the other paradigms:

- This view of translation is from the **perspective of a (figurative) translator**, not translations. No other paradigm, except perhaps parts of *Skopos* theory, has talked about the position of someone who produces language from the "between space" of languages and cultures (one could also talk about "overlaps").
- The focus on **hybridity** has something to say about the general position of translators, who by definition know two languages and probably at least two cultures, and it might say something basic about the effects that translation has on cultures, opening them to other cultures. Bhabha does not say that translations are hybrid; he locates a trans-latory discourse that enacts hybridity.
- The link with migration highlights the way translation ensues from **material move-ments**. Bhabha would not want his view of translation to be bound to any materialist determinism. Nonetheless, the framing of translation by the material movement of people seems not to have been the focus of any other paradigm.
- Bhabha sees that translatorial movements traverse **previously established borders** and thereby question them. No other paradigm has so vigorously raised the problem

of the two-side border figured by translations (see 3.5 above), although the uncertainty paradigm can certainly question the way borders produce illusory oppositions.

These are all valid points; they indicate important blind-spots in the other paradigms; they justify calling "cultural translation" a new paradigm. Perhaps more important, these points concern quite profound problems that ensue from the increasingly fragmented nature of our societies and the numerous mixes of our cultures, not all of which are due to migration (communication technologies also play a powerful role). Further, these points are raised in a way that is a little different from what we have seen in the uncertainty paradigm. Whereas Benjamin and Derrida, for example, were ultimately engaged in reading and translating *texts*, attempting to bring out multiple potential meanings, Bhabha makes rather more programmatic statements about the world, without much heed for second thoughts or clear referents (e.g. "Rushdie translates this into the migrant's dream of survival"). Rather than a hermeneutics of texts, "cultural translation" has become a way of talking about the world.

Now for some down-to-earth questions: Do we really have to go through Rushdie, Benjamin, and Derrida to reach the tenets of "cultural translation"? Or have all these things been said before, in different places, from different perspectives? And are they being said in other places as well, as different but similar responses to the underlying phenomena of globalization?

Separating the terms

After Bhabha, the term "cultural translation" might be associated with material movement, the position of the translator, cultural hybridity, the crossing of borders, and border zones as a "third space." As such, the term is not to be confused with several formulations that sound similar but mean different things. I attempt to define the differences:

- *Cultural translation (Bhabha)*: In the sense of Bhabha (1994/2004), a set of discourses that enact hybridity by crossing cultural borders, revealing the intermediary positions of (figurative) translators. This is the most general sense, the one I am using the term to describe a paradigm.
- *Cultural translation (ethnography)*: In the tradition of British social anthropology, a view of ethnography as the description of a foreign culture. That is, the ethnographer translates the foreign culture into an (English-language) ethnographic description.
- *Cultural turn*: A term proposed by Snell-Hornby (1990) and legitimated by Lefevere and Bassnett (1990) whereby Translation Studies should focus on the cultural effects of translations. For Snell-Hornby, the "translation unit" (the unit taken for each analysis) should move from the text to the culture. The thrust of this view does not challenge traditional uses of the term "translation" and has long been a part of the intellectual background of the descriptive paradigm. Other versions see the "turn" as the use of cultural variables to explain translations, which has also long been part of the descriptive paradigm.
- *Translation culture* (*Übersetzungskultur*): Term used by the Göttingen group (see Frank 1989) to describe the cultural norms governing translations within a target system, on the model of *Esskultur*, which would describe the way a certain

society eats (including all the Chinese and Indian restaurants in Germany, for example). This concept applies to what a society does with translations and expects of them; it does not challenge traditional definitions of translations and it does not focus on the translator. The concept works within the descriptive paradigm.

- **Translation culture** (*Translationskultur*): Defined by Erich Prunč as a "variable set of norms, conventions and expectations which frame the behavior of all inter-actants in the field of translation" (Prunč 2000: 59; cf. Pöchhacker 2001, who renders the term as "translation standards"), considered to be a "historically developed subsystem of a culture" (Prunč 1997: 107). This concept focuses on translators and associated social actors, but strangely does not place them near any border. Developed with clear sympathies with *Skopos* theory, the concept would like to be descriptive.

- **Cultural Studies**: A diffuse set of academic studies that adopt a critical and theorizing approach to cultural phenomena in general, emphasizing hetero-geneity, hybridity, and the critique of power. Bhabha's postcolonial use of "cultural translation" fits in with this frame. The researcher is generally implicated in the object under study (as is the case in Bhabha).

- **Culture Research**: The term preferred by Even-Zohar for the study of the way cultures develop, interact, and die. On this view, cultures are seen as systems that need transfer (exchange) for their maintenance of energy and thus survival. The researcher seeks to adopt an objective stance.

- **Professional interculture**: A cultural place where people combine elements of more than one primary culture in order to carry out crosscultural communication. For Pym (2004a), professional intercultures are the places where the borders between primary cultures are defined. They include most of the situations in which translators work. This concept is sociological.

8.3 TRANSLATION WITHOUT TRANSLATIONS: CALLS FOR A WIDER DISCIPLINE

"Cultural translation" moves beyond translations as restricted (written or spoken) texts; its concern is with general cultural processes rather than finite linguistic products. This is the sense of "translation without translations." Was this wider view invented by Bhabha in 1994? Probably not. Previous paradigms have envisaged projects for the study of transla-tion without translations, albeit without undoing the concept of "a translation" (product) as such. Here I recall just a few of those projects.

8.3.1 Mediation (*Sprachmittlung*)

The term *Sprachmittler* (language mediator) has long been present in German as a super-ordinate for translators and interpreters (cf. Pöchhacker 2006: 217). *Sprachmittlung* (language mediation) was used as a general term for all modes of cross-language commu-nication in the Leipzig school (cf. Kade 1968, 1977). In the Leipzig system, "mediation" would be the general term for everything that can be done to communicate between languages, while "translation" and "interpreting" would be specific forms that are constrained by equivalence. This did not mean there were modes of translation that escaped from equivalence constraints, but it did mean that translation should be studied within a frame wider than equivalence.

In the mid-1980s, the *Skopos* theory of translation (see 4.3 above) relaxed the criterion of equivalence, using "translatorial action" as a synonym for "mediated cross-language communication." Holz-Mänttäri (1984) was aware that translators do more than translate (they can give advice as to when not to translate, for example, or they can write new texts on command), so she proposed to study the entire range of their activity.

At the same time, however, the term "mediation" took on a slightly different meaning in research on bilingualism (cf. Pöchhacker 2006: 217). Knapp and Knapp-Potthoff (1985) used the term *Sprachmitteln* ("linguistic mediating") to describe the performances of untrained bilinguals in face-to-face communication. This is what Translation Studies had been calling "natural translation" (after Harris 1976). German experts in second-language acquisition now refer to "mediation" as the full range of what speakers can do with two languages, ranging from giving the gist of a foreign text or indicating street directions right through to translation in the narrowest of senses. The term "mediation" features prominently in this sense in the *Common European Framework of Reference for Languages* (Council of Europe 2001), where it is referred to as the **fifth main language skill**, alongside speaking, listening, writing, and reading (Council of Europe 2001).

This means that the term "translation" has gained a very restricted (and restrictive) sense in Bilingualism Studies and Language Education, at the same time as it has become virtually synonymous with "mediation" in German-language Translation Studies. Between these two meanings, translation activities have traditionally been squeezed out of additional-language classes, sometimes because translation is somehow not considered a "communicative activity."

If the case can be made that "translation" and "mediation" are effectively the same thing, then the result will not only be a wider and more diverse field of inquiry, but also a conceptual basis for the return of dynamic translation activities to the language classroom. There is more to this than confusion over words.

At the moment, many language educationists in Germany use "mediation" to mean "translation without translations."

8.3.2 Jakobson and semiosis

When discussing the development of hermeneutics within the uncertainty paradigm (6.4.6), I mentioned **Roman Jakobson**'s statement that "the meaning of any linguistic sign is its translation into some further, alternative sign" (1959/2012: 127). This is the key point of a theory of **semiosis**, where **meaning is constantly created by interpretations** and is thus never a fixed thing that could be objectified and transferred. As I noted, rather than represent a previous meaning, translation would be the active *production* of meaning. That was in 1959, from within a linguistics that at that stage wanted to become semiotics, the wider study of all kinds of signs.

Jakobson's 1959 paper attempts to draw out some of the consequences of semiosis. One of those consequences is his list of three kinds of translation, which he claims can be "intralingual" (i.e. any rewording within the one language), "interlingual" (rewording between languages), or "intersemiotic" (interpretation between different sign systems, as when a piece of music interprets a poem). Once you decide that translation is a process rather than a product, you can find evidence of that process virtually everywhere. Any use of language (or semiotic system) that rewords or reworks any other piece of language (or semiotic system) can be seen as the result of a translational process. And since languages are based precisely on the repetition of utterances in different situations, producing different but related meanings, just as all texts are made meaningful by intertextuality, **all language use can be seen as translation**. The consequences of this view are perhaps far wider and more revolutionary than what Bhabha has to say.

Perhaps the most eloquent enactment of Jakobson's semiosis is to be found in the French philosopher **Michel Serres**. His book *La Traduction* (1974) considers the ways different sciences translate concepts from each other: how philosophy is translated from formal languages, how painting can translate physics (Turner translates primitive thermo-dynamics), and how literature translates religion (Faulkner translates the Bible). Serres does not claim to be studying any set of texts called translations; he is more interested in translation as a process of communication between domains otherwise thought to be separate. His practice of "general translation" would become important for French sociology (see 8.5 below).

Jakobson, however, did not want to travel too far down that path. His typology retains the notion of "translation proper" for "interlingual translation," and his description of "intersemiotic translation" privileges verbal signs (like those of "translation proper") as the point of departure. In this, he was preceded by the Danish semiotician **Louis Hjelmslev**, whose view of intersemiotic translation was similarly directional:

> In practice, a language is a semiotic into which all other semiotics may be translated—both all other languages and all other conceivable semiotic structures. This translata-bility rests on the fact that all languages, and they alone, are in a position to form any purport whatsoever.
>
> (Hjelmslev 1943/1963: 109)

Similarly, the Italian theorist **Umberto Eco** (2001) classified translatory movements between semiotic systems, at the same time as he privileged the place of "translation proper" as a finite textual product of interlingual movements (5.4.6 above). Jakobson and Eco could both envisage a wide conceptual space for "translation without translations," yet they did not want to throw away or belittle the translations that professional translators do.

Types of translation without translations?
Roman Jakobson recognizes three kinds of translation (1959/2012: 127):

- *Intralingual translation* or rewording is an interpretation of verbal signs by means of other signs of the same language.
- *Interlingual translation* or translation proper is an interpretation of verbal signs by means of some other language.
- *Intersemiotic translation* or transmutation is an interpretation of verbal signs by means of signs of nonverbal sign systems.

These categories can be compared with the forms Umberto Eco describes for the interpretant (1977: 70):

- An equivalent sign in another semiotic system (a drawing of a dog corresponds to the word dog).
- An index directed to a single object (smoke signifies the existence of a fire).
- A definition in the same system (*salt* signifies *sodium chloride*).
- An emotive association which acquires the value of an established connotation (*dog* signifies "fidelity").
- A "translation into another language," or substitution by a synonym.

8.3.3 Even-Zohar's call for transfer theory

Jakobson's 1959 paper is one of the starting points for Itamar Even-Zohar's call to extend the scope of Translation Studies. Since all systems are heterogeneous and dynamic, Even-Zohar proposes there are always movements of "textual models" from one to another, and translation is only one type of such movements. We should thus be studying all kinds of transfer:

> Some people would take this as a proposal to liquidate translation studies. I think the implication is quite the opposite: through a larger context, it will become even clearer that "translation" is not a marginal procedure of cultural systems. Secondly, the larger context will help us identify the really particular in translation. Thirdly, it will change our conception of the translated text in such a way that we may perhaps be liberated from certain postulated criteria. And fourthly, it may help us isolate what 'translational procedures' consist of.
>
> (Even-Zohar 1990a: 74)

The term "transfer" here means that a textual model from one system is not just put into another, it is *integrated* into the relations of the host system and thereby undergoes and generates change. Thus "transfer [...] is correlated with transformation" (Even-Zohar 1990b: 20). This maps out a kind of study in which there are many movements between systems, only some of which occur as translations, and the same kinds of movements are crossing borders *within* systems as well.

This extension is comparable to Bhabha's "cultural translation," except that:

1   What is transferred here is limited to "textual models" (although Even-Zohar's more recent work refers to "goods," "technologies," and "ideational energy").
2   In these formulations there is no particular focus on the human element, on the position and role of the mediators, and thus no attention to anything like a "third space."
3   As a consequence, the model remains one of systems separated by borders, no matter how many borders (and thus sub-systems) there may be within each system.
4   As a further consequence, the human researcher remains clearly external to the systems under investigation, with all the trappings of scientific discourse.

Perhaps because of these choices, Even-Zohar's proposed "transfer theory" has had little effect on the general development of translation theory. Many of those who have opened the paths of "cultural translation" would perhaps be surprised at the extent to which Even-Zohar addressed similar problems well before them. I hasten to add that Even-Zohar's *Ideational Labor and the Production of Social Energy* (2008) does show greater interest in human intermediaries, and indeed sees transfer as necessary for cultural survival, not in Bhabha's sense of worrying about the identity of Salman Rushdie, but with respect to whole cultures disappearing for want of transfers from other cultures. That is a rather more perturbing sense of survival.

8.4 ETHNOGRAPHY AS TRANSLATION

None of the above approaches uses the term "cultural translation"; all of them can be associated with other paradigms of translation theory; none of them (barring cautious winks to Jakobson) is mentioned by the theorists of cultural translation. A more powerful antecedent, however, can be found in ethnology or "social anthropology," which is where the term "cultural translation" seems to have been coined. How might this relate to the new paradigm?

The basic idea here is that when ethnologists set out to describe distant cultures (thus technically becoming "ethnographers," writers of descriptions), they are translating the cultures into their own professional language. In some cases the translations are remarkably like the traditional cases dealt with in the equivalence paradigm: they might concern a cultural concept, a place name, or a value-laden phrase. In other instances, however, they are dealing with issues that have more to do with the philosophy and ethics of crosscultural discourse. In very basic terms, the ethnographer can neither suppose radical cultural difference (in which case no description or understanding would be possible) nor complete sameness (in which case no one would need the description). In between those two poles, the term "translation" is used.

The earlier Western anthropologists were generally unaware of their descriptions being translations, since they tended to assume that their own language was able to describe adequately whatever they found (see Rubel and Rosman 2003). **Talal Asad** (1986) notes that in the British tradition the task of social anthropology has been described as a kind of "translation" since the 1950s. Asad goes back to Walter Benjamin (he would probably have been more sure-footed going to Schleiermacher) in order to argue that good translations show the structure and nature of the foreign culture; he thus announces a "call to transform a language in order to translate the coherence of the original" (Asad 1986: 157), especially in situations where there is a pronounced asymmetry in the power relations between the languages involved.

Note that the term "cultural translation" here fundamentally means the **translation of a culture**, and translation theory (not much more than Benjamin) is being used in an argument about how this should be done. This is not quite the same sense as we have found in Bhabha, where "cultural translation" is more closely related to the problematics of hybridity and border-crossing. Asad's argument about a "better" mode of translation certainly pushes "cultural translation" toward a more hybrid kind of space, opening the more powerful language to those of the less powerful cultures being described. One hesitates, however, to equate Bhabha's usage of "cultural translation" with this simpler and more traditional sense of "describing other cultures."

Some translation theorists have taken due note of the way the term "translation" has been used in ethnography. **Wolf** (1997) allows that this is a kind of translation, but she notes that ethnographers are typically engaged in a two-stage mode of work, first interpreting the spoken discourse of informants, then adapting that interpretation for consumption in the dominant culture. Two-stage work involving oral then written mediation can of course be found in mainstream translation history (the practice was noted in Hispania in the twelfth and thirteenth centuries). The prime difference is that the ethnographer does not usually have a materially fixed text to start from. In this sense, ethnographic translation might yet fit under Bhabha's "non-substantive translation."

Some rather more interesting things have been said either within the ethnographic frame or with reference to it. **James Clifford** (especially 1997) has elaborated an approach in which **travel** becomes the prime means of contact between cultures, configuring the spaces in which cultural translation is carried out. Within literary hermeneutics, this kind of approach is seen as reducing the asymmetries of intercultural alterity and risking a tendency toward sameness (see, for example, the essays in Budick and Iser 1996, where translation theory returns to various prescriptive stances). Clifford's line of thought nevertheless remains extremely suggestive for future research. The way translations represent cultures through travel and for travelers is a huge area requiring new forms of theorization (as in Cronin 2000, 2003).

A position closer to Bhabha is announced by **Wolfgang Iser**, who sees translation as a key concept not just for "the encounter between cultures" (1994: 5) but also for interactions within cultures. Iser uses the notion of **untranslatability** not as the resistance of the migrant, as it is in Bhabha, but as the use of cultural difference to change the way descriptions are produced. In translation, says Iser, "foreign culture is not simply subsumed under one's own frame of reference; instead, the very frame is subjected to alterations in order to accommodate what does not fit" (1994: 5).

At this level, the references to ethnography as translation enter general debates about how different cultures should interrelate, and any sense of translations as a specific class of texts has been lost.

8.5 TRANSLATION SOCIOLOGY

I have mentioned the work of Michel Serres as a mode of "generalized translation." Serres' work influenced a group of French ethnographers of science, notably **Michel Callon** and **Bruno Latour**, who developed what they term a "*sociologie de la traduction*" (cf. Akrich *et al.* 2006), also known as "**actor-network theory.**" I render this as "**translation sociology**" rather than "the sociology of translation" because, for me, the "translation" part refers to the *method of analysis* rather than to the object under analysis (although the theory would reject this binary distinction). The term "the sociology of translation" has nevertheless been used in English by these same sociologists (for example in Callon 1986). These researchers are not at all concerned with explaining interlingual translations, and they are not particularly interested in the historical and ethical issues of "cultural translation" in Bhabha's sense. They have instead been using a model of translation to explain the way networks are formed between social actors, particularly with respect to power relations involving science.

For example, **Michel Callon** (1986), in a seminal paper, studies the way marine biologists sought to stop the decline in a population of scallops by influencing the social groups involved. This involved not just forming networks, but also producing and extending social discourses on the problem. At each stage in the analysis, from the actions of the scallops to those of the fishermen, of the scientists and indeed of the sociologist, there is a common process by which one actor or group is taken to represent (or speak on behalf of) others. The result is a rather poetic leveling out where the one process ("translation") applies to all, including the scallops. This is a key point, and one that should be of interest to translation theory. Translation, for Callon, is the process by which one person or group says things that are taken to be "on behalf of" or to "stand for" another person or group. That might simply be another version of Jakobson's view of linguistic meaning, of semiosis, except that in this case the representation process is seen as the formation of social power. Here, for another example, are Callon and Latour on something a little more general than scallops, namely the **social contract** sought by the seventeenth-century English philosopher Thomas Hobbes:

> The social contract is only a particular instance of the more general phenomenon known as translation. By "translation" we mean the set of negotiations, intrigues, acts of persuasion, calculations, acts of violence by which an actor or a force accords or allows itself to be accorded the authority to speak or to act in the name of another actor or force: "your interests are our interests," "do what I want," "you cannot succeed without me." As soon as an actor says "we," he or she translates other actors into a single aspiration [*volonté*] of which she or he becomes the master or spokesperson.
> (Callon and Latour 1981/2006: 12–13; my translation)

The word "translation" in this passage has a footnote referring to Serres 1974 and Callon 1975.

Seen in these terms, translation becomes the basic building block of social relations, and thereby of societies, the object of sociology. This sociology is exceptional in that it tries *not* to assume any pre-existing categories or boundaries. It would simply follow the translations, the budding nodes in networks, in order to observe the actual institution of any borders. There is no need to question *what* is being translated. Indeed, for Bruno Latour (1984/1988: 167), "[n]othing is, by itself, either knowable or unknowable, sayable or unsayable, near or far. Everything is translated." Similarly, there is no "society or social realm," only translators who generate "traceable associations" (Latour 2005: 108). Translation becomes the process through which we form social relations.

With respect to the theory of translations as texts, and indeed within the paradigm of cultural translation, translation sociology has appeal on several grounds:

1   The **refusal to recognize pre-established social and cultural boundaries** is essentially what the discourses of cultural translation would be doing when they position themselves in the in-between space of cultures. Translation sociology forces the borders to manifest themselves, as indeed would the hybrid discourses of cultural translation.
2   The emphasis on **translation as the formation of power relations** clearly also fits in with postcolonial problematics, particularly as far as problems of agency and relations between cultural groups are concerned.
3   If the building block of power relations is the process by which one social actor presumes to or is made to **"speak on behalf of another,"** is this not precisely what all

translations are presumed or made to do? This might pose the interesting question of why not all translators accrue the social power presumably gained by those who presume to speak on behalf of science.

4   The **networks** in which translators tend to work are so small, so intercultural and so marked by cultural hybridity that they are ill-served by the classical sociologies of societies or indeed sociologies of systems (as in Luhmann) and structurally defined social groups (as in Bourdieu). Translation sociology would seem well suited to such an object, as might concepts such as "micro-cosmopolitanism" (Cronin 2006).

5   The recognition that **networks extend to and include the sociologist** (or any other analyst) fits in not only with the general sense of involvement found in the theorists of cultural translation, but also with action research (largely influencing the field of translator education) and indeed psychoanalytical approaches.

This does not mean that translation sociology is automatically a part of the paradigm of cultural translation. There are many other things going on. I submit, however, that the work of Callon and Latour has responded to an increasing fragmentation of social categories, just as theorists like Bhabha have done from other perspectives. Some attempts have been made to apply translation sociology to the networks in which translators operate (e.g. Buzelin 2007), and much more can be done. It would be a sad error, however, to think that translation sociology should be applied to professional translators simply because the term "translation" appears in both. The word has very different meanings in the two places.

A more effective connection between translation sociology and cultural translation can be found in a group of Germanic sociologists and translation theorists. For example, **Joachim Renn** (2006a, 2006b) argues that our postmodern societies are so culturally fragmented that translation is the best model of the way the different groups can communicate with each other and ensure governance. "Cultural translation" can thus be associated with the way differences are maintained and negotiated within complex societies. It may concern both institution and resistance, as well as what a more traditional systems sociology would call "boundary maintenance" (after Parsons 1951). Since this kind of cultural translation generally involves the displacements of people rather than texts, it is just a few steps from there to the view of migration itself as a form of translation (Papastergiadis 2000; Cronin 2006; Vorderobermeier and Wolf 2008), which ultimately returns us to the postcolonial frame. The work of the Germanic scholars bridges across the gaps that initially separated translation sociology of Callon and Latour from the kind of cultural translation we find in Bhabha.

8.6 SPIVAK AND THE PSYCHOANALYTICS OF TRANSLATION

One final strand should be mentioned, before a general consideration of cultural translation. Quite a few authors have explored the relations between psychoanalysis and translation, although few of them have done so to make any original contribution to translation theory as such. The general idea is that psychoanalysis concerns the use of language, translation is a use of language, so in translations we can find traces of the unconscious. Other approaches consider the terms Freud used for the workings of the unconscious (Benjamin 1992), many of which can be seen as modes of translation. This effectively places translational processes anterior to meaning formation, concurring with many of the views held within the uncertainty paradigm. None of this particularly concerns cultural translation of the kind I have been considering in this chapter. An intriguing bridge is built, however, in the way the Indian theorist **Gayatri Spivak**, working from the psychoanalytical approach of Melanie Klein, describes a primal kind of translation:

> The human infant grabs on to some one thing and then things. This grabbing (*begreifen*) of an outside indistinguishable from an inside constitutes an inside, going back and forth and coding everything into a sign-system by the thing(s) grasped. One can call this crude coding a "translation".
>
> (2007: 261)

Translation, in this sense, would describe the way the infant enters culture and forms subjectivity; it is spatially a dynamic by which borders are enacted. In Spivak, this sense of translation can be applied to all subsequent entries into all further cultures. Translation is thus also the movement from indigenous cultures in Australia or Bengal to standard cultures of their regions, or indeed of any of the other cultural movements involved in "cultural translation" (although Spivak does not use the term in the paper I am citing from).

Although Spivak openly avows that this is not the literal sense of the word "translation" —"a term I use not for obscurity, but because I find it indispensable" (2007: 264)—she does stretch it to include her own work as a translator of Derrida and the Bengali writer Mahasweta Devi. This is perhaps the closest we come to a psychoanalytical description of translation from the perspective of a translator:

> When a translator translates from a constituted language, whose system of inscription, and permissible narratives are "her own", this secondary act, translation in the narrow sense, as it were, is also a peculiar act of reparation—towards the language of the inside, a language in which we are "responsible", the guilt of seeing it as one language among many.
>
> (2007: 265)

The one primal narrative thus manages to account for the various senses of the word "translation."

Part of the interest of Spivak's view of translation is not just her experience as a translator but her preparedness to experiment with modes of translation that go beyond the reproduction of sentences. Her self-reflexive and informative prefaces and peritextual material (particularly in the translations of Devi) not only make the translator highly visible but inscribe the context of a wider cultural translation. Spivak's is one of the few proposals that might relate cultural translation to the actual practice of translators.

Spivak's message, however, is not univocal. Spivak takes issue with theories that claim translation should privilege foreignness and resistance (just as she elsewhere reclaims the right to use essentialism within deconstruction):

> The toughest problem here is translation from idiom to standard, an unfashionable thing among the elite progressives, without which the abstract structures of democracy cannot be comprehended.
>
> (2007: 274)

The democracy of Bengal requires common understanding of shared standard terms. The same might be true of democracies everywhere. And standardized languages, especially when in minority situations, are not well served by foreignizing translations. This is one of the great debates with which theories of cultural translation have not sought to engage.

8.7 "GENERALIZED TRANSLATION"

Within and beyond the above frames, there is no shortage of metaphorical uses of the word "translation." Language is a translation of thought; writing translates speech; literature translates life; a reading translates a text; all metaphors are also translations (*metapherein* is one of the Greek terms for "translation"), and in the end, as the Lauryn Hill song puts it, "everything is everything." The metaphors have long been present in literary theory and they are increasingly operative in cultural theory. Here I just pick at a few threads:

- Translation is the displacement of theory from one topographic location to another (for example, Miller 1995); it is the figure of intellectual nomadism, moving from discipline to discipline (for example, Vieira 2000; West 2002), but that was already in Serres.
- Translation is "a metaphor for understanding how the foreign and the familiar are inter-related in every form of cultural production" (Papastergiadis 2000: 124).
- Translation is part of all meaning production; there is no non-translation (Sallis 2002), but that proposition was already in Jakobson and Latour.
- Translation plays a key role in the transmission of values from one generation to the next, and is part of all "literary invigoration" (Brodski 2007).
- Translation is "a means of repositioning the subject in the world and in history; a means of rendering self-knowledge foreign to itself; a way of denaturalizing citizens, taking them out of the comfort zone of national space, daily ritual, and pre-given domestic arrangements" (Apter 2006: 6).
- And a long etcetera (cf. Duarte 2005).

Such generalization may be liberating and exciting to many; it could seem dissipating and meaningless to others. Let me simply note that many (although not all) of the above references are from the United States or are in tune with the development of Literary Theory and Comparative Literature in the United States. At the same time, the United States is a country with remarkably few translator-training institutions and thus with relatively little demand for the kind of translation theory developed within the equivalence or *Skopos* paradigms, and scant development of Translation Studies as envisaged in the descriptive paradigm. In terms of academic markets, if nothing else, the United States has provided a situation where the uncertainty paradigm could flourish into several modes of generalized translation.

Most of the above discourses do not actually refer to "cultural translation," since that term has tended to propagate later. They have, however, opened huge conceptual spaces for the paradigm. Once its moorings to equivalence are severed, "translation" easily becomes a drunken boat.

8.8 FREQUENTLY HAD ARGUMENTS

The positive points of the cultural translation paradigm are roughly those we outlined with reference to Bhabha (in 8.2 above): it introduces a human dimension and sees translation from the perspective of the (figurative) translator; it concerns translation as a cultural process rather than a textual product; its focus on hybridity undoes many of the binary oppositions marking previous translation theory; it relates translation to the demographical movements that are changing the shape of our cultures; it can generally operate within all the critiques ensuing from the uncertainty paradigm.

Those are not minor virtues. The existence of "cultural translation" as a paradigm is nevertheless illustrated by the many places in which others do not see the point, or do not accept its redefinitions of basic terms. The following arguments are part and parcel of its emergence as a paradigm among paradigms.

8.8.1 "These theories only use translation as a metaphor"

Many of the theorists cited here freely recognize that they are using the term "translation" in a metaphorical way. They are drawing ideas from one area of experience (the things that translators do) to a number of other areas (the ways cultures interrelate). This can be productive and stimulating for both the fields involved. On the other hand, the generalized production of metaphors risks expanding the term "translation" until it becomes meaning-less (Duarte 2005), or indeed of losing track of the original referent. Michaela Wolf points out the risk of developing "a sociology of translation without translation" (2007: 27).

It would be dangerous, though, to defend any original or true sense of the word "translation." Is there anything really wrong with the metaphors? Is there anything new in their workings? After all, metaphors always map one area of experience onto another, and when you think about it, the words we use in European languages for the activities of translators ("translation," "Übersetzen," etc.) are no less metaphorical, since they propose images of movement across space (more than time) (see D'hulst 1992). Perhaps the problem is that they have become dead metaphors, images that we somehow accept as self-evident truths. The more conscious metaphors in "cultural translation" might help us think more critically about all kinds of translation.

8.8.2 "Cultural translation is an excuse for intellectual wandering"

Here I translate **Antoine Berman**'s term "vagabondage conceptuel" (1985/1999: 21), which he used as a complaint about the proliferation of metaphors and "generalized trans-lation" he found in George Steiner and Michel Serres. Berman recognizes that translations will always produce cultural change, and there will thus always be the temptation to asso-ciate change with translation. However, he warns against the view where everything can translate everything else, where there is "universal translatability." To oppose this, indeed to oppose excessive theorizing, he argues for a concept of "restrained translation" that respects the letter of the foreign text (cf. Godard 2002).

Berman nevertheless does not seem to account for the many theorists of cultural translation who emphasize *untranslatability*, resistance, and maintenance of foreignness in all processes of translation. That is, many would agree with his politics, but not with his strategy. Indeed, many would accept "intellectual wandering" as a compliment—was not Greek truth, *aletheia*, supposed to be "divine wandering"?

8.8.3 "Cultural translation is a space for weak interdisciplinarity"

Associated with criticism of "generalized translation" is the suspicion that the scholars dealing with cultural translation do not know anything about interlingual translation, or are not interested in it. From this perspective, the various theorists would be stealing the notion of translation, without due appreciation of any of the other paradigms of translation theory. Wolf (2009: 77–8) retorts:

> the question arises "who is the owner of the translation term?" I argue that banning a metaphorical variant of the translation notion—i.e. what has been called "cultural translation"—from the field of research of Translation Studies would ultimately mean rejecting any sort of interdisciplinary work in this respect.

Can any discipline own a word? Obviously not. Can it attempt to stop others using the word? It is difficult to see how. Yet there is an obvious question here: Why should we work with other theorists simply because they use the same word as us? If you are producing a theory of forks as tools for eating, would you have to work in an interdisciplinary way with experts in "forks in the road" or "tuning forks" or "fork" as a situation in chess? The analogy is perhaps not as far-fetched as it sounds.

One kind of solution here can be found in the difference between a word ("translation") and a term ("translation" plus a set of defining characteristics, such as the ones mentioned in 5.4 above). If a term is defined precisely, as a conceptual tool for working on a particular problem, then perhaps it can indeed be owned by a discipline. Of course, no one can then stop other disciplines from using words any way they want.

Wolf's second argument is that if we do not accept this **interdisciplinarity**, then we must refuse all interdisciplinarity. This is the kind of argument reminiscent of binary political activists: "If you are not with us, you are against us." There seems to be no reason why translation scholars might choose to work with some disciplines (perhaps Sociology, Cognitive Science, or Linguistics) and not others (Cultural Studies, Philosophy, or Psychoanalysis), as long as the cooperation is suited to the problem being worked on.

8.8.4 "Cultural translation can be studied entirely in English"

Once the term "translation" loses the interlingual element of its definition, it can be studied without reference to different languages. In fact, everything can be studied within the major languages, often just within English (or French, or German): as we have seen, Homi Bhabha was writing as a professor of English about a novel in English. The result is a paradoxical eclipse of alterity, as noted by Harish Trivedi: "Rather than help us encounter and experience other cultures, translation would have been assimilated in just one monolingual global culture" (2007: 286). This critique fits in with Berman's fear of "global translatability," and indeed with a mode of theorization where the model "postmodern society" somehow fits all societies, and the one kind of "translation correctly understood" (after reading Walter Benjamin, in English) accounts for all translation. The theories of cultural translation could be sweeping away the very otherness they claim to espouse.

8.8.5 "Cultural translation is not in touch with the translation profession"

This is a version of a general reproach made of translation theory: the people who theorize do not actually know how to translate, so they do not really know about translation. The criticism might be more acute in the case of "cultural translation" since these theorists are talking about much more than translations as texts, and there is the associated argument that they are more interested in their power in the academy than in anything to do with other minority cultures. I have noted that there is very little concern for actual translators (Rushdie's translators took the bullets for him, while Bhabha calmly declares that Rushdie's resistance is "untranslatable") and one might more generally lament that the dynamics of cultures swamp any focus on specific "translation cultures" or "professional intercultures." In a sense, the paradigm is too powerful to empower translators in any clear way.

On the other hand, some theorists are indeed translators, and very innovative ones at that (Spivak, certainly, and Venuti), and most of the others live and work across multiple cultures. They are not unaware of the kinds of situations in which translators work. More promisingly, the connection with migration helps us consider the many new translation situations, with a focus on "social needs" rather than market demands. There is no theoretical reason why the paradigm of cultural translation should exclude a closer focus on translators.

The above are real arguments, of significance for the future of translation theory. Some of them are profound enough to threaten any attempt to see cultural translation as a coherent paradigm; others are debates that ensure the dynamism and contemporary relevance of the paradigm. You might run through them and keep a scorecard of good and bad points. On balance, for me, the virtues of cultural translation merit serious attention.

SUMMARY

This chapter started from a reading of the way Homi Bhabha uses the term "cultural translation" in his chapter "How Newness Enters the World." I have then questioned how new the concept really is. I have reviewed earlier calls for a wider discipline, particularly in Jakobson and Even-Zohar, and how the term "cultural translation" developed from social anthropology. The wider view can also draw on actor-network theory (translation sociology) and German-language work on communication between different cultural groups in complex societies, particularly in contexts involving immigration. If something new has entered the world of translation, it is probably from the migrations and changes in communication patterns, to the extent that we can no longer assume separate languages and cultures. The social and cultural spaces that once set up equivalence theory are no longer there. Cultural translation might thus offer ways of thinking about the many situations in which translation now operates in the world.

SOURCES AND FURTHER READING

The third edition of *The Translation Studies Reader* (Venuti 2012) includes texts by Berman, Spivak, Appiah, and Derrida (although the last-mentioned is not highly representative of Derrida's uses of translation). Munday (2012) touches on this paradigm in three separate chapters, somehow distinguishing between culture, ideology, sociology, and philosophy. Homi Bhabha should be basic reading for anyone interested in cultural translation. Where you go from there depends very much on what you want to work on. The volume *Nation, Language, and the Ethics of Translation*, edited by Bermann and Wood (2005), gives samples of the work being done in the United States. Many of the more international strands are being brought together in the Routledge journal *Translation Studies*.

Suggested projects and activities

1   Do a web search for the term "cultural translation." How many different meanings can you find? Would they all fit into the one paradigm?
2   If a novel by Salman Rushdie can be considered an act of cultural translation because of its active use of hybridity, could the same be said of most novels? Are there any non-translational uses of language?
3   Consider the statement that "the language of the Americas is translation." Could the same be true of all languages? (Is there any language that has not been displaced?) How many different natural languages are spoken in the Americas? How many have died? What could be the ideological effect of saying that they are all really the one language? For that matter, who said that "the language of *Europe* is translation"?
4   Even-Zohar wants "transfer studies" to look at the movements from culture to culture of basic technologies like the horse or the alphabet. Should such things be considered by translation theory?
5   Locate one of Spivak's translations of Mahasweta Devi (or any literary translation that has a substantial preface by the translator). How does the translator describe the start languages for the translation processes? How many start languages are there in the content of the text (i.e. what languages are the ideas coming from)? Are the start texts assumed to be more authentic than the translations? Can the start texts be seen as translations?
6   Callon and Latour see translation as an act where someone speaks on behalf of someone else, making themselves indispensable and thus accruing power. Is this the case of all translations? Could it be the case of the relation between Bhabha and Rushdie, or Spivak and Devi?
7   Emily Apter is an American Professor of Comparative Literature and French who associates translation theory with a "new Comparative Literature" (2006). In doing so, she acknowledges the following "pioneers in the field of translation studies": "George Steiner, André Lefevere, Antoine Berman, Gregory Rabassa, Lawrence Venuti, Jill Levine, Michel Heim, Henri Meschonnic, Susan Sontag, Richard Howell, and Richard Sieburth" (2006: 6). Who are all these

people? What do they have in common? Why have so few of them been mentioned in this book?

8 Go to the website of the European Institute for Progressive Cultural Policies (eipcp) and look up its various publications and activities involving "cultural translation." Now, what kind of translation has produced this superb multilingual website? What is the relation between what the authors say about translation and the way they use translations? What language does the siglum "eipcp" make sense in? Why are there so few references to the "pioneers" mentioned by Apter?

9 Can translation be studied by looking at one language only? Should it be studied by people who know only one language?

10 In 1928, in full Surrealist swing, the Brazilian poet Oswald de Andrade proclaimed his *Manifesto antropófago* for Brazilian culture. Here is a taste:

Only Cannibalism unites us. Socially. Economically. Philosophically.
The only law of the world. Masked expression of all individualisms, of all collectivisms. Of all religions. Of all peace treaties.
Tupi, or not tupi that is the question.
Against all catechisms. And against the mother of the Gracchus brothers.
I am only interested in that which is not mine. Law of the human. Law of the cannibal.

(Andrade 1928/1980: 81; my translation)

In 1978 the Brazilian poet Augusto de Campos applied this to translation, listing his favorite foreign poets and declaring, "[m]y way of loving them is to translate them. Or to swallow them down, in accordance with Oswald de Andrade's Cannibal Law: I am only interested in that which is not mine" (1978: 7; my translation).

Compare these statements with the inner/outer dynamic described by Spivak. Are they talking about the same kind of translation? Now compare it with the guilt described by Spivak, or with the power of "speaking on behalf of" mentioned by Callon and Latour. Do the degrees of guilt or power depend on the directionality of the translation? Do they have anything to do with your own experience when translating?

11 Compare the statements by Andrade and Campos with the accounts of postcolonial cannibalism theory in Vieira (1999) or Gentzler (2008). Do the above statements actually present a translation theory? Do the commentaries by Vieira or Gentzler present much more evidence than the above? Have the commentaries somehow constructed a whole school of thought (cf. Milton and Bandia 2008: 12)?

12 Look for information on the translation services (not) provided for immigrants in your country. Are immigrants obliged to become translators themselves? What role do children play? What is the position of women with respect to the various languages? Are these problems and forms of translation addressed by any other paradigm of translation theory?

Postscript
What if they were all wrong?

I will now try to position myself with respect to the various paradigms (since there can be no neutral description), before suggesting how you might go about positioning yourself.

What do I think of the paradigms? Equivalence, for me, is an efficient social illusion. People believe in it just as they believe in the value of the money they carry in their pockets; we believe in these things even when there is no linguistic certainty behind equivalence and not enough gold to back up our coins. We have to understand the way *equivalence beliefs* work. From that point, I can accept all the other paradigms as having valid points to make about the illusory nature of equivalence. *Skopos* theory, for me, is a collection of quite evident things, unfortunately unable to solve ethical problems involving competing purposes. As for the descriptive paradigm, it stands at the center of translation research and cannot be ignored, but it must be made to reflect critically on the role of the describer. The uncertainty paradigm also has good and bad in it—I accept the lessons of deconstruction and I am looking for ways to live with them, but I do not go along with theories that assume the supremacy of the start text, and I am uneasy with the hermeneutic tradition that stares in that direction. I am more interested in the aspects of the uncertainty paradigm that can help create a future, particularly in the dynamics of risk management and cooperation (sooner or later we have to build a better world, as well as criticize bad worlds). As for localization, I am fascinated by the effects of technology, which is offering a better future, just as I am appalled by the naïve way in which equivalence has returned in that paradigm, in all its deceptive simplicity. Cultural translation then opens up new ways of thinking about translation in social contexts. For me, however, the paradigm ceases to function as translation theory when it can no longer address translations, and I suspect that much of the work done on cultural translation would be better branded as "intercultural studies."

If I can take all those positions, I clearly do not belong to just one paradigm. I do not think anyone need be situated in just one place or another. We should feel free to move between the paradigms, selecting the ideas that can help us solve problems. That is the way I think translation theories should develop.

Here, for example, is a problem that is plaguing my mind these days, and on which I need help from theories. Part of the problem is already a major institutional theory. In recent decades the Vatican has seen translation as an aspect of "inculturation," described as "the incarnation of the Gospel in autonomous cultures and at the same time the introduction of these cultures into the life of the Church" (John Paul II 1985: 21). Most translators think translation goes from one culture to another, but the Vatican, along with many proponents of cultural translation, knows better: inculturation involves, very ideally, a double movement rather than a simple one-way translation: "Through inculturation the Church makes the

Gospel incarnate in different cultures and at the same time introduces peoples, together with their cultures, into her own community" (John Paul II 1990: 52). The aim of translation is simultaneously to put Catholic culture *into* the target culture, and to bring the target culture *within* Catholic culture. Is this just for Catholics? But surely the communications of the European Union institutions have more or less this same double movement as their goal? And are not the institutions of international literature (the mergers of publishers and list of global best sellers) working in a similar way? Or something like MTV culture? Or the liberal humanism of the world university system?

My concern is not particularly how to describe the asymmetric imperialism: non-linear systems theory can handle the complex absorption of one culture by another. And there is no shortage of theories of cultural mixes. My particular problem is that the kinds of communications most operative in these movements somehow make people *want* to give up or transform their home culture—they are texts that promote aspiration and conversion. And yet, almost all of our translation theories are about rendering content, propositions, information, and we are training generations of translators and interpreters to focus on such anodyne things, rather than on the aspirations by which the world changes. Are all the theories wrong? Should we be concerned with quite a different dimension of communication? And so I go off in search of help, re-reading Meschonnic in a political frame, returning to the sociolinguistics of Gumperz and Tannen, finding their sense of "involvement" in the basic thought of Nida, and then re-reading Paul of Tarsus, the great converter, and from there, like many people these days (including Venuti 2013: 184–6), Alain Badiou and the theory of events, all the time haunted by the classical debates between rhetoric and ethics. The existing paradigms of translation theory are not of great help with this kind of problem. You have to go out searching, inquiring, questioning, seeking alternative kinds of theorization.

Here, then, is my one piece of advice: When theorizing translation, when developing your own translation theory, first identify a problem—a situation of doubt requiring action, or a question in need of an answer. Then go in search of ideas that can help you work on that problem. And be prepared to change everything. There is no need to start in any one paradigm, and certainly no need to belong to one.

References

Akrich, M., M. Callon, and B. Latour (2006) *Sociologie de la traduction. Textes fondateurs*, Paris: Presses de l'École des Mines.

Ammann, M. (1994) 'Von Schleiermacher bis Sartre. Translatologische Interpretationen,' in M. Snell-Hornby and K. Kaindl (eds) *Translation Studies: An Interdiscipline*, Amsterdam and Philadelphia: Benjamins, pp. 37–44.

Andrade, O. de (1928/1980) 'Manifesto antropófago,' in J. Schwartz (ed.) *Literatura comentada*, São Paulo: Abril, pp. 81–3.

Angelone, E. (2010) 'Uncertainty, Uncertainty Management and Metacognitive Problem Solving in the Translation Task,' in G. M. Shreve and E. Angelone (eds) *Translation and Cognition*, Amsterdam and Philadelphia: Benjamins, pp. 17–40.

Appiah, K. A. (1993/2012) 'Thick Translation,' in L. Venuti (ed.) *The Translation Studies Reader*, London and New York: Routledge, pp. 331–43.

Apter, E. (2006) *The Translation Zone: A New Comparative Literature*, Princeton and Oxford: Princeton University Press.

Arrojo, R. (1992) *Oficina de tradução. A teoria na prática*, second edition, São Paulo: Ática.

—— (1993) *Tradução, Desconstrução e Psicanálise*, Rio de Janeiro: Imago.

—— (1994) 'Fidelity and the Gendered Translation,' *TTR* 7: 147–63.

—— (1997) 'Asymmetrical Relations of Power and the Ethics of Translation,' *TEXTconTEXT* 11: 5–25.

—— (1998) 'The Revision of the Traditional Gap between Theory and Practice and the Empowerment of Translation in Postmodern Times,' *The Translator* 4: 25–48.

Asad, T. (1986) 'The Concept of Cultural Translation in British Anthropology,' in J. Clifford and G. E. Marcus (eds) *Writing Culture: The Poetics and Politics of Ethnography*, Berkeley, Los Angeles, and London: University of California Press, pp. 141–64.

Augustine of Hippo (Aurelius Augustinus) (c.400/1969) 'De catechizandis rudibus,' *Aurelii Augustini Opera*, vol. 13.2, Turnhout: Brepols.

Bascom, B. (2007) 'Mental Maps and the Cultural Understanding of Scripture,' Unpublished paper presented to the conference *Translation, Identity, and Language Heterogeneity*, San Marcos University, Lima, December 7–9 2007.

Baumgarten, S. (2009) *Translating Hitler's "Mein Kampf": A Corpus-Aided Discourse-Analytical Study*, Saarbrücken: VDM Verlag.

Bédard, C. (2000) 'Translation Memory Seeks Sentence-oriented Translator …,' *Traduire* 186: 41–9.

Benjamin, A. (1989) *Translation and the Nature of Philosophy: A New Theory of Words*, London and New York: Routledge.

—— (1992) 'Translating Origins: Psychoanalysis and Philosophy,' in L. Venuti (ed.) *Rethinking Translation: Discourse, Subjectivity, Ideology*, London: Routledge, pp. 18–41.

Benjamin, W. (1923/1977) 'Die Aufgabe des Übersetzers,' in *Illuminationen: Ausgewählte Schriften*, Frankfurt am Main: Suhrkamp, pp. 50–62.

—— (1923/2012) 'The Task of the Translator,' trans. S. Rendall, in L. Venuti (ed.) *The Translation Studies Reader*, third edition, London and New York: Routledge, pp. 75–83.

Berman, A. (1984/1992) *The Experience of the Foreign: Culture and Translation in Romantic Germany*, trans. S. Heyvaert, Albany: State University of New York Press.

—— (1985/1999) *La traduction et la lettre ou l'Auberge du lointain*, Paris: Seuil.

—— (1995) *Pour une critique des traductions: John Donne*, Paris: Gallimard.

Bermann, S., and M. Wood (eds) (2005) *Nation, Language, and the Ethics of Translation*, Princeton: Princeton University Press.

Bhabha, H. (1994/2004) *The Location of Culture*, London and New York: Routledge.

Bigelow, J. (1978) 'Semantics of Thinking, Speaking and Translation,' in F. Guenthner and M. Guenthner-Reutter (eds) *Meaning and Translation: Philosophical and Linguistic Approaches*, London: Duckworth, pp. 109–35.

Blum-Kulka, S. (1986/2004) 'Shifts of Cohesion and Coherence in Translation,' in L. Venuti (ed.) *The Translation Studies Reader*, second edition, London and New York: Routledge, pp. 290–305.

Blum-Kulka, S., and E. A. Levenston (1983) 'Universals of Lexical Simplification,' in C. Faerch and G. Casper (eds) *Strategies in Inter-language Communication*, London and New York: Longman, pp. 119–39.

Boéri, J., and C. Maier (eds) (2010) *Compromiso social y traducción/interpretación: Translation/Interpreting and Social Activism*, Granada: ECOS.

Brislin, R. W. (1981) *Cross-Cultural Encounters: Face-to-Face Interaction*, New York: Pergamon.

Brodski, B. (2007) *Can these Bones Live? Translation, Survival, and Cultural Memory*, Stanford: Stanford University Press.

Budick, S., and W. Iser (eds) (1996) *The Translatability of Cultures: Figurations of the Space Between*, Stanford: Stanford University Press.

Bühler, K. (1934/1982) *Sprachtheorie: Die Darstellungsfunktion der Sprache*, Stuttgart and New York: Gustav Fischer.

Burge, T. (1978) 'Self-Reference and Translation,' in F. Guenther and M. Guenther-Reutter (eds) *Meaning and Translation: Philosophical and Linguistic Approaches*, London: Duckworth, pp. 137–53.

Buzelin, H. (2007) 'Translations "in the Making",' in M. Wolf and A. Fukari (eds) *Constructing a Sociology of Translation*, Amsterdam and Philadelphia: John Benjamins, pp. 135–60.

Callon, M. (1975) 'L'opération de traduction,' in Pierre Roquepio (ed.) *Incidence des rapports sociaux sur le développement des sciences et des techniques*, Paris: Cordes, pp. 105–41.

—— (1986) 'Some Elements for a Sociology of Translation: Domestication of the Scallops and the Fishermen of St-Brieuc Bay,' in J. Law (ed.) *Power, Action and Belief: A New Sociology of Knowledge?* London: Routledge, pp. 196–223.

Callon, M., and B. Latour (1981/2006) 'Unscrewing the Big Leviathan; or How Actors Macrostructure Reality, and How Sociologists Help Them to Do So,' in K. D. Knorr and A. Cicourel (eds) *Advances in Social Theory and Methodology: Toward an Integration of Micro and Macro Sociologies*, London: Routledge and Kegal Paul, pp. 277–303.

Campbell, S. (2001) 'Choice Network Analysis in Translation Research,' in M. Olohan (ed.) *Intercultural Faultlines: Research Models in Translation Studies I: Textual and Cognitive Aspects*, Manchester: St. Jerome, pp. 29–42.

Campos, A. de (1978) 'Verso, reverso, controverso,' in *Verso, reverso e controverso*, São Paulo: Perspectiva, pp. 7–8.

Campos, H. de (1962/1976) 'Da tradução como criação e como crítica,' reprinted in *Metalinguagem*, São Paulo: Cultrix, pp. 35–36.

Catford, J. C. (1965) *A Linguistic Theory of Translation*, London: Oxford University Press.

Chau, Simon S. C. (Chau Suicheong) (1984) 'Hermeneutics and the Translator: The Ontological Dimension of Translating,' *Multilingua* 3(2): 71–7.

Chesterman, A. (1996) 'On Similarity,' *Target* 8(1): 159–63.

— (1997) *Memes of Translation: The Spread of Ideas in Translation Theory*, Amsterdam and Philadelphia: Benjamins.

— (1999) 'The Empirical Status of Prescriptivism,' *Folia Translatologica* 6: 9–19.

— (2005) 'Where is Similarity?' in S. Arduini and R. Hodgson (eds) *Similarity and Difference in Translation*, Rimini: Guaraldi, pp. 63–75.

— (2006) 'Interpreting the Meaning of Translation,' in M. Suominen, A. Arppe, A. Airola, O. Heinämäki, M. Miestamo, U. Määttä, J. Niemi, K. K. Pitkänen, and K. Sinnemäki (eds) *A Man of Measure: Festschrift in Honour of Fred Karlsson on his 60th Birthday*, Turku: Linguistic Association of Finland, pp. 3–11.

— (2009) 'The Name and Nature of Translator Studies,' *Hermes* 42: 13–22.

— (2010) 'Skopos Theory: A Retrospective Assessment,' in W. Kallmeyer, E. Reuter, and J. F. Schopp (eds) *Perspektiven auf Kommunikation: Festschrift für Liisa Tittula zum 60. Geburtstag*, Berlin: SAXA Verlag, pp. 209–25.

Chesterman, A., and R. Arrojo (2000) 'Forum: Shared Ground in Translation Studies,' *Target* 12(1): 151–60

Chomsky, N. (1980) *Rules and Representations*, New York: Columbia University Press.

Cicero, M. T. (46CE/1996) 'De optimo genere oratorum,' in F. Lafarga (ed.) *El discurso sobre la traducción en la historia*, bilingual edition, Barcelona: EUB, pp. 32–44.

Clifford, J. (1997) *Routes: Travel and Translation in the Late Twentieth Century*, Cambridge, MA: Harvard University Press.

Coseriu, E. (1978) 'Falsche und richtige Fragenstellungen in der Übersetzungstheorie,' in L. Grähs, G. Korlén, and B. Malmberg (eds) *Theory and Practice of Translation*, Bern, Frankfurt am Main, and Las Vegas: Peter Lang, pp. 17–32.

Council of Europe (2001) *Common European Framework of Reference for Languages: Learning, Teaching, Assessment*, Strasbourg: Council of Europe, Cambridge University Press.

Croce, B. (1902/1922) *Aesthetic as a Science of Expression and General Linguistic*, London: Noonday.

Cronin, M. (2000) *Across the Lines: Travel, Language, Translation*, Cork: Cork University Press.

— (2003) *Translation and Globalization*, London and New York: Routledge.

— (2006) *Translation and Identity*, London and New York: Routledge.

— (2013) *Translation in the Digital Age*, London and New York: Routledge.

Crystal, D. (2006) *Words, Words, Words*, Oxford: Oxford University Press.

Davis, K. (2001) *Deconstruction and Translation*, Manchester and Northhampton, MA: St Jerome.

Delabastita, D. (2008) 'Status, Origin, Features: Translation and beyond,' in A. Pym, M. Shlesinger, and D. Simeoni (eds) *Beyond Descriptive Translation Studies*, Amsterdam and Philadelphia: Benjamins, pp. 233–46.

Delabastita, D., L. D'hulst, and R. Meylaerts (2006) *Functional Approaches to Culture and Translation: Selected Papers by José Lambert*, Amsterdam and Philadelphia: Benjamins.

Delisle, J. (1988) *Translation: An Interpretive Approach*, trans. P. Logan and M. Creery, Ottawa: University Press.

— (1993) 'Traducteurs médiévaux, traductrices féministes: une même éthique de la traduction?' *TTR* 6(1): 203–30.

de Man, P. (1986) *The Resistance to Theory*, Minneapolis: University of Minnesota Press.

Derrida, J. (1967) *De la grammatologie*, Paris: Minuit.

— (1968) 'La pharmacie de Platon,' *Tel Quel* 32: 3–48; 33: 18–59.

— (1972) *Marges de la philosophie*, Paris: Minuit.

— (1979) 'Living On: Border Lines,' in H. Bloom (ed.) *Deconstruction and Criticism*, New York: Seabury, pp. 75–176.

— (1982/1985) *The Ear of the Other: Otobiography, Transference, Translation*, trans. P. Kamuf, New York: Schocken.

— (1985) 'Des Tours de Babel' (French and English versions), in J. F. Graham (ed.) *Difference in Translation*, Ithaca, NY: Cornell University Press, pp. 165–207, 209–48.

— (1993) *Spectres de Marx*, Paris: Galilée.

— (2005) *Qu'est-ce qu'une traduction « relevante »?* Paris: L'Herne.

D'hulst, L. (1992) 'Sur le rôle des métaphores en traductologie contemporaine,' *Target* 4(1): 33–51.

Duarte, J. Ferreira (2005) 'Para uma crítica de retórica da tradução em Homi Bhabha,' in A. G. Macedo and M. E. Keating (eds) *Colóquio de Outono: Estudos de tradução – Estudos pós-coloniais*, Braga: Universidade do Minho, pp. 89–100.

Dunne, K. J. (ed.) (2006) *Perspectives on Localization*, Amsterdam and Philadelphia: Benjamins.

Eco, U. (1977) *A Theory of Semiotics*, London and Basingstoke: Macmillan.

— (2001) *Experiences in Translation*, trans. A. McEwan, Toronto, Buffalo, and London: University of Toronto Press.

Eco, U., with R. Rorty, J. Culler, and C. Brooke-Rose (1992) *Interpretation and Overinterpretation*, Cambridge: Cambridge University Press.

Eliot, T. S. (1933/1975) 'The Use of Poetry and the Use of Criticism,' in F. Kermode (ed.) *Selected Prose of T. S. Eliot*, Orlando: Harcourt, pp. 79–96.

Englund Dimitrova, B. (2005) *Expertise and Explicitation in the Translation Process*, Amsterdam and Philadelphia: Benjamins.

Esselink, B. (2000) *A Practical Guide to Localization*, Amsterdam and Philadelphia: Benjamins.

Even-Zohar, I. (1978) 'The Position of Translated Literature within the Literary Polysystem,' in J. S Holmes, J. Lambert, and R. van den Broeck (eds) *Literature and Translation*, Leuven: Acco, pp. 117–27. Cited here from I. Even-Zohar *Papers in Historical*

Poetics, Tel Aviv: Porter Institute, 1978. http://www.tau.ac.il/~itamarez/. Visited May 2013.

—— (1986) 'The Quest for Laws and its Implications for the Future of the Science of Literature,' in G. M. Vajda and J. Riesz (eds) *The Future of Literary Scholarship*, Frankfurt am Main: Peter Lang, pp. 75–9.

—— (1990a) 'Translation and Transfer,' *Poetics Today* 11(1): 73–8.

—— (1990b) 'Polysystem Theory,' *Poetics Today* 11(1): 9–26.

—— (2008) *Ideational Labor and the Production of Social Energy: Intellectuals, Idea Makers and Culture Entrepreneurs*, Tel Aviv: Porter Chair of Semiotics.

Fawcett, P. (1997) *Translation and Language: Linguistic Theories Explained*, Manchester: St Jerome.

Fedorov, A. V. (1953) *Vvedenie b teoriu perevoda*, Moscow: Literaturi na inostrannix iazikax.

Folkart, B. (1989) 'Translation and the Arrow of Time,' *TTR* 2(1): 19–50.

—— (1991) *Le Conflit des énonciations: Traduction et discours rapporté*, Montreal: Balzac.

Frank, A. P. (1989) 'Translation as System and *Übersetzungskultur*, On Histories and Systems in the Study of Literary Translation,' *New Comparison* 8: 85–98.

Fraser, J. (1996) 'Professional versus Student Behaviour,' in C. Dollerup and V. Appel (eds) *Teaching Translation and Interpreting 3: New Horizons*, Amsterdam and Philadelphia: Benjamins, pp. 243–50.

Freeman, D. (1999) *The Fateful Hoaxing of Margaret Mead*, Boulder: Westview.

Gadamer, H. G. (1960/1972) *Wahrheit und Methode: Grundzüge einer philosophischen Hermeneutik*, Tübingen: Mohr.

García, I. (2010) 'Is Machine Translation Ready Yet?' *Target* 22(1): 7–21.

Genette, G. (1976) *Mimologiques: Voyage en Cratylie*, Paris: Seuil.

Gentzler, E. (1993/2001) *Contemporary Translation Theories*, revised version, Clevedon: Multilingual Matters.

—— (2008) *Translation and Identity in the Americas*, London and New York: Routledge.

Godard, B. (2002) 'L'Éthique du traduire: Antoine Berman et le « virage éthique » en traduction,' *Meta* 14(2): 49–82.

Gorlée, D. L. (1994) *Semiotics and the Problem of Translation*, Amsterdam and Atlanta: Rodopi.

Gouadec, D. (2007) *Translation as a Profession*, Amsterdam and Philadelphia: Benjamins.

Grice, H. P. (1975) 'Logic and Conversation,' in P. Cole and J. L. Morgan (eds) *Syntax and Semantics*, vol. 3, New York: Academic Press, pp. 41–58.

Gutt, E.-A. (1991/2000) *Translation and Relevance: Cognition and Context*, second edition, Manchester: St Jerome.

Halverson, S. (1998) 'Translation Studies and Representative Corpora: Establishing Links between Translation Corpora, Theoretical/Descriptive Categories and a Conception of the Object of Study,' *Meta* 43(4): 459–514.

—— (2007) 'Translations as Institutional Facts: An Ontology for "Assumed Translation",' in A. Pym, M. Shlesinger, and D. Simeoni (eds) *Beyond Descriptive Translation Studies*, Amsterdam and Philadelphia: Benjamins, pp. 343–62.

Harris, B. (1976) 'The Importance of Natural Translation,' *Working Papers in Bilingualism* (Toronto) 12: 96–114.

Hatim, B., and I. Mason (1990) *Discourse and the Translator*, London: Longman.

—— (1997) *The Translator as Communicator*, London and New York: Routledge.

Heidegger, M. (1927/1953) *Being and Time*, trans. J. Stambaugh, Albany: State University of New York Press.

—— (1957) *Der Satz vom Grund*, Pfullingen: Neske.

Hemmungs Wirtén, E. (1998) *Global Infatuation: Explorations in Transnational Publishing and Texts*, Uppsala: Uppsala University.

Hermans, T. (1997) 'Translation as Institution,' in M. Snell-Hornby, Z. Jettmarová, and K. Kaindl (eds) *Translation as Intercultural Communication*, Amsterdam and Philadelphia: Benjamins, pp. 3–20.

—— (1999) *Translation in Systems: Descriptive and Systemic Approaches Explained*, Manchester: St Jerome.

Hermans, T. (ed.) (1985) *The Manipulation of Literature: Studies in Literary Translation*, London and Sydney: Croom Helm.

Hjelmslev, L. (1943/1963) *Prolegomena to a Theory of Language*, trans. F. J. Whitfield, Madison: University of Wisconsin.

Hoffman, E. (1989) *Lost in Translation: Life in a New Language*, New York: Penguin.

Holmes, J. S (1970) 'Forms of Verse Translation and the Translation of Verse Form,' in J. S Holmes, F. de Haan, and A. Popovič (eds) *The Nature of Translation: Essays in the Theory and Practice of Literary Translation*, The Hague and Paris: Mouton de Gruyter, pp. 91–105.

Holmes, J. S, F. de Haan, and A. Popovič (eds) (1970) *The Nature of Translation: Essays in the Theory and Practice of Literary Translation*, The Hague and Paris: Mouton de Gruyter.

Holmes, J. S, J. Lambert, and R. van den Broeck (eds) (1978) *Literature and Translation*, Louvain: Acco.

Holz-Mänttäri, J. (1984) *Translatorisches Handeln: Theorie und Methode*, Helsinki: Academia Scientiarum Fennica.

—— (1990) 'Funktionskonstanz—eine Fiktion?' in H. Salevsky (ed.) *Übersetzungswissenschaft und Sprachmittlerausbildung*, vol. I, Berlin: Humboldt-Universität zu Berlin, pp. 66–74.

Hönig, H. G. (1997) 'Positions, Power and Practice: Functionalist Approaches and Translation Quality Assessment,' *Current Issues in Language and Society* 4(1): 6–34.

Hönig, H. G., and P. Kussmaul (1982/1996) *Strategie der Übersetzung: Ein Lehr-und Arbeitsbuch*, Tübingen: Narr.

House, J. (1997) *Translation Quality Assessment: A Model Revisited*, Tübingen: Narr.

Iser, W. (1994) 'On Translatability,' *Surfaces* 4: 5–13.

Jääskeläinen, R. (1999) *Tapping the Process: An Exploratory Study of the Cognitive and Affective Factors Involved in Translating*, Joensuu: University of Joensuu Publications in the Humanities.

Jääskeläinen, R., and S. Tirkkonen-Condit (1991) 'Automatised Processes in Professional vs. Non-Professional Translation: A Think-aloud Protocol Study,' in S. Tirkkonen-Condit (ed.) *Empirical Research in Translation and Intercultural Studies*, Tübingen: Narr, pp. 89–110.

Jakobs, C. (1975) 'The Monstrosity of Translation,' *Modern Language Notes* 90: 755–66.

Jakobsen, A. L. (2002) 'Translation Drafting by Professional Translators and by Translation Students,' in G. Hansen (ed.) *Empirical Translation Studies: Process and Product*, Copenhagen: Samfundslitteratur, pp. 181–204.

Jakobsen, A. L., and K. T. H. Jensen (2008) 'Eye Movement Behaviour across Four Different Types of Reading Task,' in S. Göpferich, A. L. Jakobsen, S. Göpferich, and I. M. Mees (eds) *Looking at Eyes: Eye-Tracking Studies of Reading and Translation Processing*, Copenhagen: Samfundslitteratur, pp. 103–24.

Jakobson, R. (1959/2012) 'On Linguistic Aspects of Translation,' in L. Venuti (ed.) *The Translation Studies Reader*, third edition, London and New York: Routledge, pp. 126–31.

—— (1960) 'Closing Statement: Linguistics and Poetics,' in T. A. Sebeok (ed.) *Style in Language*, Cambridge, MA, New York, and London: MIT Press, John Wiley and Sons, pp. 350–77.

Jensen, A. (1999) 'Time Pressure in Translation,' in G. Hansen (ed.) *Probing the Process in Translation: Methods and Results*, Copenhagen: Samfundslitteratur, pp. 103–19.

Jensen, A., and A. L. Jakobsen (2000) 'Translating under Time Pressure: An Empirical Investigation of Problem-solving Activity and Translation Strategies by Non-professional and Professional Translators,' in A. Chesterman, N. Gallardo San Salvador, and Y. Gambier (eds) *Translation in Context*, Amsterdam and Philadelphia: Benjamins, pp. 105–15.

John Paul II (1985) *Slavorum Apostoli*, encyclical epistle, June 2, 1985, Rome: Libreria Editrice Vaticana.

—— (1990) *Redemptoris Missio: On the Permanent Validity of the Church's Missionary Mandate*, encyclical epistle, December 7, 1990, Rome: Libreria Editrice Vaticana.

Kade, O. (1968) *Zufall und Gesetzmässigkeit in der Übersetzung*, Leipzig: VEB Verlag Enzyklopädie.

—— (1977) 'Zu einigen Grundpositionen bei der theoretischen Erklärung der Sprachmittlung als menschlicher Tätigkeit,' in O. Kade (ed.) *Vermittelte Kommunikation, Sprachmittlung, Translation*, Leipzig: Enzyklopädie, pp. 27–43.

Kamenická, R. (2007) 'Explicitation Profile and Translator Style,' in A. Pym and A. Perekrestenko (eds) *Translation Research Projects 1*, Tarragona: Intercultural Studies Group, pp. 117–30.

Katan, D. (1999) *Translating Cultures*, Manchester: St. Jerome.

—— (2000) 'Language Transfer: What Gets Distorted or Deleted in Translation,' *Mostovi* 34: 29–37.

Katz, J. (1978) 'Effability and Translation,' in F. Guenthner and M. Guenthner-Reutter (eds) *Meaning and Translation: Philosophical and Linguistic Approaches*, London: Duckworth, pp. 191–234.

Kiraly, D. C. (2000) *A Social Constructivist Approach to Translator Education: Empowerment from Theory to Practice*, Manchester: St Jerome.

Klaudy, K. (2001) 'The Asymmetry Hypothesis: Testing the Asymmetric Relationship between Explicitations and Implicitations,' paper presented to the *Third International Congress of the European Society for Translation Studies*, Copenhagen.

Knapp, K., and Knapp-Potthoff (1985) 'Sprachmittlertätigkeit in der interkulturellen Kommunikation,' in J. Rehbein (ed.) *Interkulterelle Kommunikation*, Tübingen: Gunter Narr, pp. 450–63.

Koller, W. (1979/1992) *Einführung in die Übersetzungswissenschaft*, Heidelberg and Wiesbaden: Quelle & Meyer.

Krings, H. P. (1988) 'Blick in die "Black Box" – eine Fallstudie zum Übersetzungsprozeß bei Berufsübersetzern,' in R. Arntz (ed.) *Textlinguistik und Fachsprache*, Hildesheim: Olms, pp. 393–411.

Kuhn, T. (1962) *The Structure of Scientific Revolutions*, Chicago: University of Chicago Press.

Künzli, A. (2001) 'Experts *versus* Novices: l'utilisation de sources d'information pendant le processus de traduction,' *Meta* 46(3): 507–23.

—— (2004) 'Risk Taking: Trainee Translators vs. Professional Translators. A Case Study,' *The Journal of Specialised Translation* 2: 34–49.

Kussmaul, P. (1995) *Training the Translator*, Amsterdam: Benjamins.

—— (2000) 'Types of Creative Translating,' in A. Chesterman, N. Gallardo San Salvador, and Y. Gambier (eds) *Translation in Context*, Amsterdam and Philadelphia: Benjamins, pp. 117–26.

Lakoff, G. (1987) *Women, Fire and Dangerous Things: What Categories Reveal about the Mind*, Chicago: The University of Chicago Press.

Latour, B. (1984/1988) *The Pasteurization of France*, Cambridge, MA and London: Harvard University Press.

—— (2005) *Reassembling the Social: An Introduction to Actor-Network Theory*, Oxford: Oxford University Press.

Laygues, A. (2006) 'Pour une réaffirmation de l'« être-ensemble » par la traduction,' *Meta* 51: 838–47.

Lefevere, A. (1992) *Translation, Rewriting, and the Manipulation of Literary Fame*, London and New York: Routledge.

Lefevere, A., and S. Bassnett (1990) 'Introduction: Proust's Grandmother and the Thousand and One Nights: The "Cultural Turn" in Translation Studies,' in S. Bassnett and A. Lefevere (eds) *Translation, History and Culture*, London and New York: Pinter, pp. 1–13.

Leuven-Zwart, K. van (1989) 'Translation and Original: Similarities and Dissimilarities, I,' *Target* 1(2): 151–82.

—— (1990) 'Translation and Original: Similarities and Dissimilarities, II,' *Target* 2(1): 69–96.

Levý, J. (1963/2011) *Umění překladu*; translated into German as *Die literarische Übersetzung: Theorie einer Kunstgattung*, Frankfurt am Main: Athenäum, 1969; translated into English as *The Art of Translation*, Amsterdam and Philadelphia: Benjamins.

—— (1967/2004) 'Translation as a Decision Process,' in L. Venuti (ed.) *The Translation Studies Reader*, second edition, London and New York: Routledge, pp. 148–59.

Lewis, P. E. (1985/2012) 'The Measure of Translation Effects,' in L. Venuti (ed.) *The Translation Studies Reader*, third edition, London and New York: Routledge, pp. 220–39.

Locke, John (1690/1841) *An Essay Concerning Human Understanding*, London: Tegg.

Longa, V. M. (2004) 'A Non Linear Approach to Translation,' *Target* 16(2): 201–26.

Lörscher, W. (1991) *Translation Performance, Translation Process, and Translation Strategies: A Psycholinguistic Investigation*, Tübingen: Narr.

Lotman, Y., and B. Uspenski (1971/1979) 'Sobre el mecanismo semiótico de la cultura,' trans. N. Méndez, *Semiótica de la cultura*, Madrid: Cátedra, pp. 67–91.

Luhmann, N. (1985) *A Sociological Theory of Law*, trans. E. King and M. Albrow, London: Routledge and Kegan Paul.

Luther, M. (1530/2002) *Sendbrief von Dolmetschen / Del arte de traducir*, ed. T. Brandenberger, Madrid: Caparrós.

Malblanc, A. (1944/1963) *Stylistique comparée du français et de l'allemand: Essai de représentation linguistique comparée et étude de traduction*, Paris: Didier.

Malmkjær, K. (1997) 'Linguistics in Functionland and through the Front Door: A Response to Hans G. Hönig,' *Current Issues in Language and Society* 4(1): 70–74.

Malone, J. L. (1988) *The Science of Linguistics in the Art of Translation: Some Tools from Linguistics for the Analysis and Practice of Translation*, Albany: State University of New York Press.

Marais, K. (J.) (2009) 'Wisdom and Narrative: Dealing with Complexity and Judgement in Translator Education,' *Acta Theologica Supplementum* 12: 219–33.

— (2013) *Translation Theory and Development Studies: A Complexity Theory Approach*, London and New York: Routledge.

Mayoral, R. (2003) *Translating Official Documents*, Manchester: St. Jerome.

Meschonnic, H. (1973) 'Propositions pour une poétique de la traduction,' *Pour la poétique II*, Paris: Gallimard, pp. 305–16.

— (1999) *Poétique du traduire*, Lagrasse: Verdier.

— (2003) 'Texts on Translation,' trans. A. Pym, *Target* 15(2): 337–53.

— (2011) *Ethics and Politics of Translating*, trans. P.-P. Boulanger, Amsterdam and Philadelphia: Benjamins.

Miko, F. (1970) 'La théorie de l'expression et la traduction,' in J. S Holmes, F. de Haan, and A. Popovi (eds) *The Nature of Translation: Essays in the Theory and Practice of Literary Translation*, The Hague and Paris: Mouton de Gruyter, pp. 61–77.

Miller, J. H. (1995) *Topographies*, Stanford: Stanford University Press.

Milton, J., and P. Bandia (2008) 'Introduction: Agents of Translation and Translation Studies,' in J. Milton and P. Bandia (eds) *Agents of Translation*, Amsterdam and Philadelphia: Benjamins, pp. 1–18.

Monacelli, C., and R. Punzo (2001) 'Ethics in the Fuzzy Domain of Interpreting: A "Military" Perspective,' *The Translator* 7(2): 265–82.

Mounin, G. (1963) *Les Problèmes théoriques de la traduction*, Paris: Gallimard.

Munday, J. (2012) *Introducing Translation Studies: Theories and Applications*, third edition, London and New York: Routledge.

Muñoz Martín, R. (1998) 'Translation Strategies: Somewhere over the Rainbow,' paper presented to the *4th International Congress on Translation*, Universitat Autònoma de Barcelona.

Newmark, P. (1988) *A Textbook of Translation*, New York: Prentice Hall.

— (1997) 'The Customer as King,' *Current Issues in Language and Society* 4(1): 75–77.

Nida, E. (1964) *Toward a Science of Translating, with Special Reference to Principles and Procedures involved in Bible Translating*, Leiden: E. J. Brill.

Nida, E., and C. Taber (1969) *The Theory and Practice of Translation*, Leiden: Brill.

Nord, C. (1988/1991) *Text Analysis in Translation: Theory, Method, and Didactic Application of a Model for Translation-Oriented Text Analysis*, Amsterdam and Atlanta: Rodopi.

— (1997) *Translating as a Purposeful Activity: Functionalist Approaches Explained*, Manchester: St. Jerome Publishing.

—— (2001) 'Loyalty Revisited: Bible Translation as a Case in Point,' in A. Pym (ed.) *The Return to Ethics*, special issue of *The Translator* 7(2): 185–202.

—— (2002/2003) 'Übersetzen als zielgerichtete Handlung,' *Interaktiv. Newsletter der German Language Division der American Translators Association*, 6–12, 5–10.

Olohan, M., and M. Baker (2000) 'Reporting *that* in Translated English: Evidence for Subconscious Processes of Explicitation?' *Across Languages and Cultures* 1(2): 141–58.

Papastergiadis, N. (2000) *The Turbulence of Migration: Globalization, Deterritorialization and Hybridity*, Cambridge: Polity Press.

Parsons, T. (1951) *The Social System*, London: Routledge & Kegan Paul.

Peirce, C. S. (1931/1958) *Collected Papers*, Cambridge, MA: Harvard University Press.

Plato (c.400BCE/1977) *Cratylus*, in *Plato in Twelve Volumes*, trans. H. N. Fowler, Loeb Classical Library, London: Heinemann, vol. 4, pp. 6–191.

Pöchhacker, F. (2001) 'Translationskultur im Krankenhaus,' in G. Hebenstreit (ed.) *In Grenzen erfahren – sichtbar machen – überschreiten*, Frankfurt am Main: Peter Lang, pp. 339–54.

—— (2004) *Introducing Interpreting Studies*, London and New York: Routledge.

—— (2006) ' "Going Social"? On Pathways and Paradigms in Interpreting Studies,' in A. Pym, M. Shlesinger, and Z. Jettmarová *et al.* (eds) *Sociocultural Aspects of Translating and Interpreting*, Amsterdam and Philadelphia: John Benjamins, pp. 215–32.

Pöchhacker, F., and M. Shlesinger (eds) (2001) *The Interpreting Studies Reader*, London and New York: Routledge.

Popovič, A. (1968/1970) 'The Concept "Shift of Expression" in Translation Analysis,' in J. S Holmes, F. de Haan, and A. Popovič (eds) *The Nature of Translation: Essays in the Theory and Practice of Literary Translation*, The Hague and Paris: Mouton de Gruyter, pp. 78–87.

Prunč E. (1997) 'Translationskultur (Versuch einer konstruktiven Kritik des translator-ischen Handelns),' *TEXTconTEXT* 11: 99–127.

—— (2000) 'Vom Translationsbiedermeier zur Cyber-translation,' *TEXTconTEXT* 14: 3–74.

Pym, A. (1992a/2010) *Translation and Text Transfer: An Essay on the Principles of Intercultural Communication*, Frankfurt am Main, Berlin, Bern, New York, Paris, and Vienna: Peter Lang. Page references are to the 2010 revised edition: http://usuaris. tinet.cat/apym/publications/TTT_2010.pdf.

—— (1992b) 'Translation Error Analysis and the Interface with Language Teaching,' in C. Dollerup and A. Loddegaard (eds) *The Teaching of Translation*, Amsterdam: Benjamins, pp. 279–88.

—— (1998) *Method in Translation History*, Manchester: St. Jerome.

—— (2003) 'Alternatives to Borders in Translation Theory,' in S. Petrilli (ed.) *Translation Translation*, Amsterdam and New York: Rodopi, pp. 451–63.

—— (2004a) 'Propositions on Cross-Cultural Communication and Translation,' *Target* 16(1): 1–28.

—— (2004b) *The Moving Text: Translation, Localization, and Distribution*, Amsterdam and Philadelphia: Benjamins.

—— (2005) 'Text and Risk in Translation,' in K. Aijmer and C. Alvstad (eds) *New Tendencies in Translation Studies*, Göteborg: Göteborg University, pp. 69–82.

—— (2007a) 'On History in Formal Conceptualizations of Translation,' *Across Languages and Cultures* 8(2): 153–66.

— (2007b) 'On Shlesinger's Proposed Equalizing Universal for Interpreting,' in F. Pöchhacker, A. L. Jakobsen, and I. M. Mees (eds) *Interpreting Studies and Beyond: A Tribute to Miriam Shlesinger*, Copenhagen: Samfundslitteratur Press, pp. 175–90.

— (2008) 'On Toury's Laws of How Translators Translate,' in A. Pym, M. Shlesinger, and D. Simeoni (eds) *Beyond Descriptive Translation Studies: Investigations in Homage to Gideon Toury*, Amsterdam & Philadelphia: Benjamins, pp. 311–28.

— (2009) 'Using Process Studies in Translator Training: Self-discovery through Lousy Experiments,' in S. Göpferich, F. Alves, and I. M. Mees (eds) *Methodology, Technology and Innovation in Translation Process Research*, Copenhagen: Samfundslitteratur, pp. 135–56.

— (2011) 'Translation Theory as Historical Problem-solving,' *Intercultural Communication Review* 9: 49–61.

— (2012) *On Translator Ethics: Principles for Mediation between Cultures*, Amsterdam and Philadelphia: Benjamins.

Pym, A., M. Shlesinger, and D. Simeoni (eds) (2008) *Beyond Descriptive Translation Studies: Investigations in Homage to Gideon Toury*, Amsterdam and Philadelphia: Benjamins.

Quine, W. V. O. (1960) *Word and Object*, Cambridge, MA: MIT Press.

— (1969) 'Linguistics and Philosophy,' in S. Hook (ed.) *Language and Philosophy: A Symposium*, New York: New York University Press, pp. 95–8.

Reiss, K. (1971/2000) *Translation Criticism: Potential and Limitations. Categories and Criteria for Translation Quality Assessment*, trans. E. F. Rhodes, Manchester: St. Jerome.

— (1976) 'Texttypen, Übersetzungstypen und die Beurteilung von Übersetzungen,' *Lebende Sprachen* 22(3): 97–100.

Reiss, K., and H. J. Vermeer (1984) *Grundlegung einer allgemeinen Translationstheorie*, Tübingen: Niemeyer. Trans. C. Nord as *Towards a General Theory of Translational Action: Skopos Theory Explained*, Manchester: St. Jerome, 2013. Page numbers herein are to the German version.

Remesal, A. de (1966) *Historia general de las Indias occidentales y particular de la gobernación de Chiapa y Guatemala*, ed. C. Saenz de Santa María, Madrid: Atlas.

Rendall, S. (1997) 'Notes on Zohn's Translation of Benjamin's "Die Aufgabe des Übersetzers",' *TTR : traduction, terminologie, rédaction* 10(2): 191–206.

Renn, J. (2006a) *Übersetzungsverhältnisse: Perspektiven einer pragmatistischen Gesellschaftstheorie*, Weilerswist: Velbrück.

— (2006b) 'Indirect Access: Complex Settings of Communication and the Translation of Governance,' in A. Parada and O. Díaz Fouces (eds) *Sociology of Translation*, Vigo: Universidade de Vigo, pp. 193–210.

Retsker, Y. I. (1974) *Teoria perevoda i perevodcheskaia praktika*, Moscow: Mezhdunarodnii otnoshenia.

Ricœur, P. (2004) *Sur la traduction*, Paris: Bayard.

Robinson, D. (2001) *Who Translates? Translator Subjectivities beyond Reason*, Albany, NY: State University of New York Press.

Rosa, A. A. (2003) 'What about a Section on Translation in that Literary History Volume? Readership, Literary Competence and Translation,' *Current Writing* 14(2): 175–91.

Rose, M. G. (1997) *Translation and Literary Criticism: Translation as Analysis*, Manchester: St. Jerome.

Rubel, P. G., and A. Rosman (2003) 'Introduction: Translation and Anthropology,' in P. G. Rubel and A. Rosman (eds) *Translating Cultures: Perspectives on Translation and Anthropology*, Oxford and New York: Berg, pp. 1–22.

Sallis, J. (2002) *On Translation*, Bloomington: Indiana University Press.

Saussure, F. de (1916/1974) *Course in General Linguistics*, trans. W. Baskin, Glasgow: Fontana Collins.

Schäler, R. (2006) 'Reverse Localization,' *Multilingual* 17(3): 82.

Schleiermacher, F. (1813/1963) 'Ueber die verschiedenen Methoden des Uebersezens,' in H. J. Störig (ed.) *Das Problem des Übersetzens*, Darmstadt: Wissenschaftliche Buchgesellschaft, pp. 38–70.

Seleskovitch, D., and M. Lederer (1984) *Interpréter pour traduire*, Paris: Didier.

Serres, M. (1974) *Hermès III. La Traduction*, Paris: Minuit.

Shlesinger, M. (1989) *Simultaneous Interpretation as a Factor in Effecting Shifts in the Position of Texts on the Oral-Literate Continuum*, MA thesis, Tel Aviv University.

Shveitser, A. D. (1973/1987) *Übersetzung und Linguistik*, Berlin: Akademie.

Simeoni, D. (1998) 'The Pivotal Status of the Translator's Habitus,' *Target* 10(1): 1–39.

Simon, S. (1996) *Gender in Translation: Cultural Identity and the Politics of Transmission*, London and New York: Routledge.

Snell-Hornby, M. (1988) *Translation Studies: An Integrated Approach*, Amsterdam and Philadelphia: Benjamins.

—— (1990) 'Linguistic Transcoding or Cultural Transfer? A Critique of Translation Theory in Germany,' in S. Bassnett and A. Lefevere (eds) *Translation, History and Culture*, London and New York: Pinter, pp. 79–86.

Sperber, D., and D. Wilson (1988) *Relevance: Communication and Cognition*, Cambridge, MA: Harvard University Press.

Spivak, G. C. (2007) 'Translation as Culture,' in P. St-Pierre and P. C. Kar (eds) *In Translation – Reflections, Refractions, Transformations*, Amsterdam and Philadelphia: Benjamins, pp. 263–76.

Stecconi, U. (2004) 'Interpretive Semiotics and Translation Theory: The Semiotic Conditions to Translation,' *Semiotica* 150: 471–89.

Steiner, G. (1975) *After Babel: Aspects of Language and Translation*, London, Oxford, and New York: Oxford University Press.

Swaan, A. de (2002) *Words of the World: The Global Language System*, Cambridge: Polity Press.

Tirkkonen-Condit, S. (1989) 'Professional versus Non-professional Translation: A Think-aloud Protocol Study,' in Candace Séguinot (ed.) *The Translation Process*, Toronto: HG Publications, pp. 73–85.

—— (1992) 'The Interaction of World Knowledge and Linguistic Knowledge in the Processes of Translation: A Think-aloud Protocol Study,' in B. Lewandowska-Tomaszczyk and M. Thelen (eds) *Translation and Meaning, Part 2*, Maastricht: Rijkshogeschool Maastricht, pp. 433–40.

—— (1997) 'Who Verbalises What: A Linguistic Analysis of TAP Texts,' *Target* 9(1): 69–84.

—— (2004) 'Unique Items – Over- or Under-represented in Translated Language?' in A. Mauranen and P. Kujamäki (eds) *Translation Universals: Do they Exist?* Amsterdam and Philadelphia: Benjamins, pp. 177–86.

Toury, G. (1980) *In Search of a Theory of Translation*, Tel Aviv: Porter Institute for Poetics and Semiotics.

—— (1986) 'Monitoring Discourse Transfer: A Text-case for a Developmental Model of Translation,' in J. House and S. Blum-Kulka (eds) *Interlingual and Intercultural Communication*, Tübingen: Narr, pp. 79–94.

—— (1992) '"Everything has its Price": An Alternative to Normative Conditioning in Translator Training,' *Interface* 6(2): 60–72.

—— (1995) 'The Notion of "Assumed Translation" – An Invitation to a New Discussion,' in H. Bloemen, E. Hertog, and W. Segers (eds) *Letterlijkheid, Woordelijheid / Literality, Verbality*, Antwerp and Harmelen: Fantom, pp. 135–47.

—— (1995/2012) *Descriptive Translation Studies – and beyond*, revised edition, Amsterdam and Philadelphia: Benjamins.

—— (2004) 'Probabilistic explanations in translation studies. Welcome as they are, would they count as universals?' in A. Mauranen and P. Kujamäki (eds) *Translation Universals. Do they exist?*, Amsterdam and Philadelphia: Benjamins, pp. 15–32.

Trivedi, H. (2007) 'Translating Culture vs. Cultural Translation,' in P. St-Pierre and P. C. Kar (eds) *In Translation – Reflections, Refractions, Transformations*, Amsterdam and Philadelphia: Benjamins, pp. 277–87.

Van den Broeck, R. (1990) 'Translation Theory after Deconstruction,' in P. N. Chaffey, A. F. Rydning, and S. S. Ulriksen (eds) *Translation Theory in Scandinavia*, Oslo: University of Oslo, pp. 24–57.

Vázquez-Ayora, G. (1977) *Introducción a la traductología*, Washington, DC: Georgetown University Press.

Venuti, L. (1995) *The Translator's Invisibility: A History of Translation*, London and New York: Routledge.

—— (1998) *The Scandals of Translation: Towards an Ethics of Difference*, London and New York: Routledge.

—— (2013) *Translation Changes Everything*, London and New York: Routledge.

Venuti, L. (ed.) (2012) *The Translation Studies Reader*, third edition, London and New York: Routledge.

Vermeer, H. J. (1989a) *Skopos und Translationsauftrag*, Heidelberg: Institut für Übersetzen und Dolmetschen.

—— (1989b/2012) 'Skopos and Commission in Translational Action,' in L. Venuti (ed.) *The Translation Studies Reader*, third edition, London and New York: Routledge, pp. 191–202.

—— (1996) *Übersetzen als Utopie: Die Übersetzungstheorie des Walter Bendix Schoenflies Benjamin*, Heidelberg: TEXTconTEXT.

—— (1998) 'Didactics of Translation,' in M. Baker (ed.) *Routledge Encyclopedia of Translation Studies*, London and New York: Routledge, pp. 60–63.

Vieira, E. (1999) 'Liberating Calibans: Readings of Antropofagia and Haroldo de Campos' Poetics of Transcreation,' in S. Bassnett and H. Trivedi (eds) *Post-Colonial Translation: Theory and Practice*, London and New York: Routledge, pp. 95–113.

—— (2000) 'Cultural Contacts and Literary Translation,' in O. Classe (ed.) *Encyclopedia of Literary Translation into English*, vol. 1, London and Chicago: Fitzroy Dearborn, pp. 319–21.

Vinay, J.-P., and J. Darbelnet (1958/1972) *Stylistique comparée du français et de l'anglais: méthode de traduction*, Paris: Didier.

von Flotow, L. (1997) *Translation and Gender: Translating in the 'Era of Feminism,'* Manchester: St. Jerome.

Vorderobermeier, G., and M. Wolf (eds) (2008) *"Meine Sprache grenzt mich ab ..." Transkulturalität und kulturelle Übersetzung im Kontext von Migration*, Münster: LIT.

West, R. (2002) 'Teaching Nomadism: Inter/Cultural Studies in the Context of Translation Studies,' in S. Herbrechter (ed.) *Cultural Studies, Interdisciplinarity and Translation*, Amsterdam and New York: Rodopi, pp. 161–76.

Wilss, W. (1982) *The Science of Translation: Problems and Methods*, Tübingen: Gunter Narr.

Wittgenstein, L. (1958) *Philosophical Investigations*, Oxford: Blackwell.

Wolf, M. (1997) 'Translation as a Process of Power: Aspects of Cultural Anthropology in Translation,' in M. Snell-Hornby, Z. Jettmarová, and K. Kaindl (eds) *Translation as Intercultural Communication*, Amsterdam and Philadelphia: Benjamins, pp. 123–33.

— (2007) 'Introduction: The Emergence of a Sociology of Translation,' in M. Wolf and A. Fukari (eds) *Constructing a Sociology of Translation*, Amsterdam and Philadelphia: Benjamins, pp. 1–36.

— (2009) 'The Implications of a Sociological Turn – Methodological and Disciplinary Questions,' in A. Pym and A. Perekrestenko (eds) *Translation Research Projects 2*, Tarragona: Intercultural Studies Group, pp. 73–9.

Zellermayer, M. (1987) 'On Comments Made by Shifts in Translation,' *Indian Journal of Applied Linguistics* 13(2): 75–90.

Index